IMAGES
of America

EARLY WOODS COUNTY

On the Cover: The Capron home of John and Elina Nelson is pictured in 1906. On the porch are Elina Nelson and Carrie Cameron. The Cameron children are seated and are, from left to right, John (professor of physics, North Western Oklahoma State University), Charlie (professor of electrical engineering, Oklahoma State University), Orville (vice president of legal department, Eastern Airlines) and Tom (died in an accident at age 18). (Courtesy of Joy (Cameron) Sherman.)

IMAGES
of America

EARLY WOODS COUNTY

Beverly Kinzie

ARCADIA
PUBLISHING

ISBN 978-0-7385-8310-5

Published by Arcadia Publishing
Charleston, South Carolina

Printed in the United States of America

Library of Congress Control Number: 2010939911

For all general information, please contact Arcadia Publishing:
Telephone 843-853-2070
Fax 843-853-0044
E-mail sales@arcadiapublishing.com
For customer service and orders:
Toll-Free 1-888-313-2665

Visit us on the Internet at www.arcadiapublishing.com

This volume is dedicated to all Woods County pioneers.
Their efforts transformed this virgin prairie into what it is today.

Contents

Acknowledgments

To my husband, Wayne, whose mother, Audrey (Bainum) Kinzie wrote notes about everyday life from the time she learned to write in the late 1890s through the 1980s. Her notes have provided a wealth of knowledge of the early days in Woods County. To my friend Lorraine (Nelson) Malzahn, whose grandmother left a written and pictorial history of coming from Denmark to Woods County in the 1890s; to Joy (Cameron) Sherman, whose parents and grandparents left a written and pictorial history of settlement in Woods County; to Warren Little, whose parents and grandparents left a written and pictorial history of northwest Woods County; and to the Alva Public Library and Cherokee Strip Museum for information and pictures they had available for public use. Images in this book belong to the author unless otherwise labeled.

INTRODUCTION

Present-day Woods County, Oklahoma, is quite different than the Woods County of the period between 1893 and 1907. In the late 1800s and early 1900s, there were approximately 67 townsites and over 223 one-room schools. Woods County today consists of six towns, of which Alva, the county seat, is the largest. Of all the states in the Union, none has a background as colorful and unique as Oklahoma. Although one of the younger states, Oklahoma has developed with remarkable speed. Woods County, in the northwestern part of the state, contributed its full share in Oklahoma's development preparatory to statehood.

For two long centuries, it was a toss-up whether the Spanish, French, or the English, by right of exploration, would win control of the vast territory that extended from what is now Canada to the Gulf of Mexico. With financial reverses at home and increasing fear of war with England, Napoleon began to cast his eyes about in search of funds. To the consternation of his people but the relief of President Jefferson, Napoleon decided to sell the land held by France in North America to the United States. The Louisiana Purchase of 1803 resulted in the acquisition of territory (including Oklahoma) far greater in area than the whole United States at the time.

A new treaty in 1828 gave the Cherokee Indians seven million acres in northern Oklahoma. They also received an "outlet," a strip of land 58 miles wide extending west to the 100th meridian. Known as the Cherokee Outlet or Cherokee Strip, it was created so the Indians could reach the hunting grounds of the Great Plains. In 1838, President Jackson ordered Gen. Winfield Scott to move the remaining Cherokees from the eastern United States to Oklahoma. This westward migration was called the "Trail of Tears," as it was a forced march during which many Cherokees died. The Cherokees were the predominant civilized tribe to come into northwest Oklahoma. In the Choctaw tongue, Oklahoma translates as "land of the red people."

Various things worked toward giving white men a glimpse into what is now Oklahoma. Strange tales of the "Wild West," that fabulous land of the Indian and abundant game, were repeated around firesides. If fathers did not feel the urge to move westward, their sons probably did. Even Washington Irving paid the area a visit, afterward publishing an account of his travels on the frontier. There were deer, wolves, antelopes, coyotes, bobcats, and panthers. Pelicans and snowy herons abounded, as did great flocks of wild geese and ducks. To the hunter and trapper, this was a veritable paradise. Fur traders found it good business to haul buffalo hides to market. When the railroads brought more people to the area, however, it was not long until the herds were depleted. Naturally, the Indians resented the pointless slaughter.

For years, this wild country had furnished asylum to fugitives from justice and continued to do so long after the land openings. In addition to the outlaws, soldiers, traders, and cowboys also came. Prior to the introduction of the railroad, it was necessary to drive cattle to market. Of the trails resulting from cattle drives, only the Chisholm Trail crossed what is now Woods County. A strong Cherokee Strip Livestock Association was formed and reigned supreme, resisting any move toward opening the area to settlement.

With so many white men seeing the fertile virgin soil and the plentiful game of the area, it was inevitable that they began clamoring for openings. Leaders began to emerge and organize groups to cross over into the forbidden country and build homes. Among these, Capt. David L. Payne was the most persistent. A born organizer, he spent over five years leading groups across the border and being chased out by soldiers. He did, however, succeed in making the name Oklahoma a household word.

Indians and cattlemen kept lobbyists in Washington to prevent the land being opened to settlement. Of course, the licensed traders and whiskey peddlers did not want their profits curtailed, either. Discovery of coal made agitators all the more persistent. Finally, with the coming of the railroads, the fight for statehood commenced in Washington. The struggle was hard and long, but the Oklahoma "boomers" would not accept defeat. At last, they tacked a rider on to the Indian Appropriation Bill, providing that lands in so-called Oklahoma should be opened to settlement. In that form, on March 3, 1889, the bill passed. Exciting years followed, when people settled in parts of the territory that had been thrown open to settlement by the government. However, the Cherokee Strip had still not been settled. After nearly four years of negotiation, the Cherokee nations ceded it to the United States, which paid them $8,300,000, effectively purchasing it twice.

In "M" (Woods) County, as with other counties in the Cherokee Strip, people had arrived from almost all areas of the United States. Some settlers came from other countries. In general, the people were industrious, frugal, and sober.

Homesteaders helped each other, often out of necessity. Many undertakings required the aid of one's neighbors. The most pressing needs were shelter and water. Several families could use one well until there was time to dig more. The first buildings in "M" County were made with whatever lay at hand. Some, whose claims included a creek or draw, cut into the bank and built a dugout. In some places, sod shanties were built, using blocks of sod turned over by the plow or spade. In a few instances, two- or three-room buildings were moved to the claim from Kansas.

Only by using whatever was at hand could the settlers stay on their claims. The summer of 1894 was so hot and dry that very little was raised. The railroad furnished free seed wheat to many who could not buy it, taking notes that were payable when and if a crop could be raised. In 1897, the summer season brought rain, and never was anything more appreciated. With the crops doing well, it was time to think of education. Life was centered on school and the church.

Early Woods County covers the period from 1893 to 1907, the year that Oklahoma gained statehood. It does not attempt to be a comprehensive history of the county and towns within the county, but does present an overview of what life was like for the early settlers.

One

Cherokee Outlet

Provision for the organization of the Oklahoma Territory was made in the Organic Act of May 2, 1890. The governor appointed a full set of county officers for each county. The statutes of Nebraska were to be those of the territory until otherwise provided.

Before the opening of the Cherokee Strip, there had been two territorial governors, both appointed by Pres. Benjamin Harrison. George W. Steele of Indiana served from 1890 to 1891 and Abraham J. Seay of Kingfisher served from 1891 to 1893. After Woods County came into being, there followed a string of governors as follows: William C. Renfrow of Norman was appointed by President Cleveland and served from 1893 to 1897, Cassius M. Barnes of Guthrie was appointed by President McKinley and served from 1897 to 1901, William M. Jenkins of Guthrie was also appointed by President McKinley and served from May to November of 1901, and Thompson B. Ferguson of Watonga was appointed by President Roosevelt and served from 1901 to 1906.

Western Woods County is the site of the Battle of Turkey Springs. This armed conflict pitted the US 4th Cavalry against Dull Knife and warriors of the Cheyenne. The engagement lasted from September 13 to September 14, 1878, and occurred 25 miles northwest of Alva. This has been depicted in a mural in Alva, Oklahoma.

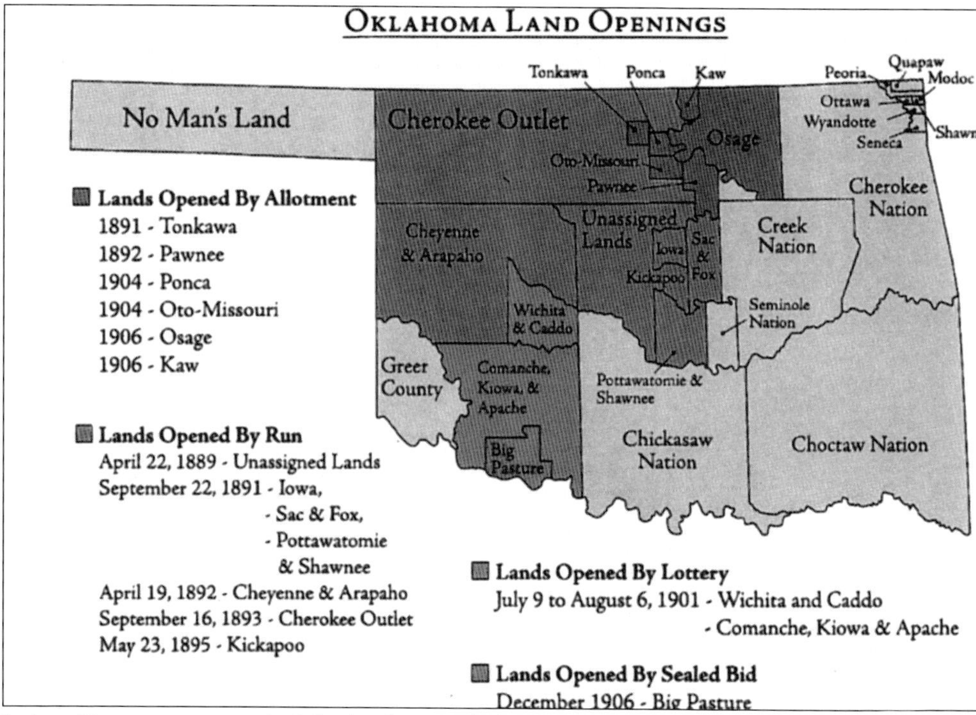

Indian Territory consisted of the land set aside for Native Americans. The Free Home Bill was passed in June of 1900. It cancelled the $1 per acre debt that settlers owed for their land. The US Congress passed the Omnibus Statehood Bill on June 14, 1906, admitting Oklahoma and Indian Territory as one state. President Roosevelt approved the constitution as adopted, designating Saturday, November 16, 1907, as the inauguration day of the new state government.

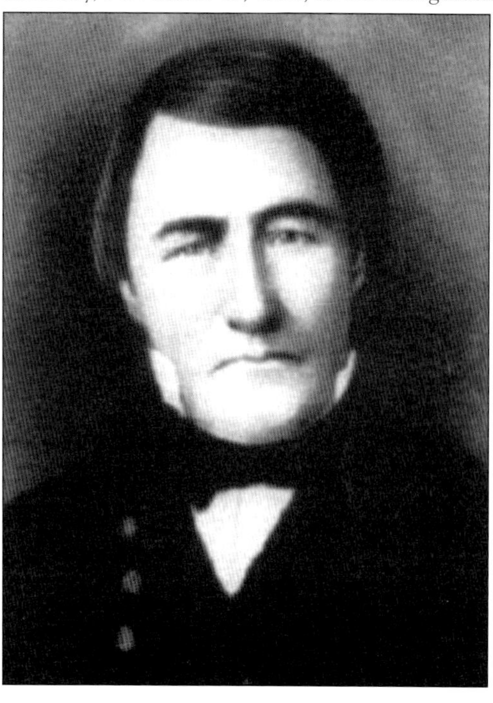

Capt. Nathan Boone, the youngest son of Daniel Boone (a captain in the 1st Regiment of US Dragoons), was commissioned by Pres. Zachary Taylor to explore and map present-day Oklahoma. In 1843, he spent time in the western part of what would become Woods County, crossing the salt flats. A historical marker has been placed along Highway 64 telling of his journey though the area.

In 1832, Washington Irving traveled to Indian Territory on a surveying mission with the commissioner of Indian affairs. Upon returning to the east, he wrote *A Tour on the Prairie*, which fed readers' imaginations with visions of life in the west.

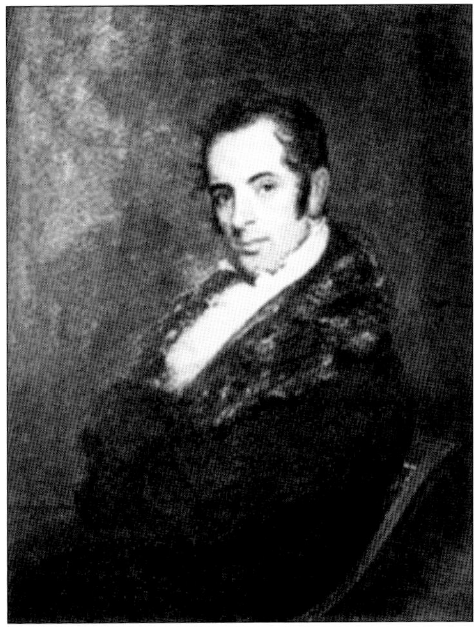

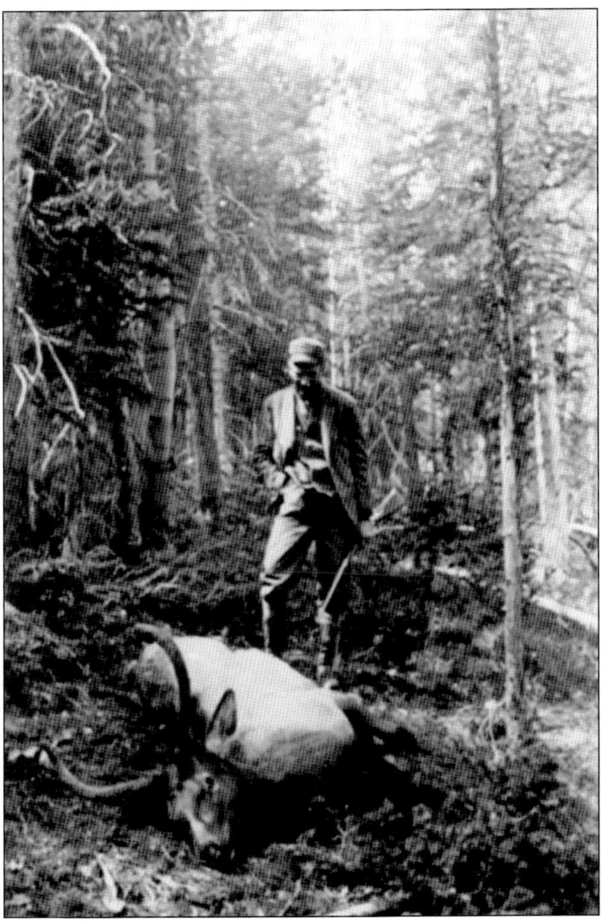

This image reflects some of what Washington Irving saw in Indian Territory, including the timber and wildlife. (Courtesy of Oklahoma Historical Society.)

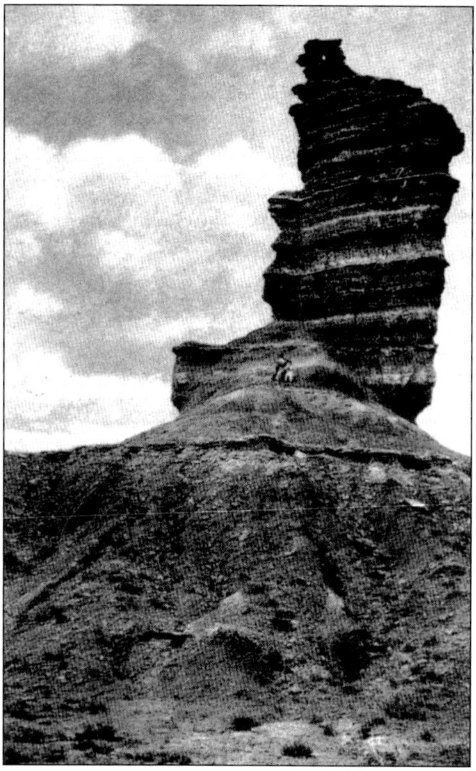

Chimney Rock is located in southwestern Woods County. It stood for centuries until a strong windstorm blew it over in the mid-1990s. Western Woods County contains rolling to rough ranch land, while the eastern portion is made up primarily of level farmland. When the pioneers came to this part of the Oklahoma Territory, this is what the land would have looked like. (Courtesy of Alva Post Card Company.)

This image shows what is known as the Gloss Mountains. Southeast of Waynoka, they were originally in "M" County but are now a part of Major County. This is another example of the rough terrain the early settlers encountered when settling the Cherokee Strip.

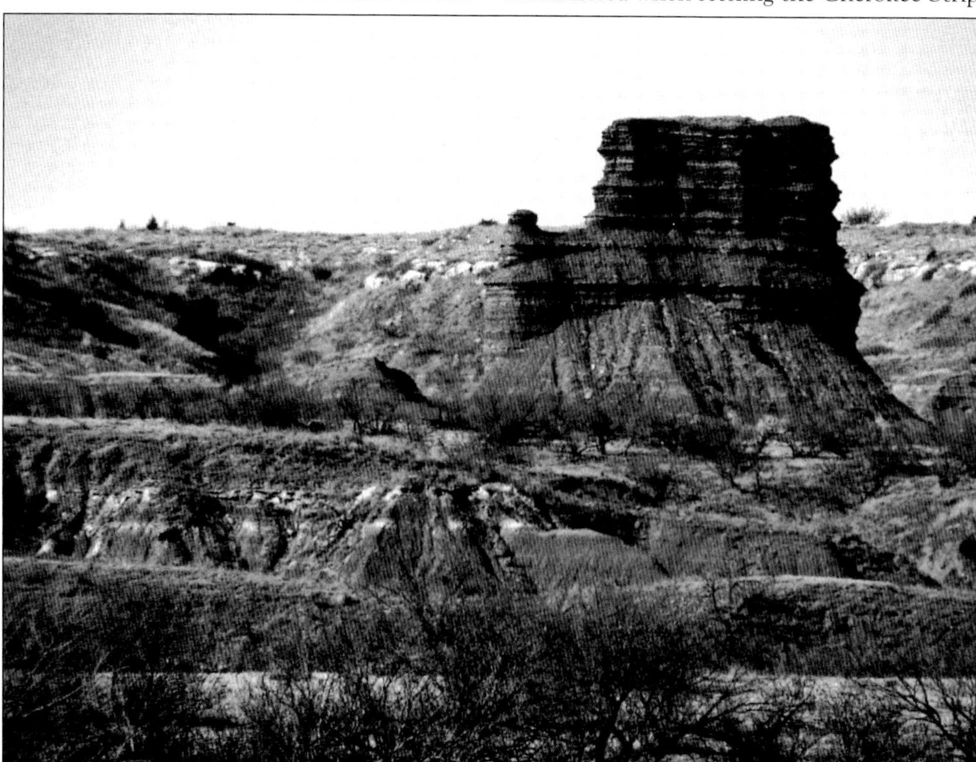

Two

"M" County Becomes Woods County

"M" County was a creation of the Oklahoma territorial government, a 48-by-58 mile area. In preparation for statehood, its boundaries were shuffled and disappeared into the counties of Alfalfa, Major, Woodward, and Woods. Woods County received the majority of the land and retained the county seat of Alva.

September 16, 1893, was the day set by the government for the run into the Cherokee Strip. This was also the year of a national depression. There were serious labor troubles back east, with many out of work. The bottom had fallen out of farm prices, and countless people came to Oklahoma. They had "dried out" in Kansas, the vital topsoil having been stripped from the land, and a move was necessary. Others came for adventure and the excitement of living in a new country. Both the educated and uneducated flooded into the area. Doctors, lawyers, blacksmiths, storekeepers, and laborers came, providing the skills and services that a new community needed.

After paying the filing fee of $14, most homesteaders had little cash left. Families suddenly found themselves sitting out alone on the wide expanse of prairie, unbroken by a single building or even trees, unless they were near a creek. They often had only a team and wagon, a cow, or a few chickens. If lucky, they might also have a plow and tools such as a spade or hoe.

Some men left their families with relatives in Kansas while improving their new property as best they could. Some plowed a few furrows to keep within the law and then hurried back home for a few months' work.

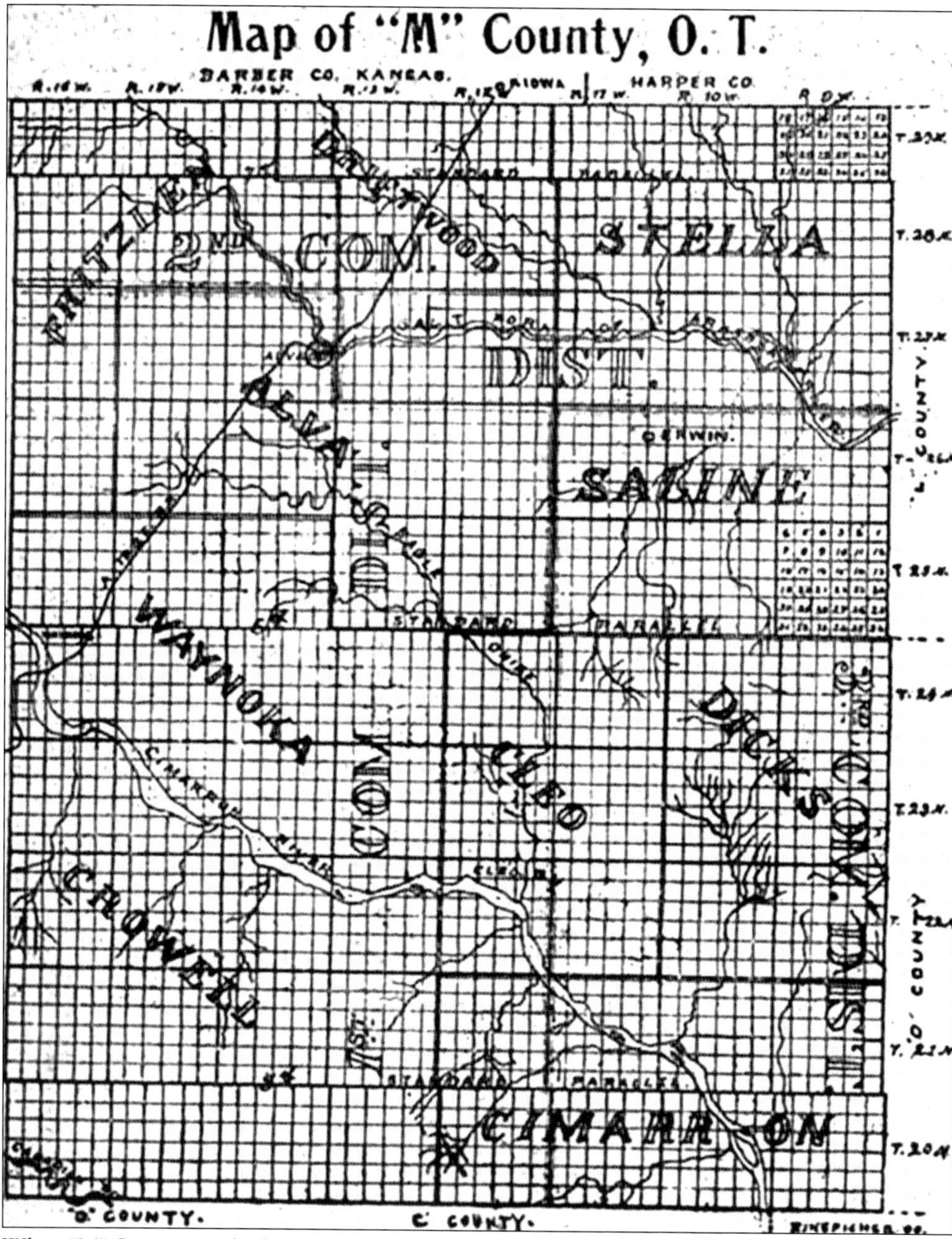

When "M" County was laid out in 1893 it was 48 miles wide and 58 miles from north to south. It was known as "M" County and remained this size until statehood in 1907; Alva was its county seat.

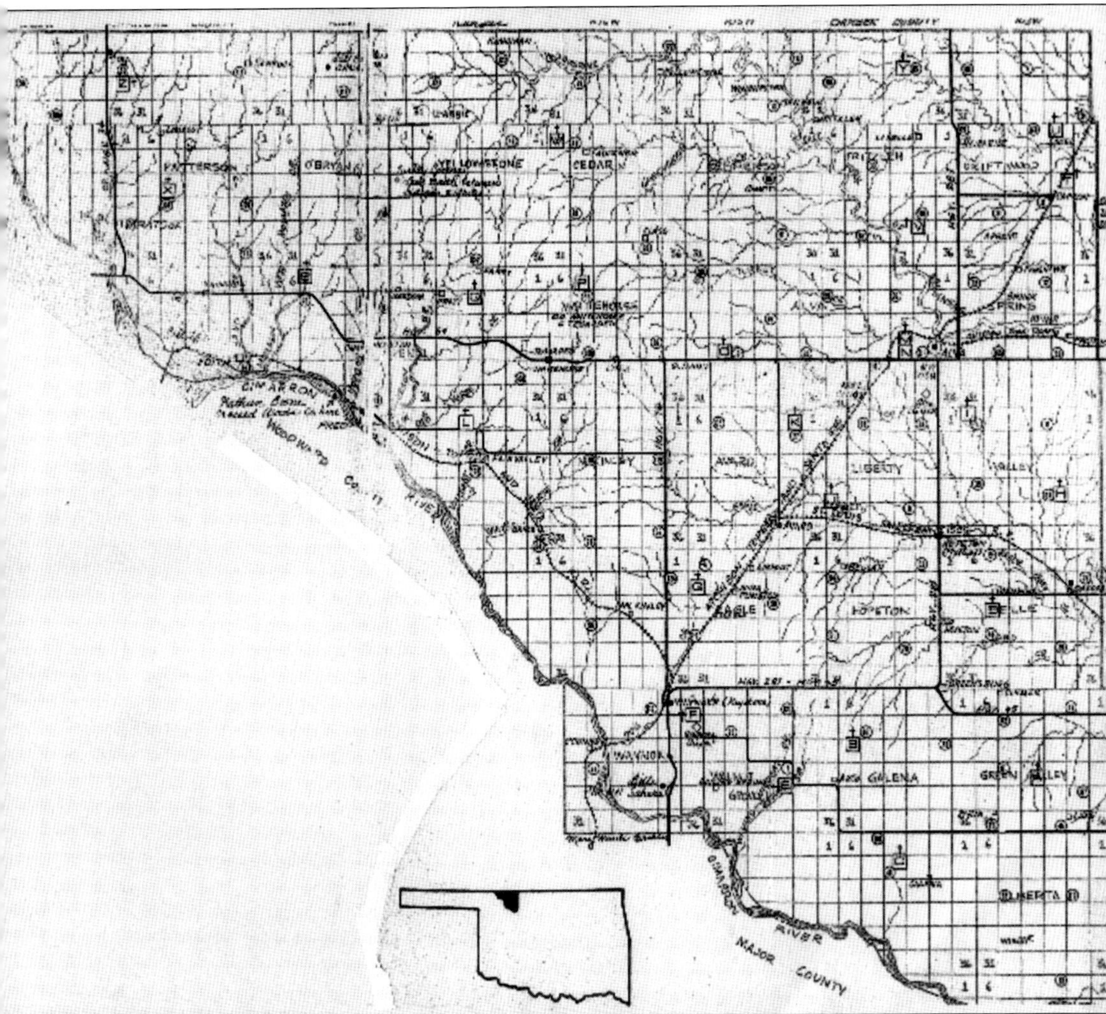

At statehood in 1907, Woods County was created mostly out of "M" County but with different boundaries. Alva remained the county seat.

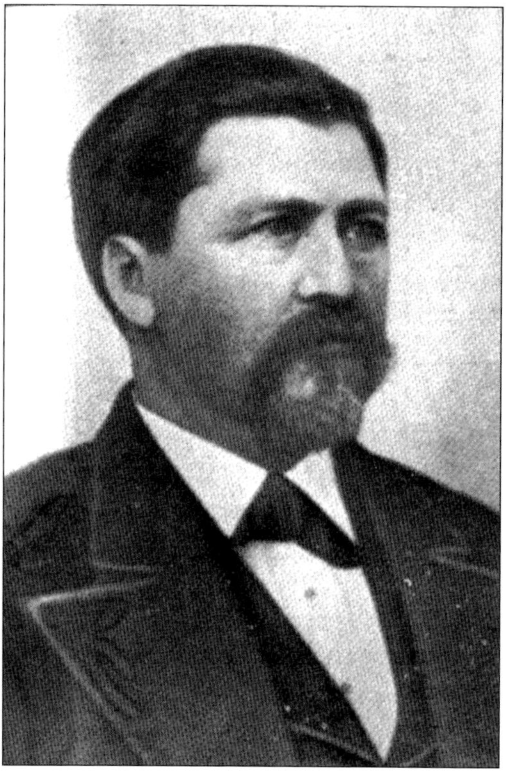

Samuel Wood, a lawyer by profession, was one of the early organizers of the Santa Fe Railroad. Wood joined the Union army at the beginning of the Civil War and fought in several battles in Missouri and Arkansas. An advocate for women's suffrage, Wood served in several Kansas state offices and was therefore familiar to pioneers from Kansas who moved to Oklahoma.

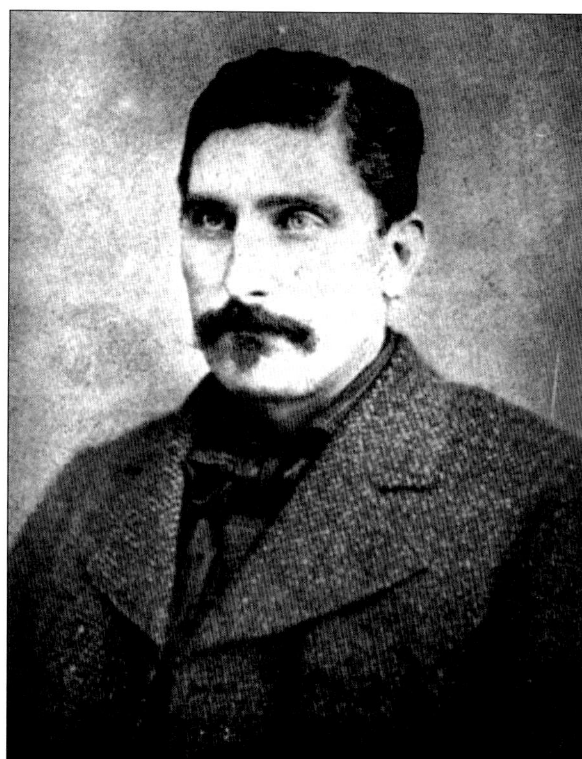

David Payne was an American soldier and pioneer. He was known as the "Father of Oklahoma" because of his work opening the state to settlement. He organized, trained, and led the "Boomer Army" on its forays into the unassigned lands. Between May 1880 and August 1882, he was arrested four times within Indian Territory. Once he was escorted to its borders and released, and three times he was jailed—either by army or civilian authorities.

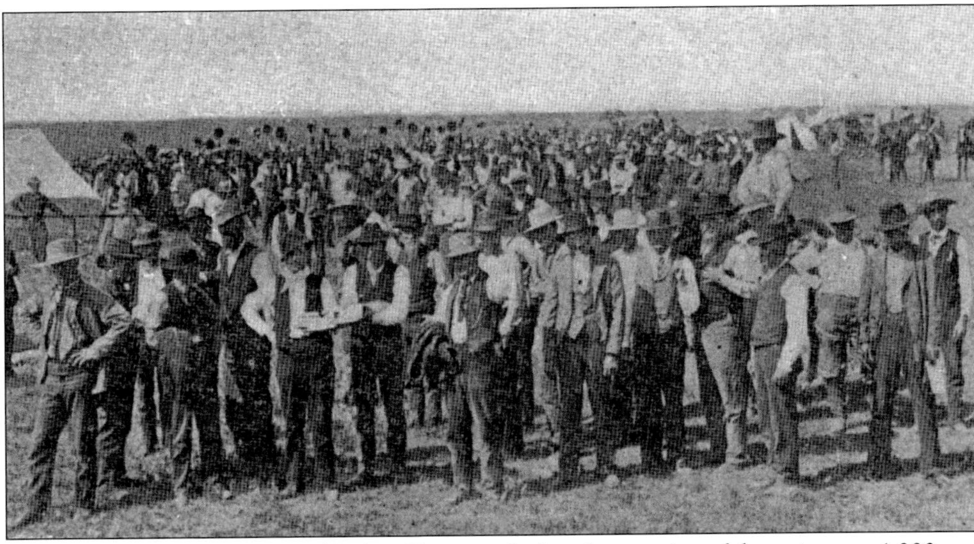

Along the border of Kansas and Indian Territory, before the opening of the strip, over 1,000 men and women got in line to register for the land run. This image is thought to have been taken outside of Kiowa, Kansas, one of the run's official starting points.

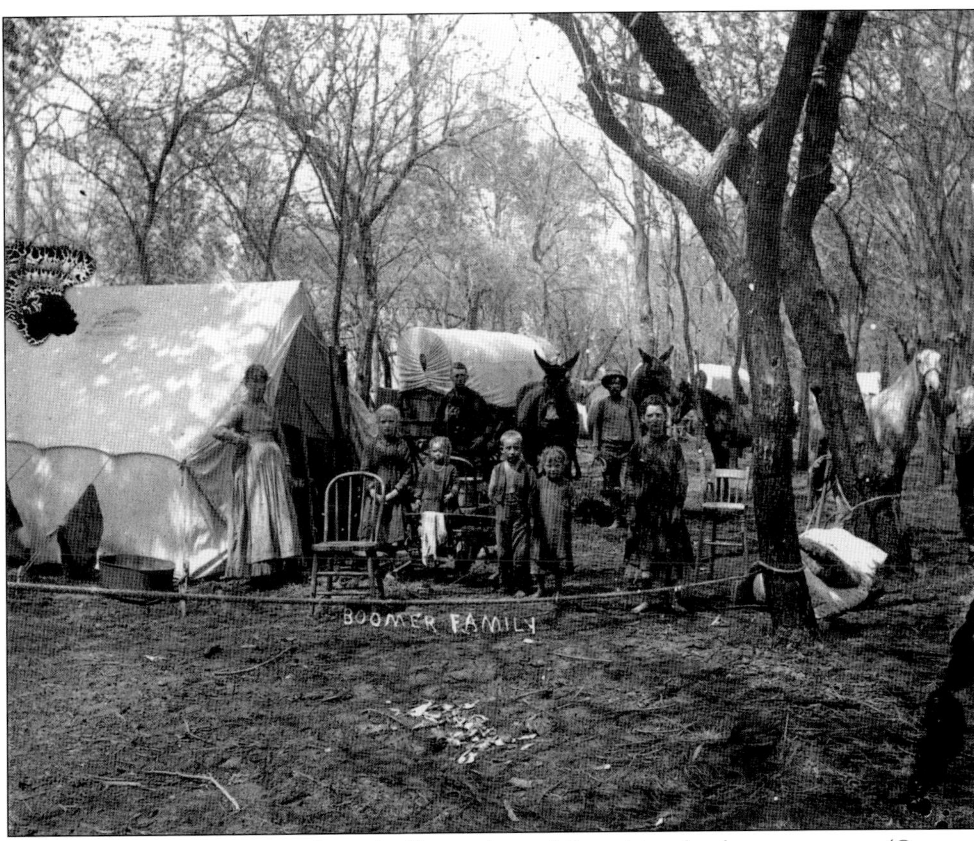

Families are shown camping along the Kansas line while waiting for the run to start. (Courtesy of Western History Collection, University of Oklahoma Press.)

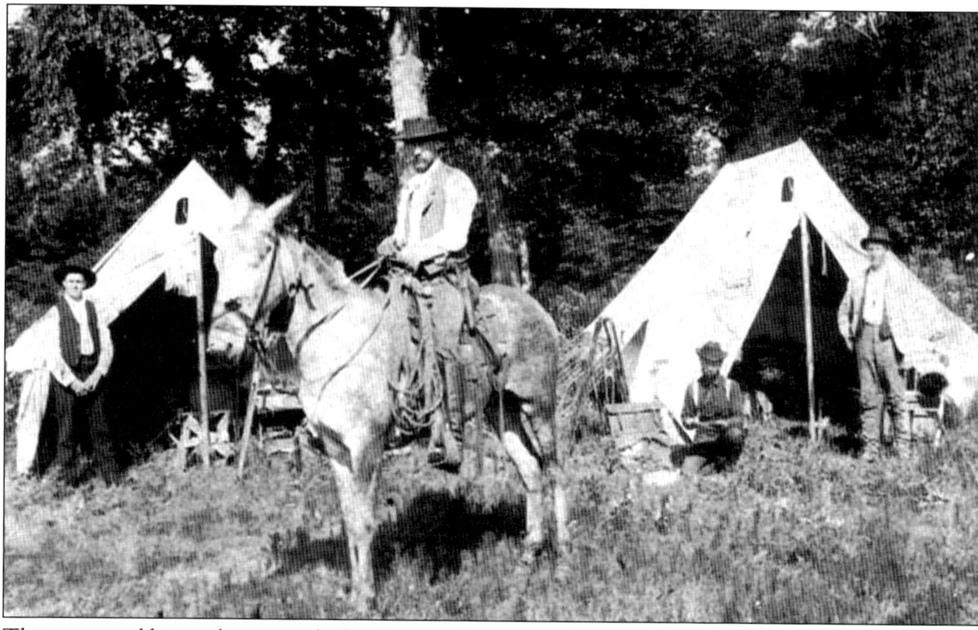

This man and his mule are ready for the run. Some people camped for days before the run started. As the important day neared, frustration grew and tempers flared. Many settlers carried guns. (Courtesy of Western History Collection, University of Oklahoma Press.)

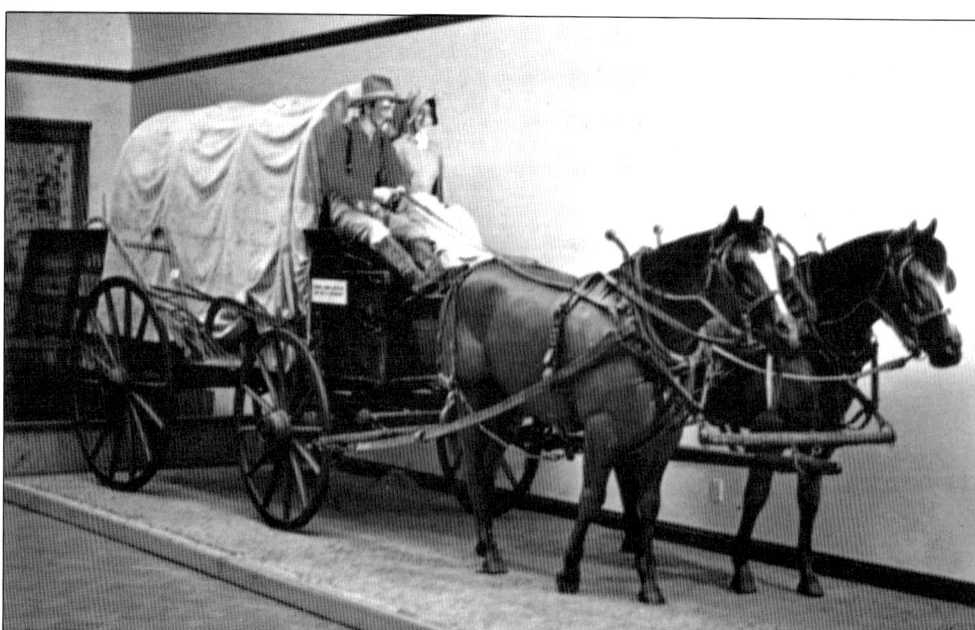

Shown here is the type of covered wagon used for the run of 1893. Wooden boxes, barrels, buckets, shovels, and a supply of hay were the staples settlers would load on prairie schooners when preparing for the Cherokee Strip land run. (Courtesy of the Oklahoma Historical Society.)

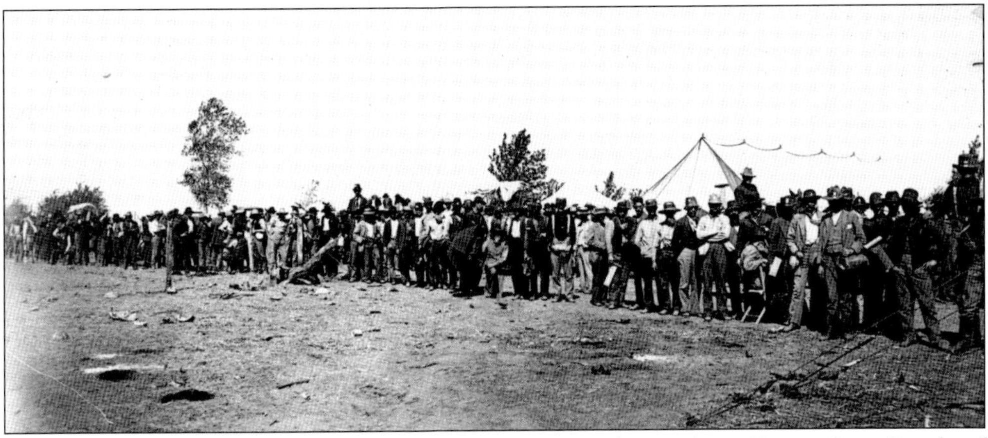

On September 16, 1893, a diverse crowd gathered along the southern Kansas line. People of every age and description were drawn there by the prospect of securing a home in this promised land. Included in this group were boomers in covered wagons, townsmen in buggies and carts, cowboys with their ponies, and people on foot and on bicycles. At 12:00 p.m., the signal was fired by soldiers who were posted at intervals along the line.

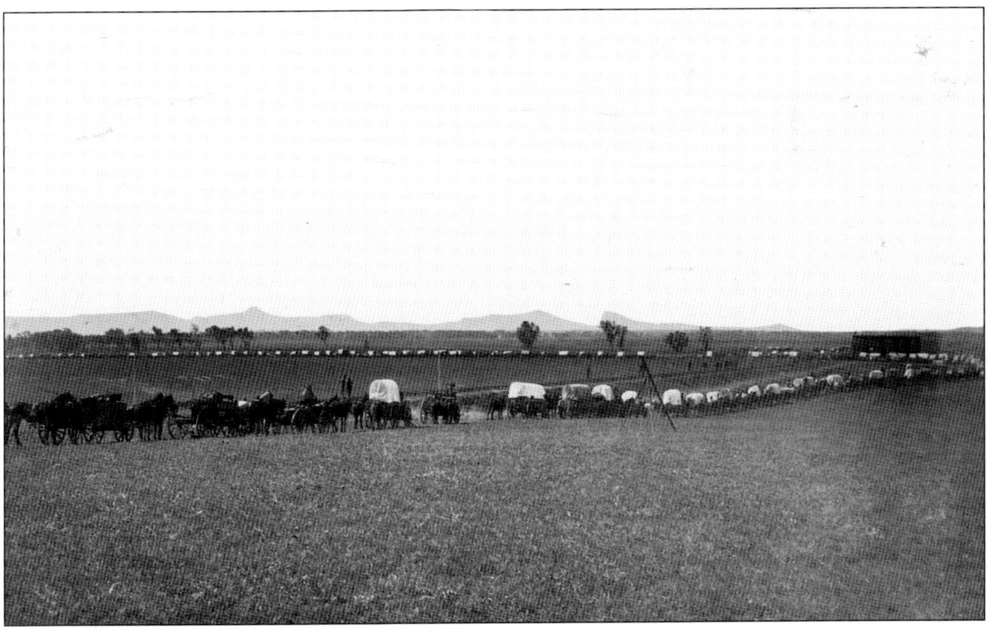

It was recorded that there were over 4,000 covered wagons lined up for the run. (Courtesy of Western History Collection, University of Oklahoma Press.)

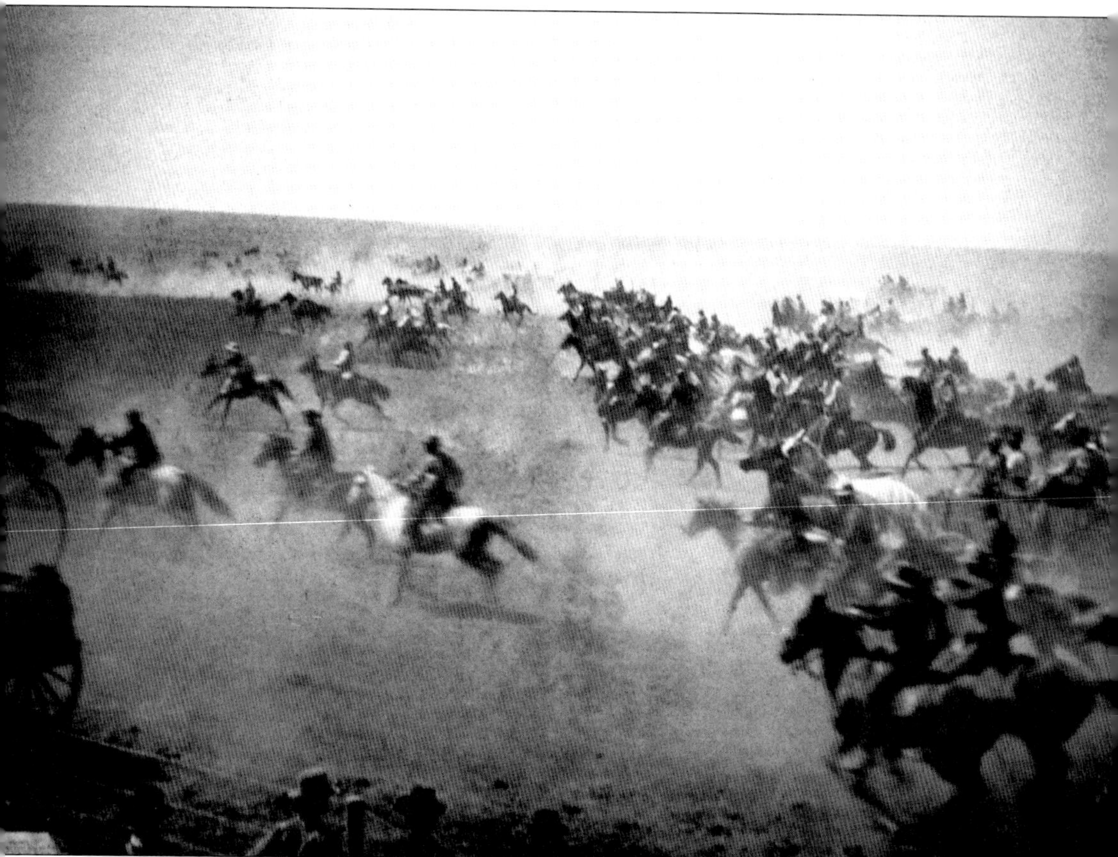

The land run of 1893 began the most remarkable race in the annals of history. There was a strong wind blowing from the south, and the dry earth was soon beaten to powder by a myriad of hooves and wheels. The scene resembled the route of a retreating army, the strong taking the lead and leaving the stragglers enveloped in a cloud of choking dust. (Courtesy of the Alva Cherokee Strip Museum.)

Three

The Homestead and Its Pioneers

As soon as possible, homesteaders began getting the land ready for crops. With winter so nearly upon them, not much could be done except plowing. However, the turning of tough virgin soil was no easy task. The roots of the native buffalo grass had matted the soil securely. No common moldboard plow could be used on such terrain, but a new kind of plow came into existence. Known by some as sod plows, they consisted of a steel shear to slide under the sod, a vertical rolling cutter to slice it, and steel rods to flip it over. Still, plowing remained hard work.

The spring of 1894 found the pioneer families busily planting. Every inch of ground they had succeeded in plowing was planted with something. Gardens were planted much as they had been in Kansas, except it was more difficult in newly plowed ground. Fruit trees and grapes were set out whenever possible and water was carried from creeks to keep the gardens alive.

Food was not plentiful during these difficult first years, but ingenuity and hard work managed to keep something on the table. As they could be found most anywhere, wild plums were picked by families and used for butters or jellies. Many people who lived near the Kansas line crossed over for peaches, apples, and other fruit when it was available. While some canning was done, drying was the most practical means of preserving food. Glass jars were used but broke so easily that food could not be canned at temperatures hot enough to preserve it. Tin cans were sometimes used. Butters, jams, and jellies were among the foodstuffs that were put into brown stone jars for storing. These jars, which probably held a quart or so, had lids that were airtight when fastened on with melted sealing wax. Fruit and other foods were stored in cellars where it was cool. Butter was often hung down the well to be kept cool.

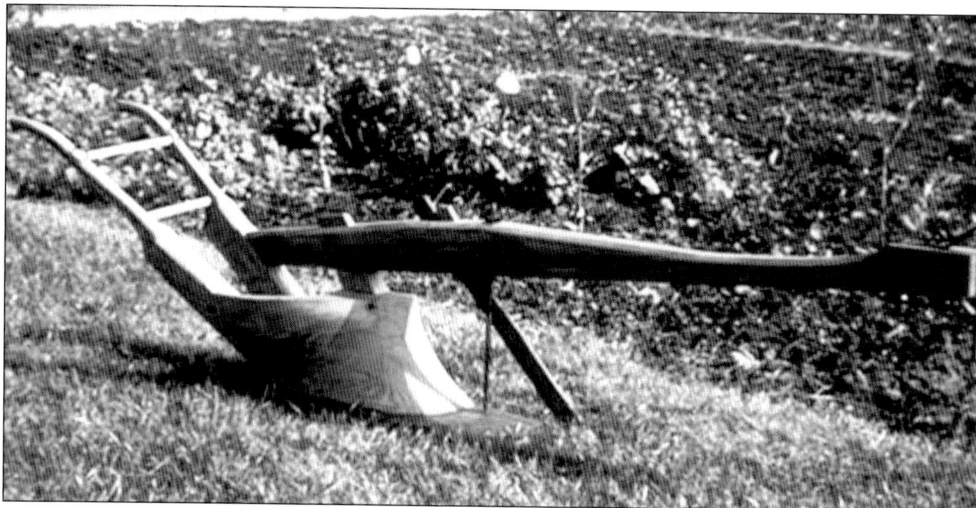

After observing them in Europe, Thomas Jefferson introduced the moldboard plow to the United States in 1788. Jefferson improved on the design he had seen abroad, but it wasn't until 1873, when John Deere added the steel plow shear, that they became so highly effective. Deere's plows were capable of turning the hard sod, and that made it possible for the early settlers to plant crops.

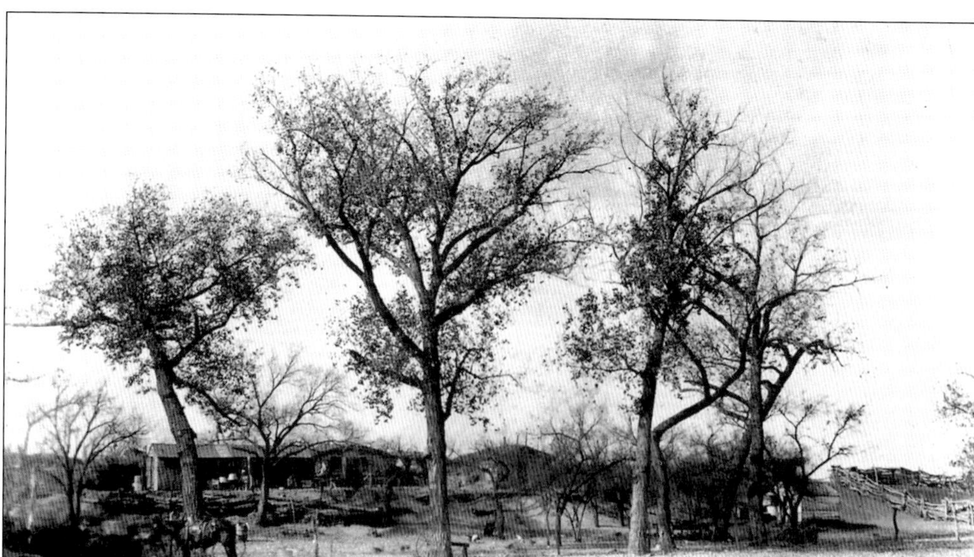

Shown in this photograph, taken some years after the run, is the claim of Orange Scott Cummins, near Winchester. The original dugout home is visible between two tall trees. Many people lived in such "soddies" for a few years following the run. Since this was a dry cycle, the fear of floods before something better could be built was not high. (Courtesy of Joy (Cameron) Sherman.)

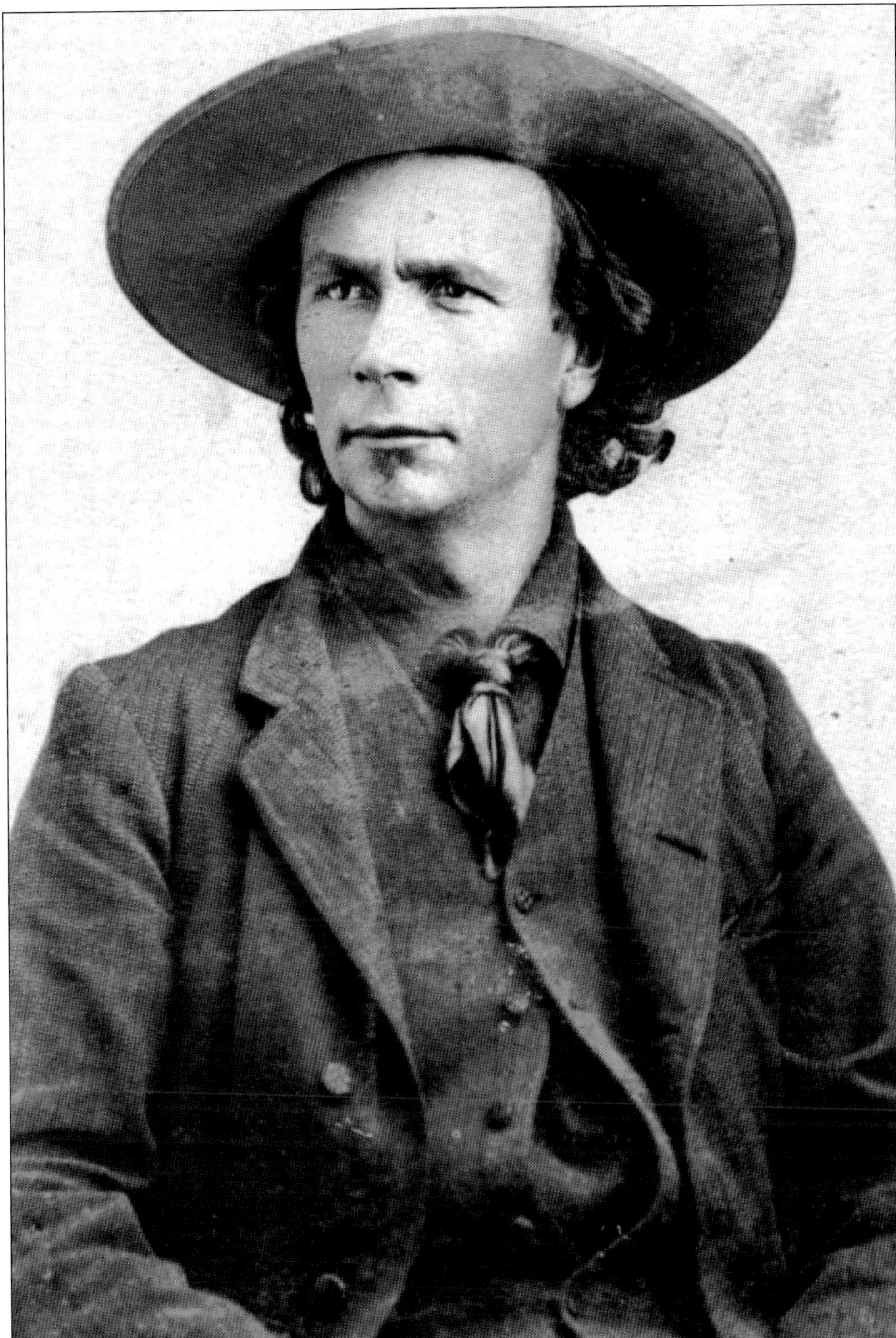

Orange Scott Cummins, also known as the Pilgrim Bard, wrote many poems (or musings, as he called them) about the early days in Oklahoma Territory. (Courtesy of Joy (Cameron) Sherman.)

My Dugout Home by Pilgrim Bard (Scott Cummins)

Surrounded by many a stately tree,
Where the whippoorwill sings in the twilight's gloam,
And the mocker warbles his notes of glee,
As a morning orison to me—
Here in my humble Dugout Home

No, it don't loom up so might grand,
Not like the Cathedral of ancient Rome;
Yet not a millionaire in the land,
With wealth and splendor on every hand,
Is prouder than I of my Dugout Home.

The earth my carpet, and earth o'erhead.
And earth each wall of the lowly dome;
The howling tempest is shorn of dread—
Calmly I sleep on my rustle bed,
When the door is closed in my Dugout Home.

From *Pilgrim Valley, O.T.*, October 6, 1894, "My Dugout Home" is indicative of the classic style and humility of Pilgrim Bard's poetry. (Courtesy of Joy (Cameron) Sherman.)

Wife says some day when we get the "stuff,"
When the "Ship" sails in through fortune's foam;
We'll build a dwelling that ain't so rough,
But then I'll bet that a cyclone puff
Would make us scoot for our Dugout Home.

We have sand in our craw and lots of pluck,
We have acres broke in the mellow loam;
In spite of the drouth we raised some truck—
And to tell the truth I'm powerfully stuck
On county "M" and my Dugout Home.

Stranger or friend if you pass this way,
"Round too" In welcome we bid you come;
Shelter or food by night or day—
Hungry and cold ye need not stray—
The latch string's out at my Dugout Home.

I have wandered about for many a day,
From youth a "pilgrim," my lot to roam
Now my stakes are set, I have come to stay—
When I "pass the Watches" my lifeless clay
Must find repose near my Dugout Home.

The last four stanzas of "My Dugout Home" are pictured above. (Courtesy of Joy (Cameron) Sherman.)

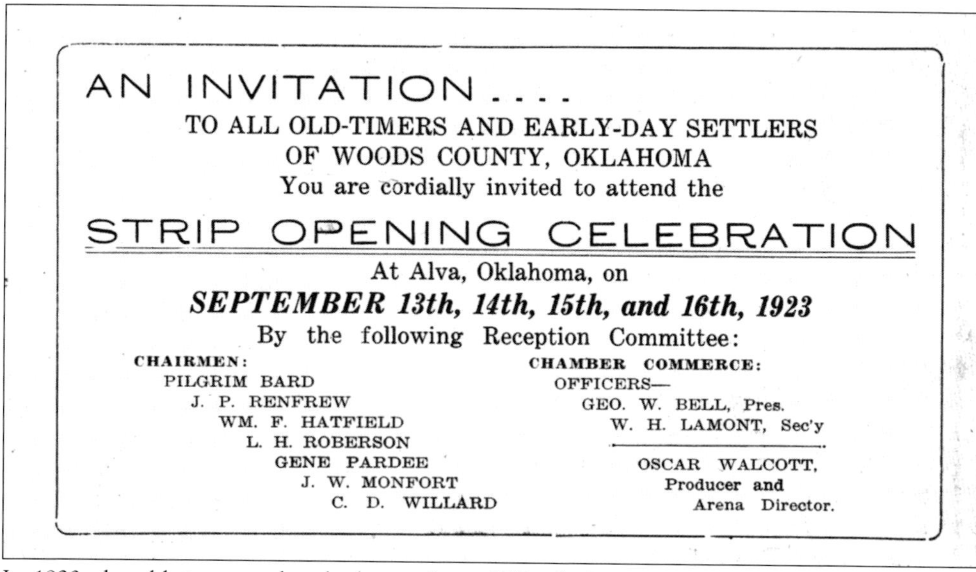

AN INVITATION . . . .

TO ALL OLD-TIMERS AND EARLY-DAY SETTLERS
OF WOODS COUNTY, OKLAHOMA
You are cordially invited to attend the

STRIP OPENING CELEBRATION

At Alva, Oklahoma, on

SEPTEMBER 13th, 14th, 15th, and 16th, 1923

By the following Reception Committee:

CHAIRMEN:
PILGRIM BARD
J. P. RENFREW
WM. F. HATFIELD
L. H. ROBERSON
GENE PARDEE
J. W. MONFORT
C. D. WILLARD

CHAMBER COMMERCE:
OFFICERS—
GEO. W. BELL, Pres.
W. H. LAMONT, Sec'y

OSCAR WALCOTT,
Producer and
Arena Director.

In 1923, the old-timers and early-day settlers of Woods County were celebrating the Cherokee Strip run. Notice the names of the committee: they were all early settlers of Alva and Woods County. (Courtesy of Joy (Cameron) Sherman.)

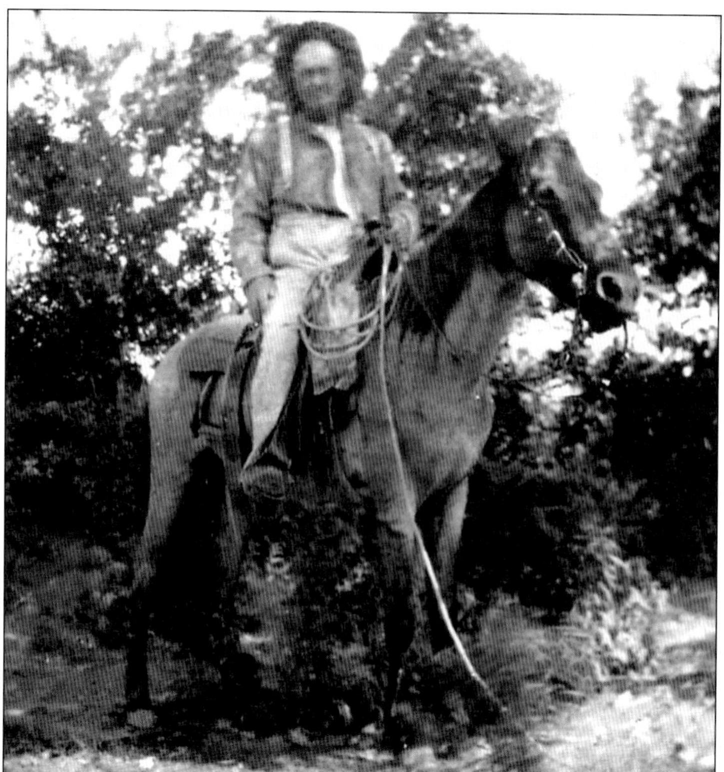

Scott Cummins was photographed near his claim in northwestern "M" (Woods) County. (Courtesy of Joy (Cameron) Sherman.)

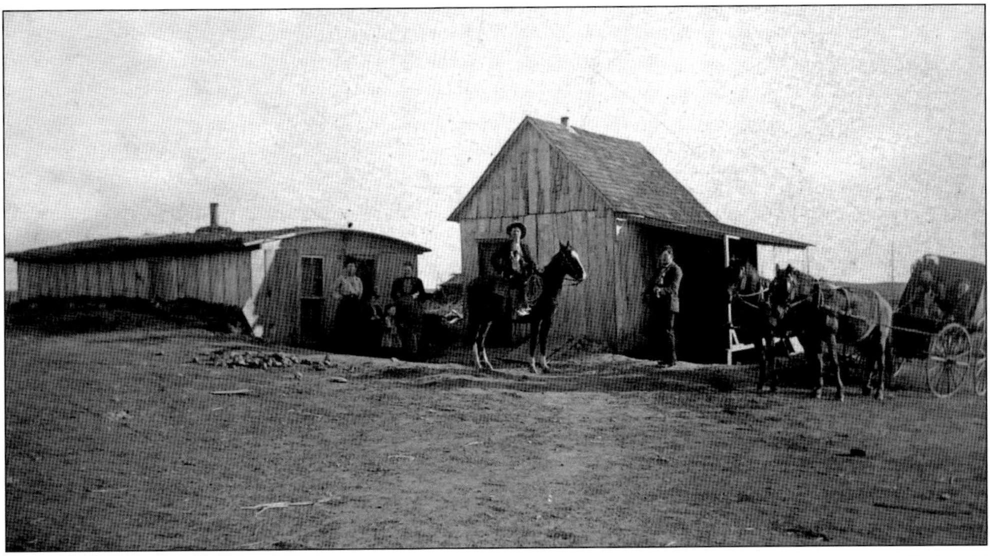

In the 1890s, a traveling photographer took this image northeast of Waynoka. It shows a dugout and a timber shed beside it. The upper half of the walls and the roof were of wood. Good windows and doors were used. (Courtesy of the Alva Cherokee Strip Museum.)

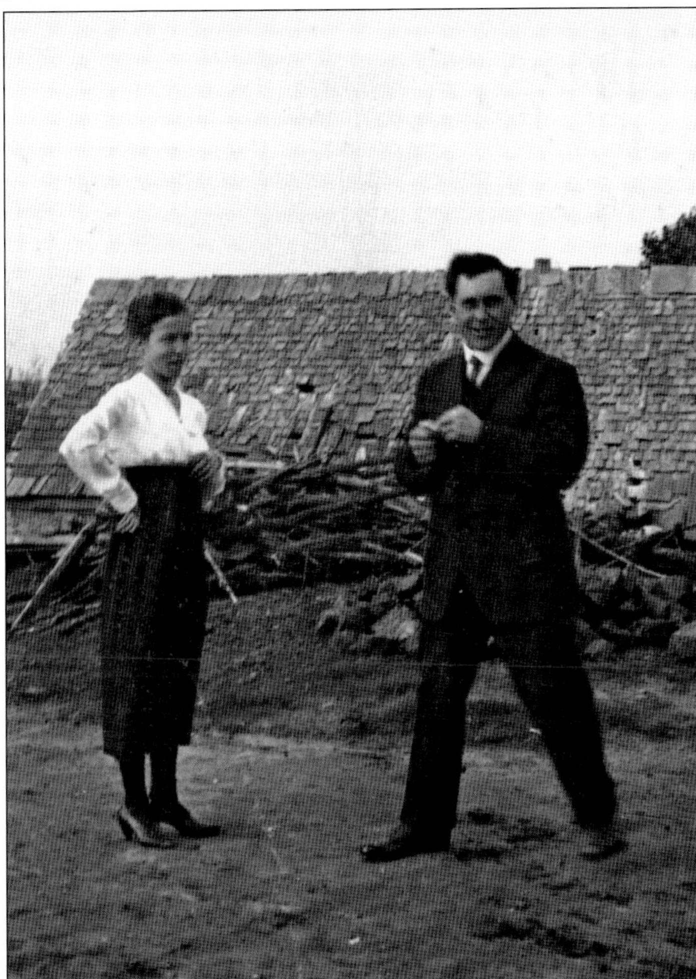

This image is of Guy and Audrey (Bainum) Kinzie in 1918. The Bainums built this dugout in the early 1890s and lived there for many years with their seven children. For roofs, soddies had cottonwood poles and brush covered with sod or dirt.

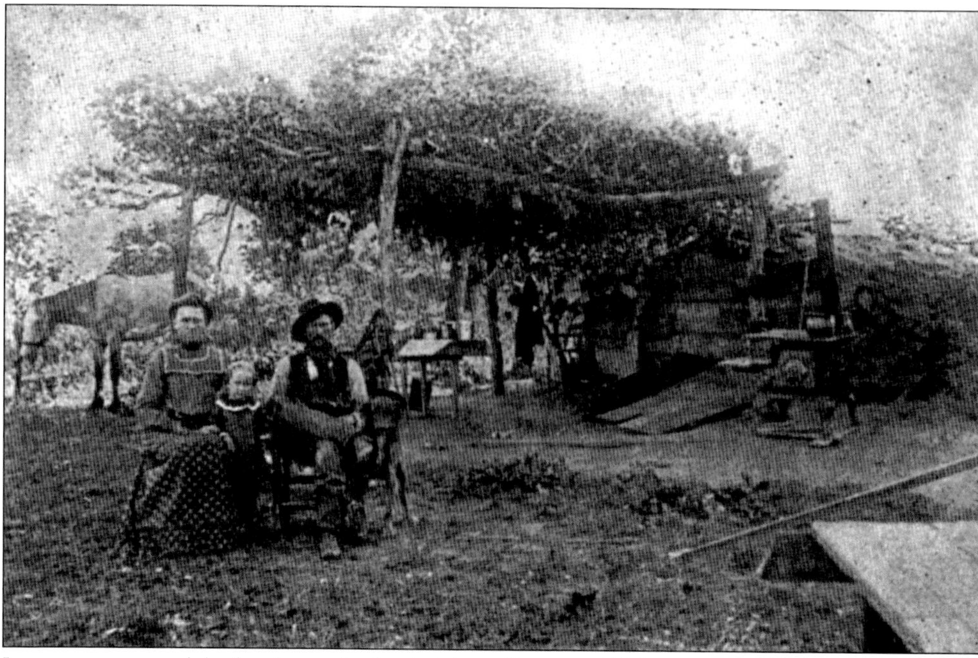

It was not unusual for lumber to be hauled from Kansas. Old houses would be bought and torn down and the wood brought to Cherokee Outlet for house construction.

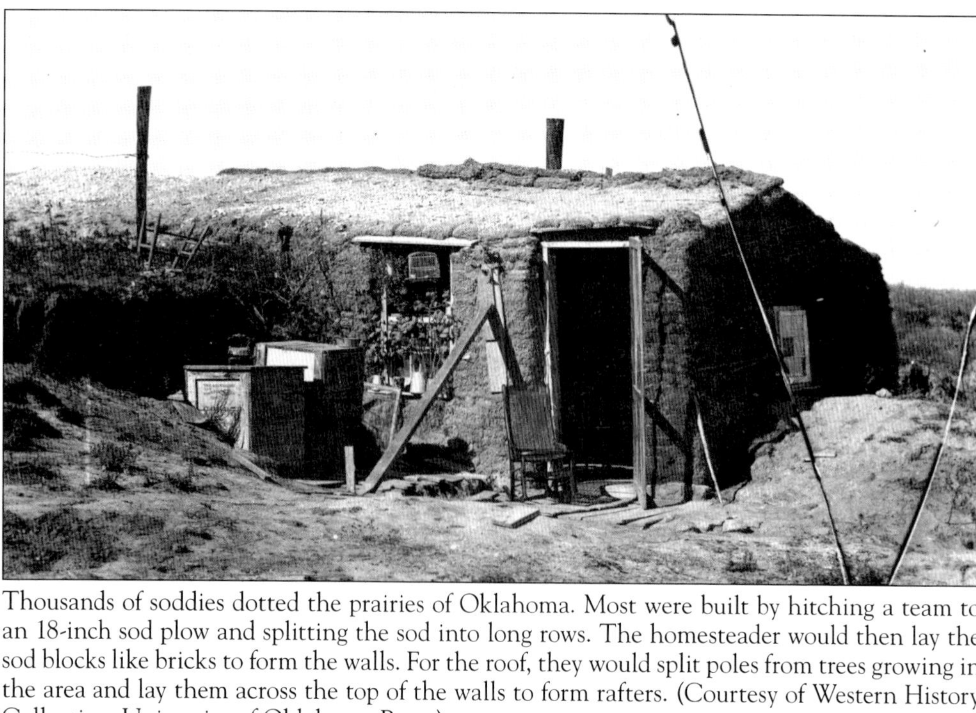

Thousands of soddies dotted the prairies of Oklahoma. Most were built by hitching a team to an 18-inch sod plow and splitting the sod into long rows. The homesteader would then lay the sod blocks like bricks to form the walls. For the roof, they would split poles from trees growing in the area and lay them across the top of the walls to form rafters. (Courtesy of Western History Collection, University of Oklahoma Press.)

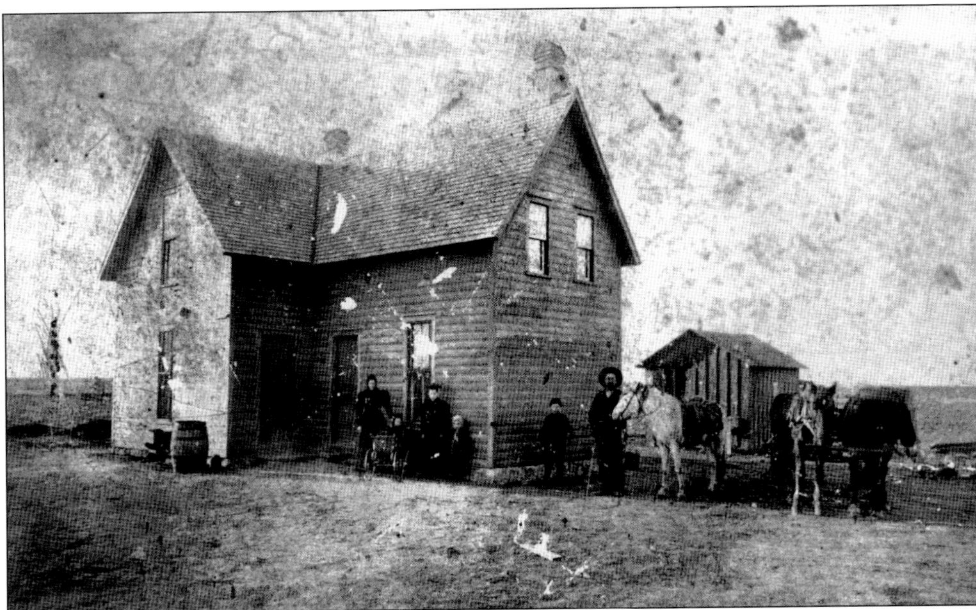

The following is an excerpt from the diary of Mable (Dyer) Cameron: "My family lived nine miles north of Hardener, Kansas. [On the] day of the 'Run,' Mother and the children came to the Kansas state line and had a picnic dinner with father and other relatives who were making the race. My father (Tom Dyer) made the run on his cow pony staking a claim 10 miles north of Alva." (Courtesy of Joy (Cameron) Sherman.)

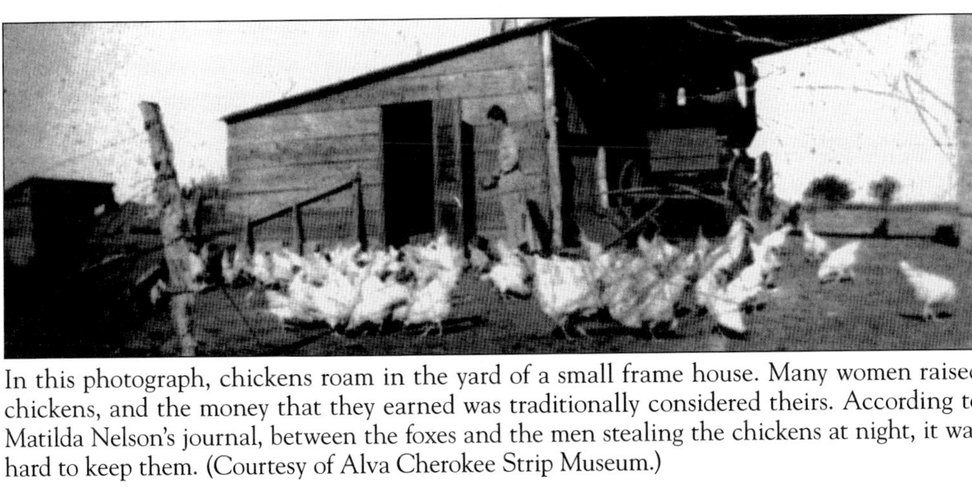

In this photograph, chickens roam in the yard of a small frame house. Many women raised chickens, and the money that they earned was traditionally considered theirs. According to Matilda Nelson's journal, between the foxes and the men stealing the chickens at night, it was hard to keep them. (Courtesy of Alva Cherokee Strip Museum.)

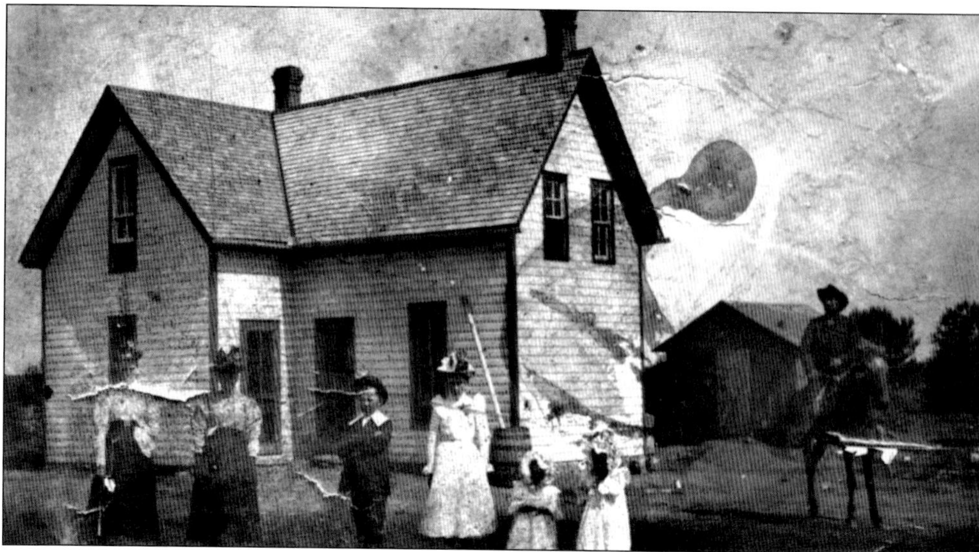

The following is an excerpt from Mable Cameron's diary: "After the 'Run' Mother returned home, spent [the] night preparing food, filling water jugs. [We] set out in covered wagon loaded with food. Drove along through [a] cloud of dust that still blanketed [the] prairie, located father and his friends . . . they were sitting on their claims afraid to move lest someone should jump them. Delighted to see the food and water, [as they] had not eaten since the day before." (Courtesy of Joy (Cameron) Sherman.)

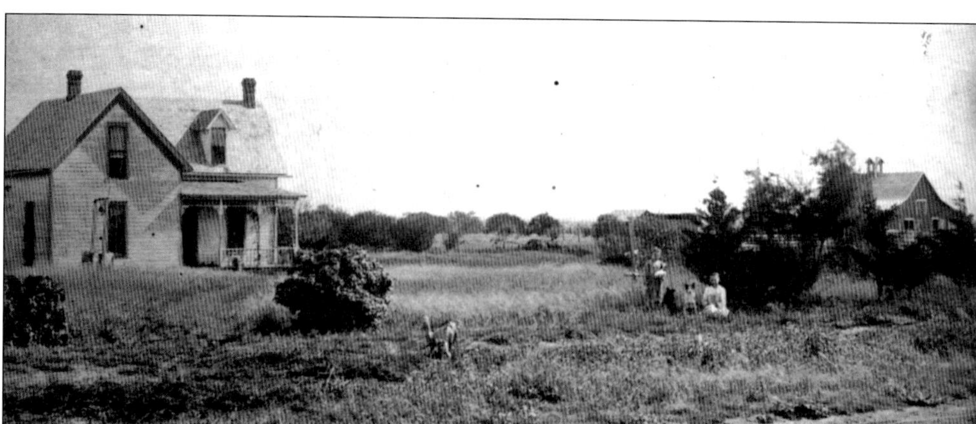

This photograph of the Tom Dyer Farm, 10 miles north of Alva, was taken before Rural Free Delivery was established by the US postal service. Included in the scene are Byrdic (sitting) and Mabel (standing, with a doll) and the dogs Snippy and Topsy. The doll now sits in a place of honor at the home of Joy Sherman. (Courtesy of Joy (Cameron) Sherman.)

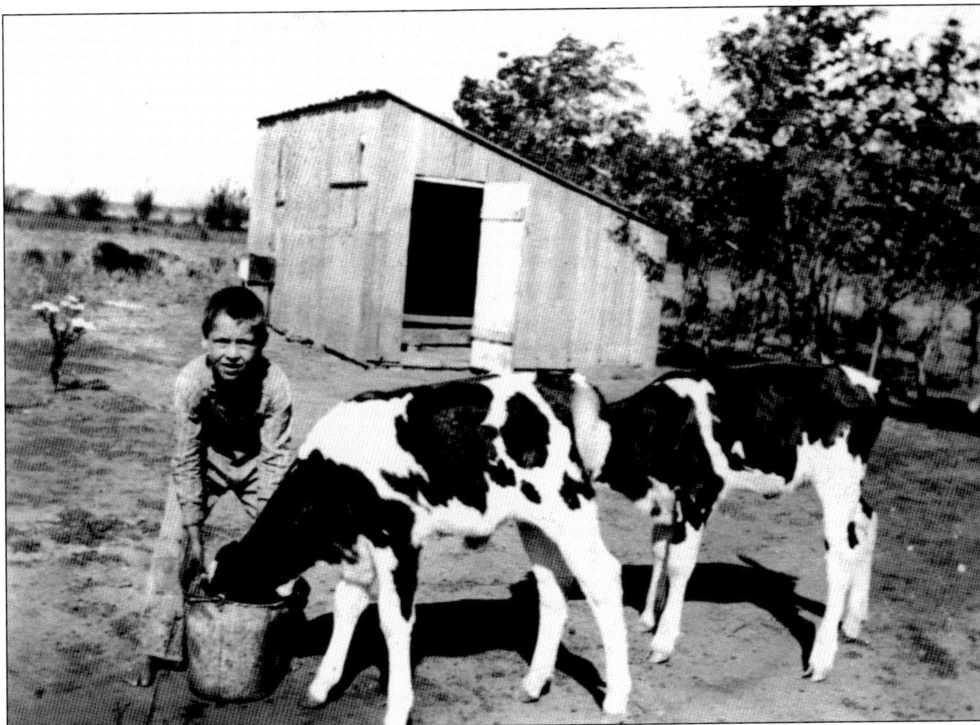

A young boy feeds the new calves on the homestead in this photograph from around 1900. Everyone helped with the work, as this was the only way that a family could survive.

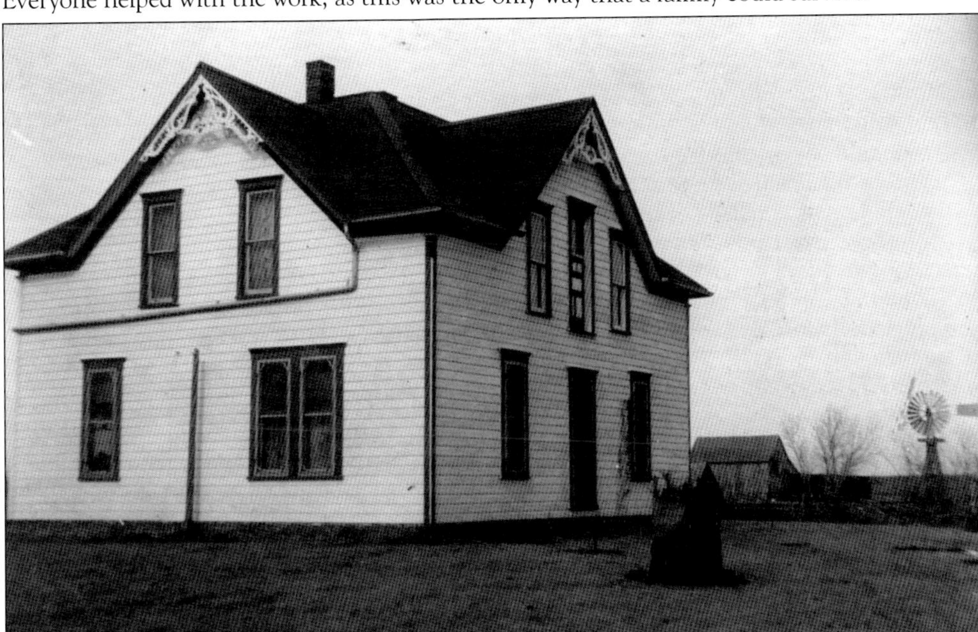

The roof peaks of this farmhouse, built about 1903, are adorned with gingerbread embellishments. The original plan was to build a second-story porch, which explains the door upstairs. After years of living in a dugout, C.E. Bainum worked on his homestead and in Avard in order to make enough money to build his family a 10-room home.

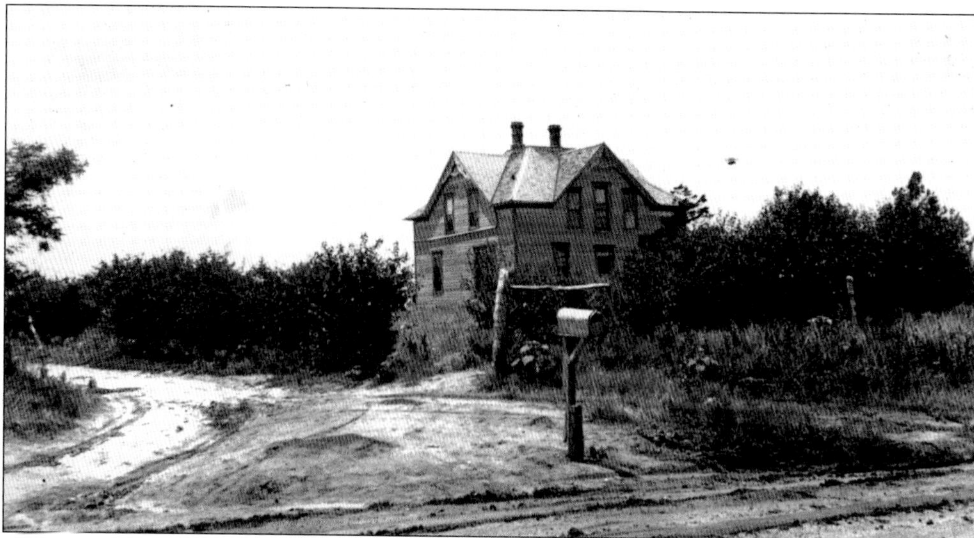

This photograph shows the Bainum home. After the dustbowl and Depression, C.E. and Jennie moved to Wichita to live close to members of their family.

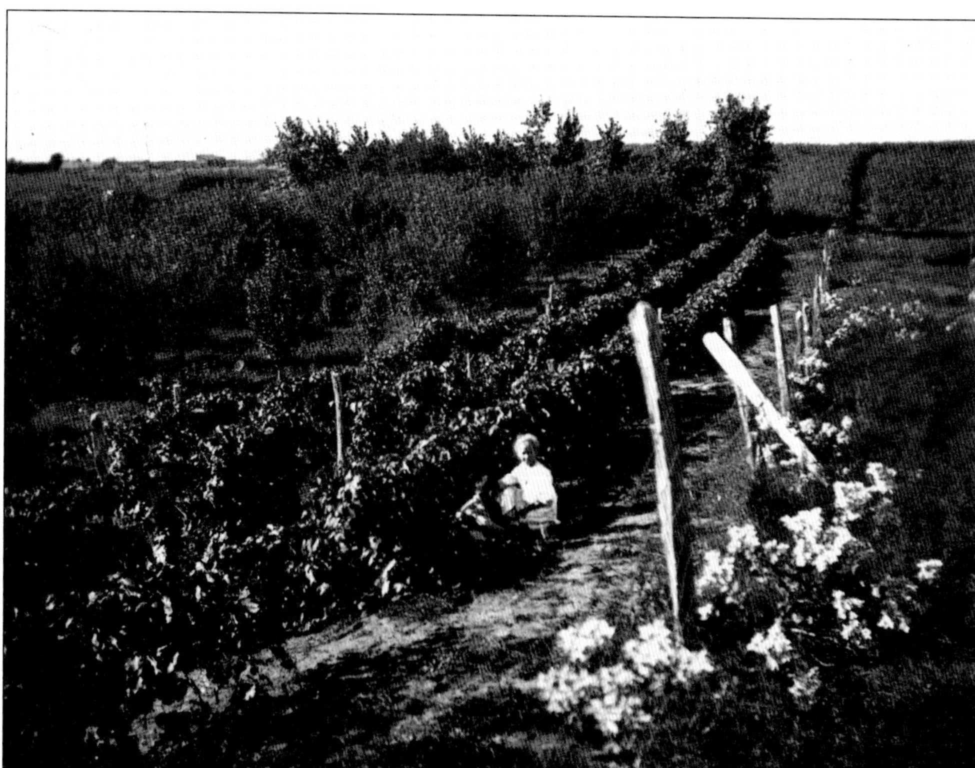

The spring of 1894 found the homesteaders busy planting gardens; they found it more difficult in newly plowed ground. Fruit trees and grapes were also set out whenever possible. Cash crops such as corn, cain, or wheat were sown by hand.

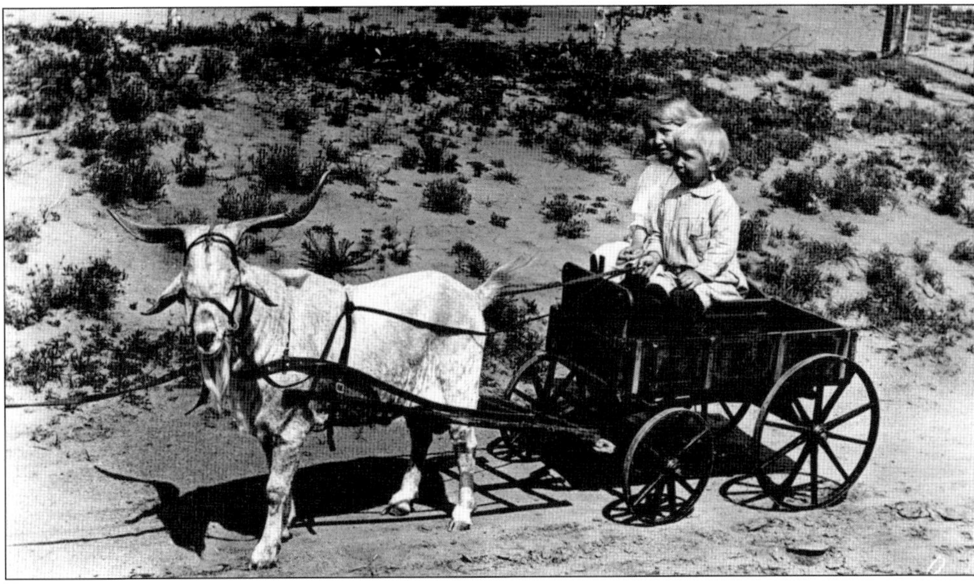

During the early years, children played with whatever was handy. These young girls were fortunate to have a billy goat and a wagon to ride in while their parents worked.

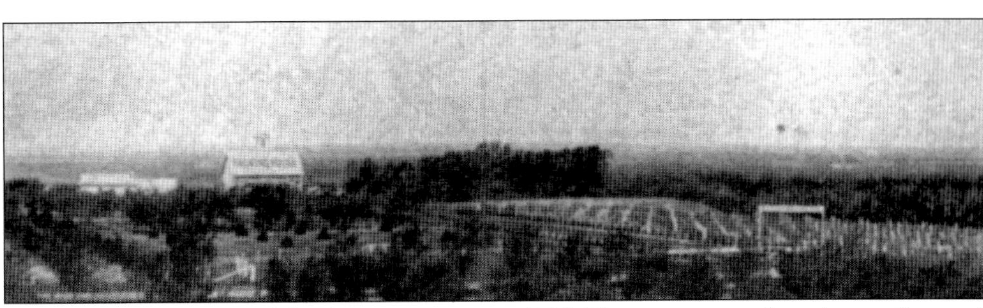

This is a bird's-eye view of the Orton nurseries in 1906. The image was taken three miles north of Burlington, Oklahoma.

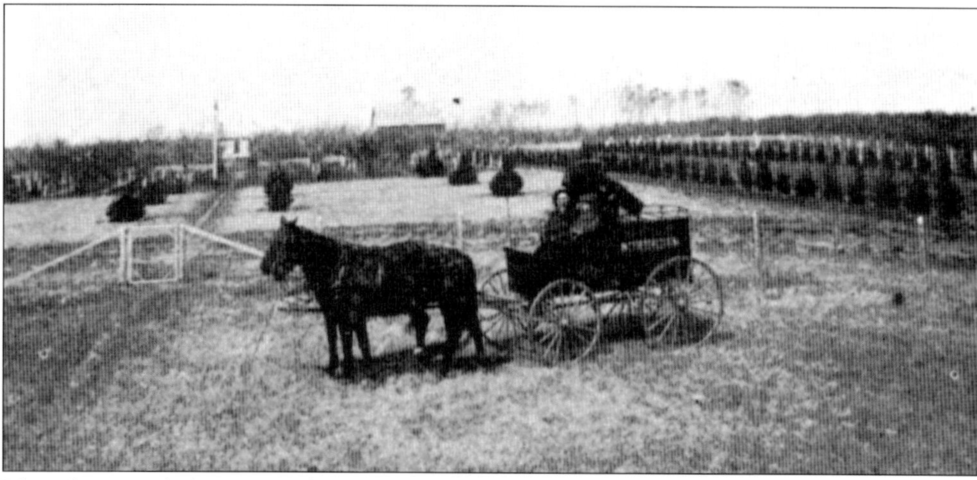

This photograph from 1906 shows the Frank Orton family in a buggy, with their home in the background. They owned and operated the Orton nurseries, a source for the pioneer families to obtain trees and plants for their homesteads.

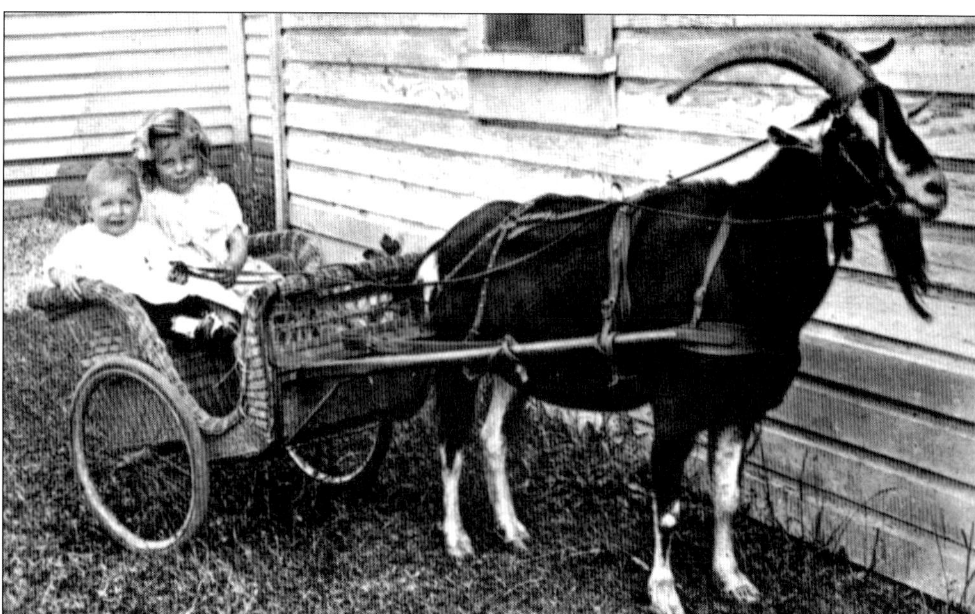

This wicker wagon was pulled by a large billy goat, a good way to cart the little ones around the homestead.

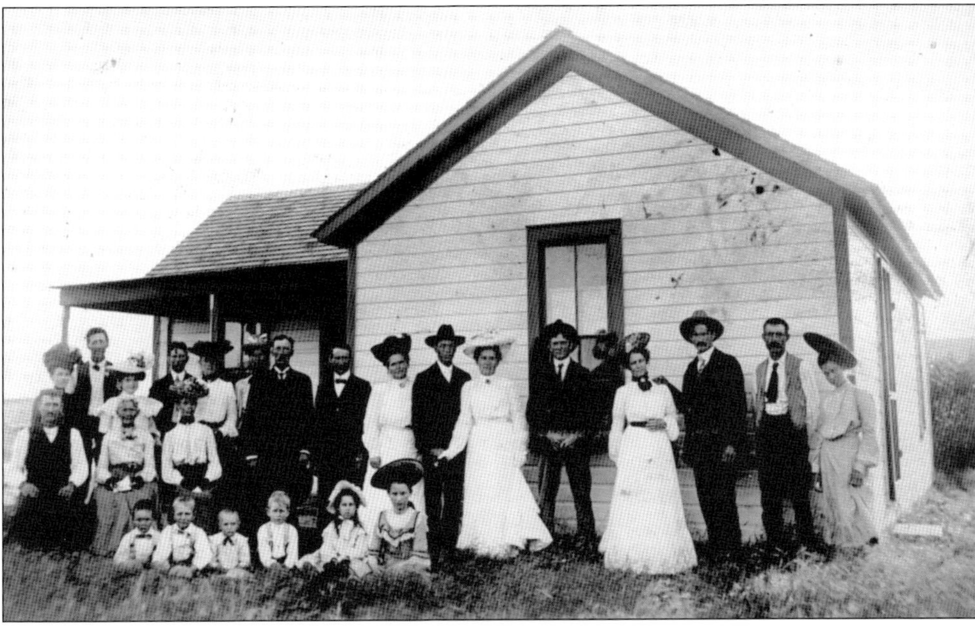

At this early-day country wedding, the bride and groom were photographed holding hands. The wedding took place southeast of Alva in the Avard area, sometime around 1900. The bride is Miss Lewis and the groom is John Bentz. The minister was C.E. Bainum, the father of Audrey (Bainum) Kinzie.

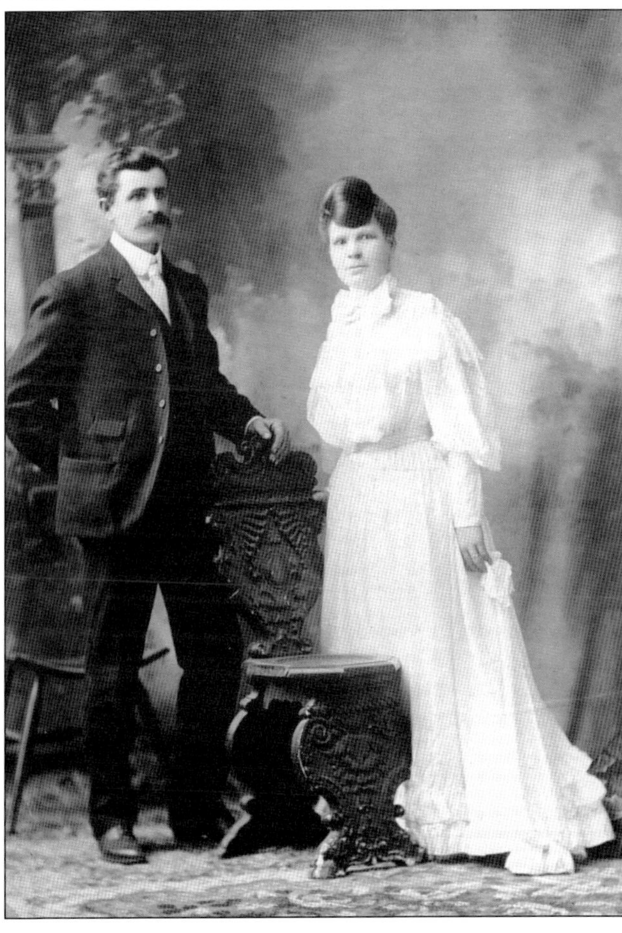

Clarence and Dora Cline farmed northwest of Alva on Turkey Creek, but they lived in Alva when not farming or threshing wheat. Clarence Cline was also an early-day Alva businessman.

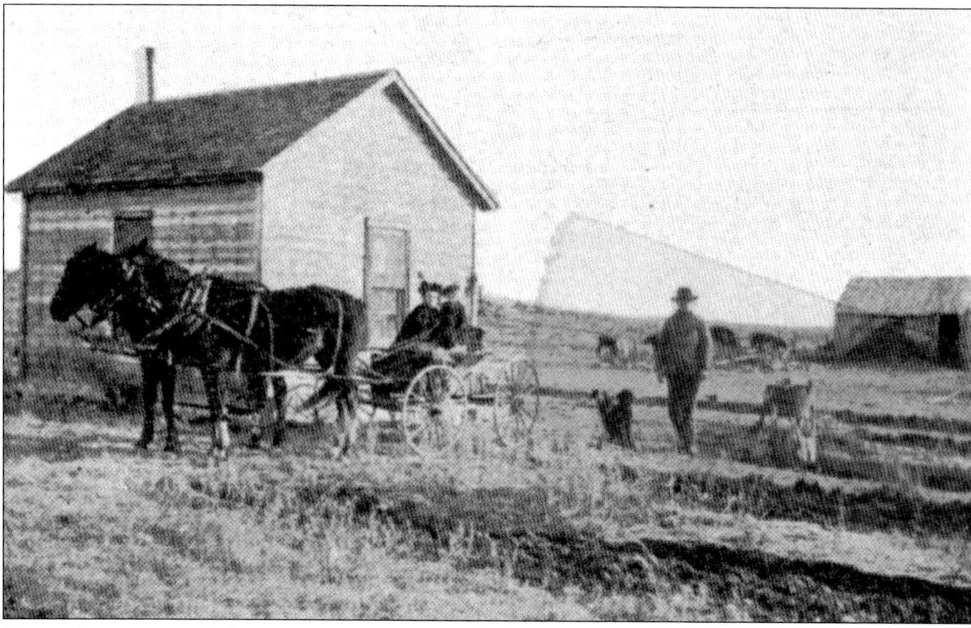

Shown here is an early homestead with a small house and outbuildings. The family was fortunate to have horses and a small buggy to take to town. (Courtesy of the Alva Cherokee Strip Museum.)

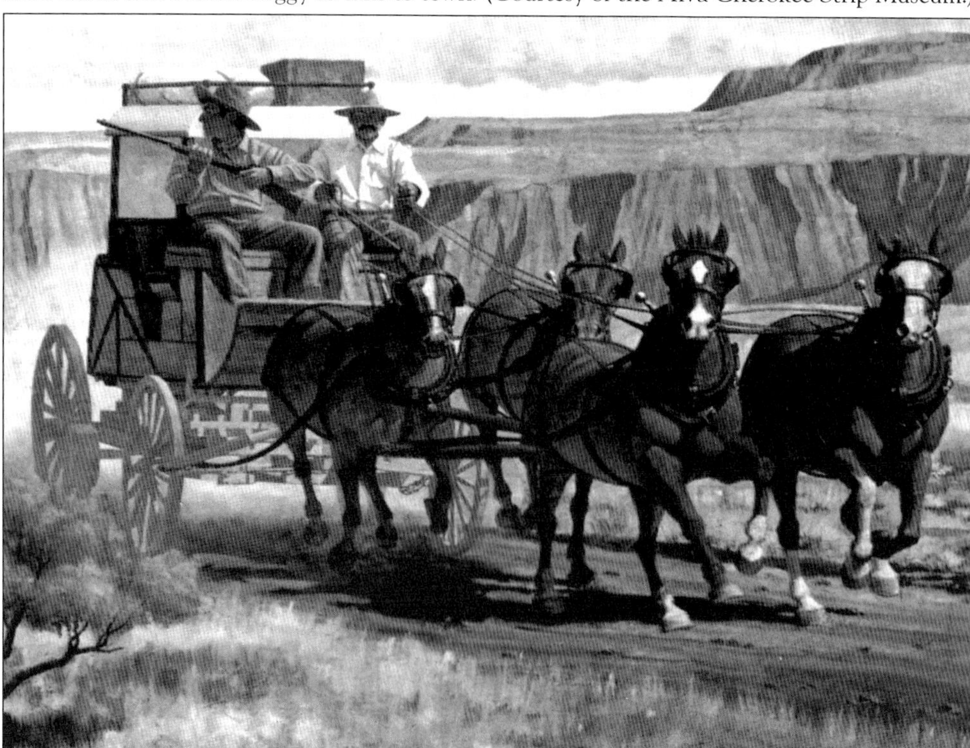

Between 1885 and 1890, a stagecoach traveled six days a week carrying supplies and mail between Kiowa, Kansas and Camp Supply, Oklahoma. It made stops at small stations along the way. This mural, located on the square in Alva, depicts the stagecoach. (Courtesy of the Alva Mural Society.)

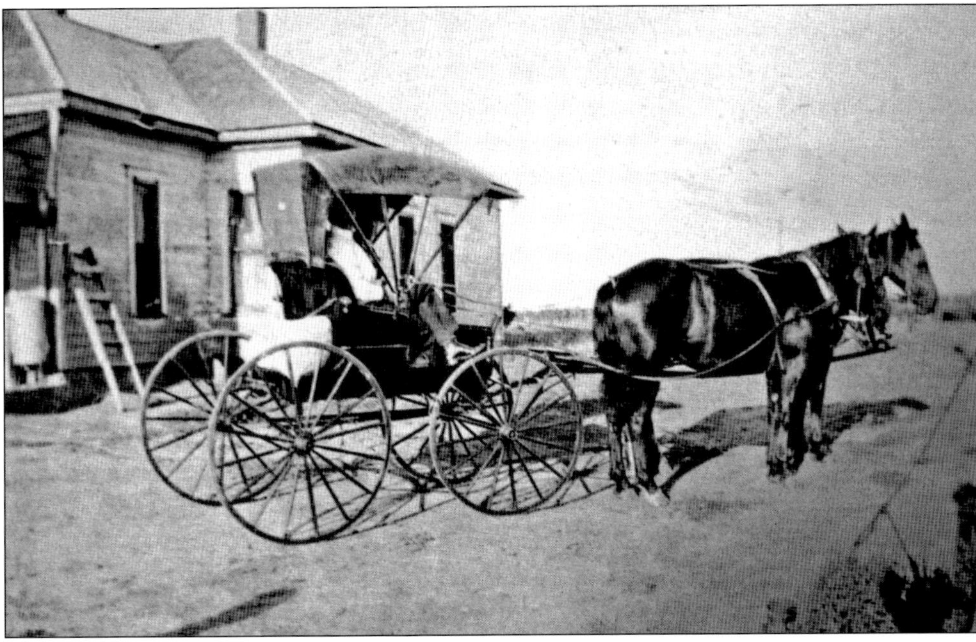

This photograph shows a type of horse and buggy that the pioneers used. (Courtesy of the Alva Cherokee Strip Museum.)

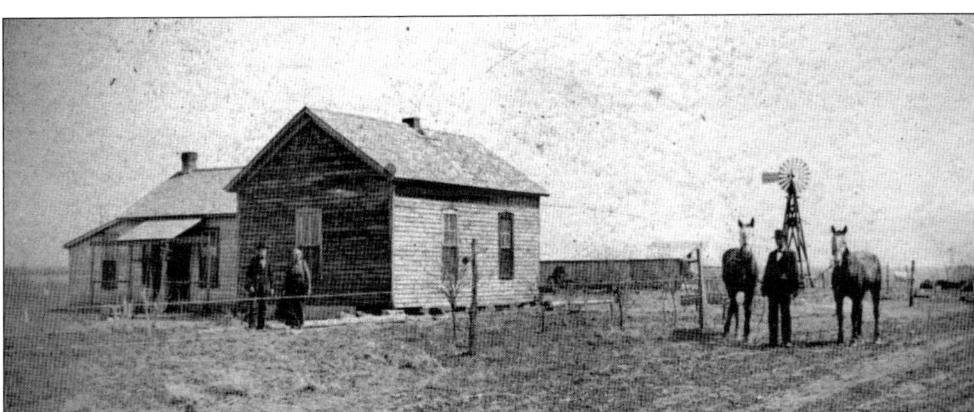

Charlie Nelson was photographed standing with horses next to John Nelson's farmhouse, four and a half miles north of Capron. John Nelson is standing in his yard with his wife, Elina. (Courtesy of Joy (Cameron) Sherman.)

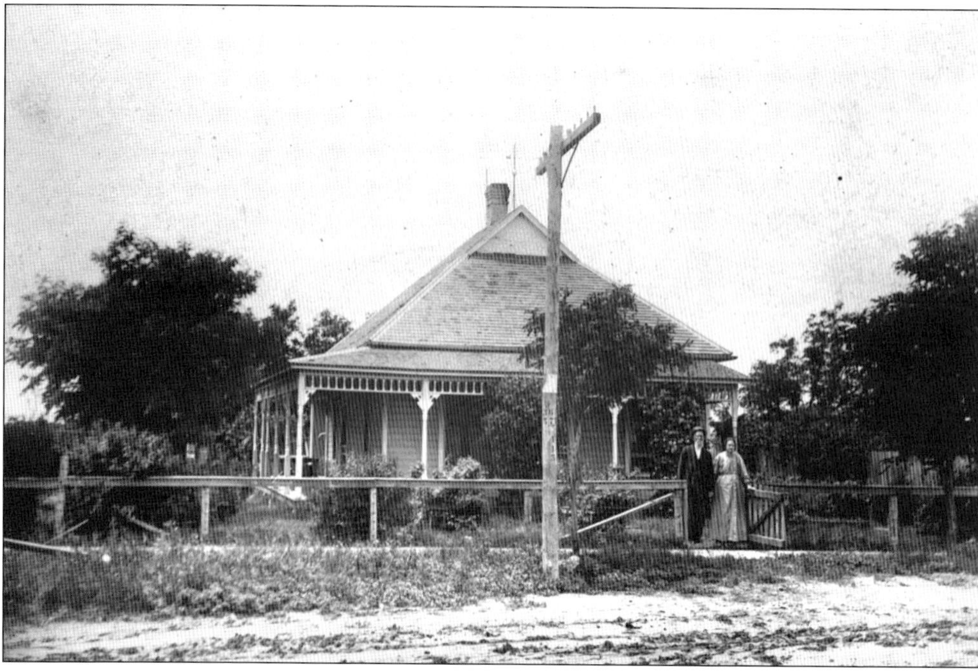

John and Elina Nelson were photographed at home before the Capron tornado of 1939. (Courtesy of Joy (Cameron) Sherman.)

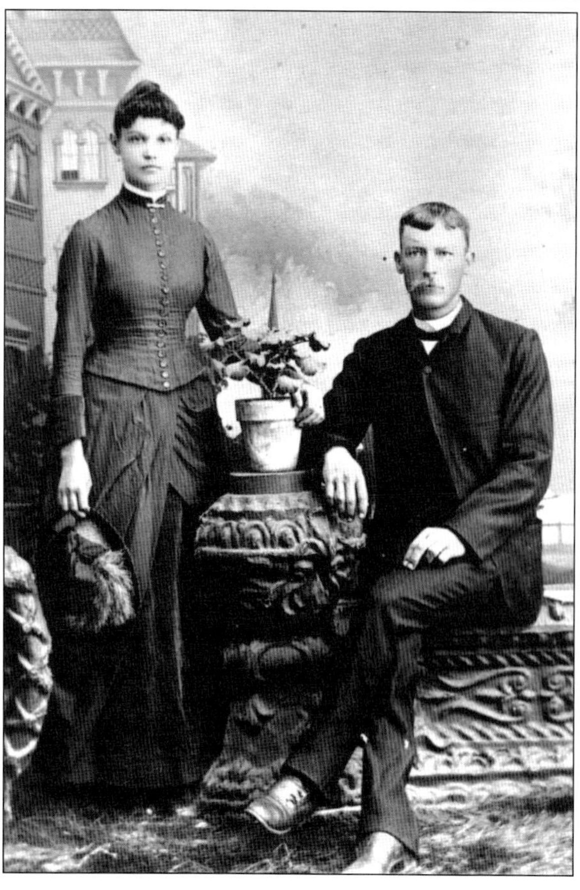

C.E. and Jennie Bainum were married on March 1, 1887, in Kingman, Kansas. Before the run of 1893, C.E. came to the Avard area to work. He later set up a homestead northeast of Avard, where he stayed until the 1930s.

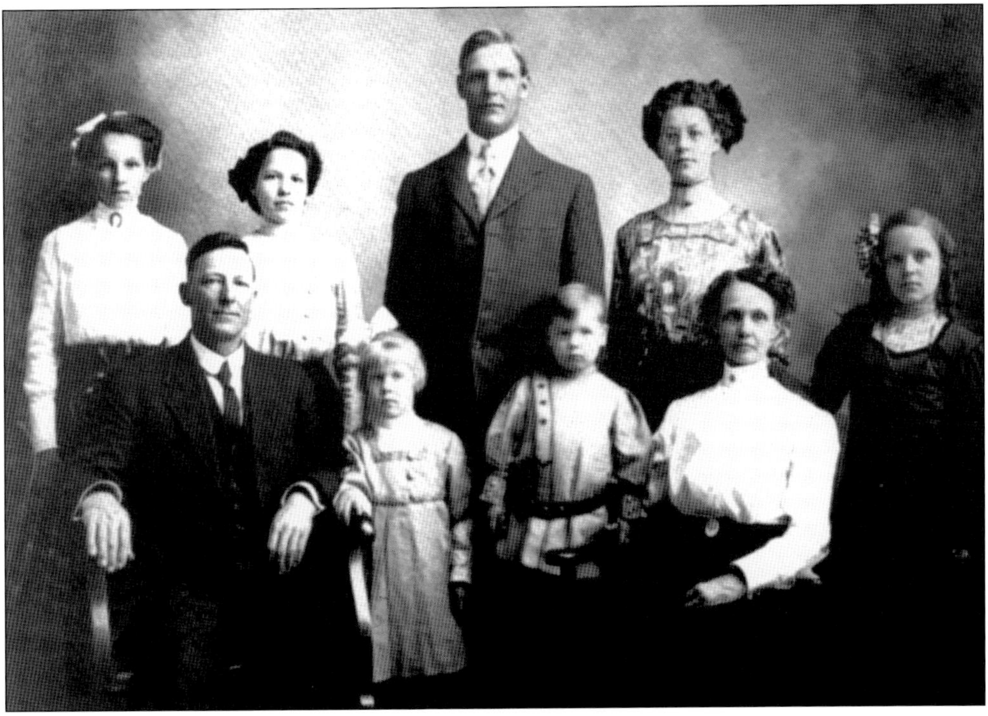

The Bainum family is shown here. From left to right, they are (first row) C.E., Thelma, Evan, Jennie, and Lorena; (second row) Lera, Audrey, Vesper, and Zaida.

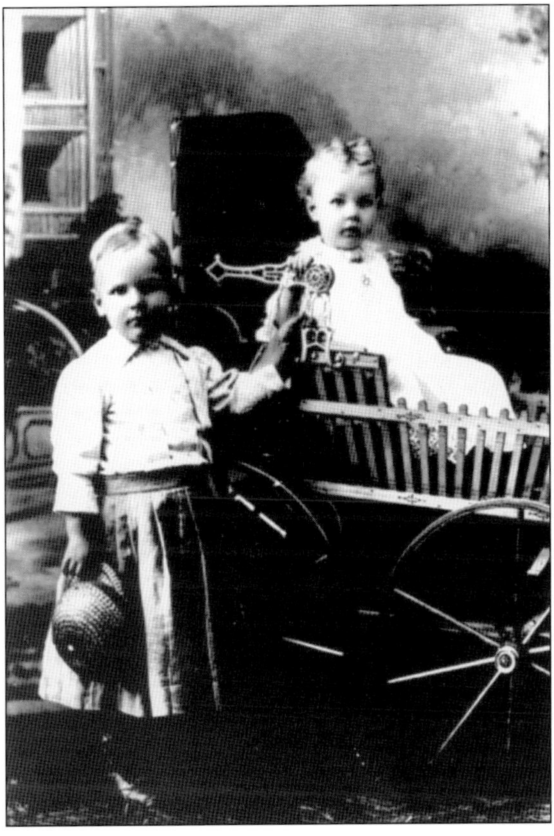

It was a very special occasion when children were taken to a photographer in town. In this c. 1893 portrait, the boy standing is Vesper Bainum, born in 1888, and the baby is Zaida Bainum, born in 1892.

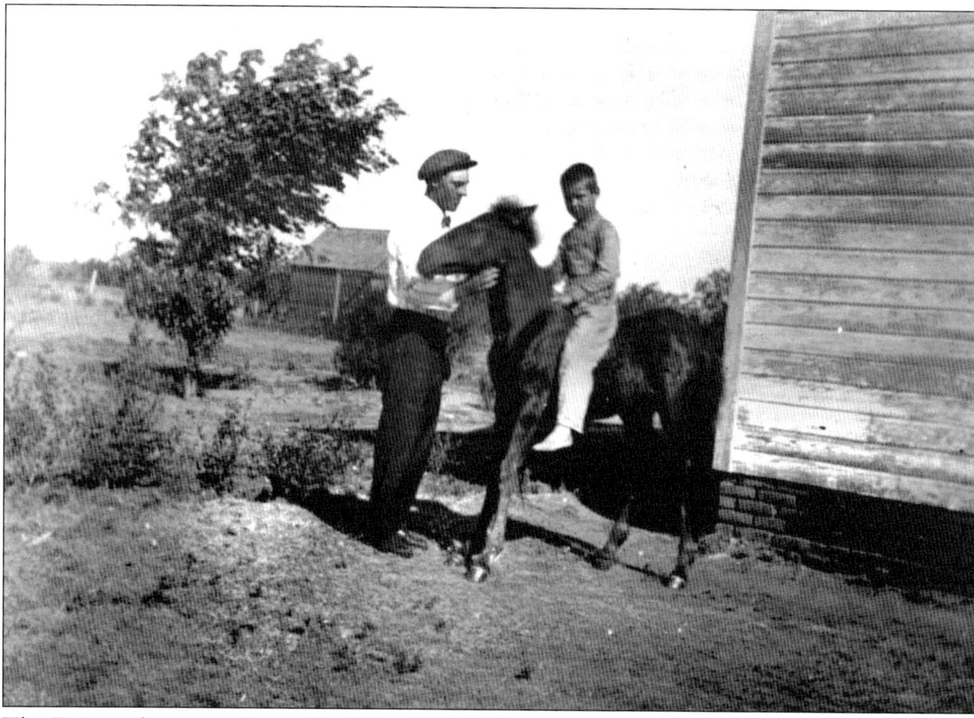

The Bainum homestead outside of Avard was the site of this photograph. The boy on the pony is Evan Bainum.

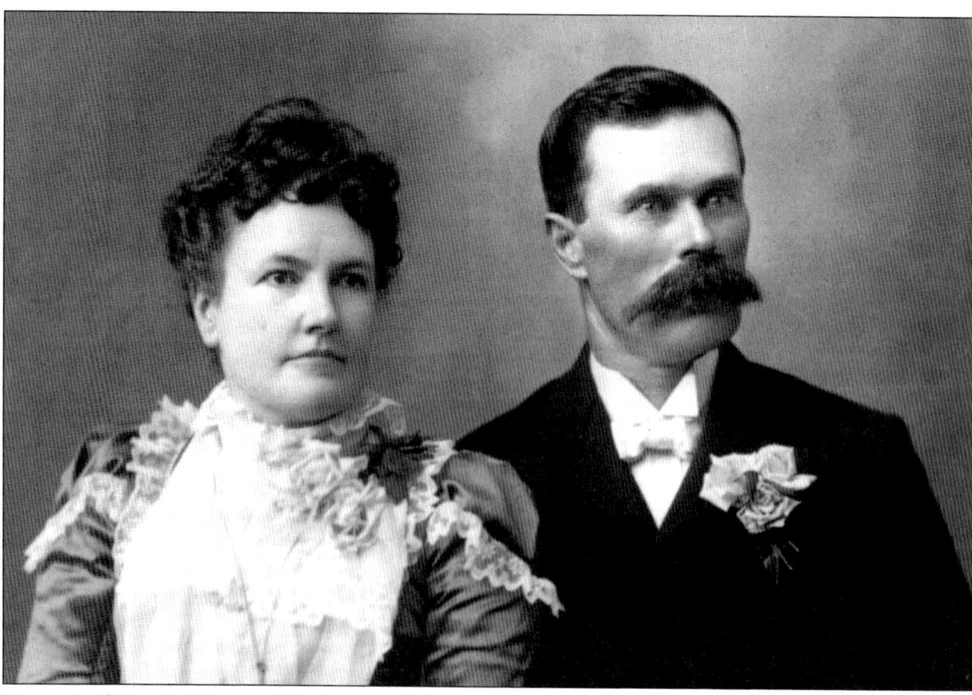

Linten and Mattie (Warren) Little were the great-grandparents of Warren Little. Prior to statehood, Linten founded the Little Ranch northwest of Alva in "M" (Woods) County. The original Little Ranch was two miles by three miles. (Courtesy of Warren Little.)

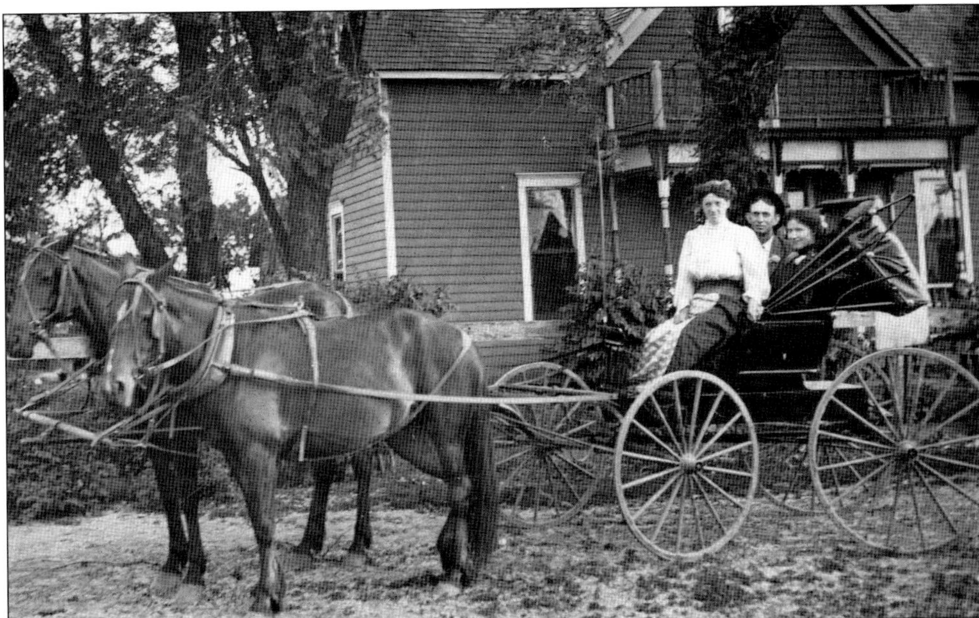

The Little family lived in Iowa before coming to the Oklahoma Territory around 1900. Linten Little built and ran an electric power plant in Iowa that he sold to fund the Little Ranch. He also had Studebaker wagon liveries in Laverne and Alva. Located in the same general area along Yellow Stone Creek were the Little Post Office, the Little School, and the Little General Store. (Courtesy of Warren Little.)

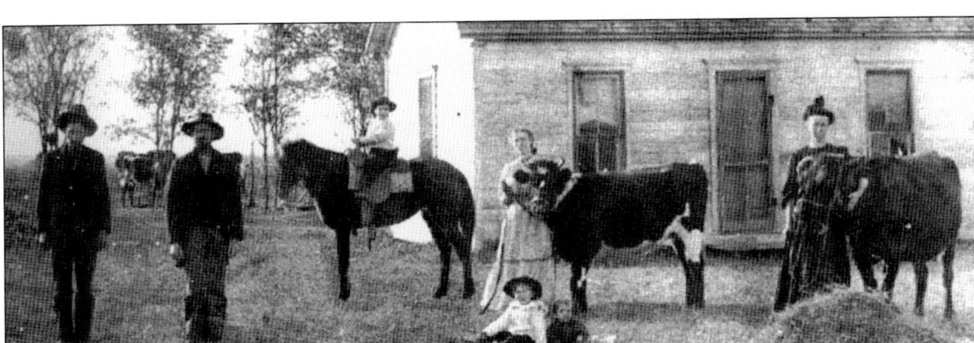

This photograph of a family gathered with their prize animals outside of Alva was taken by a traveling photographer.

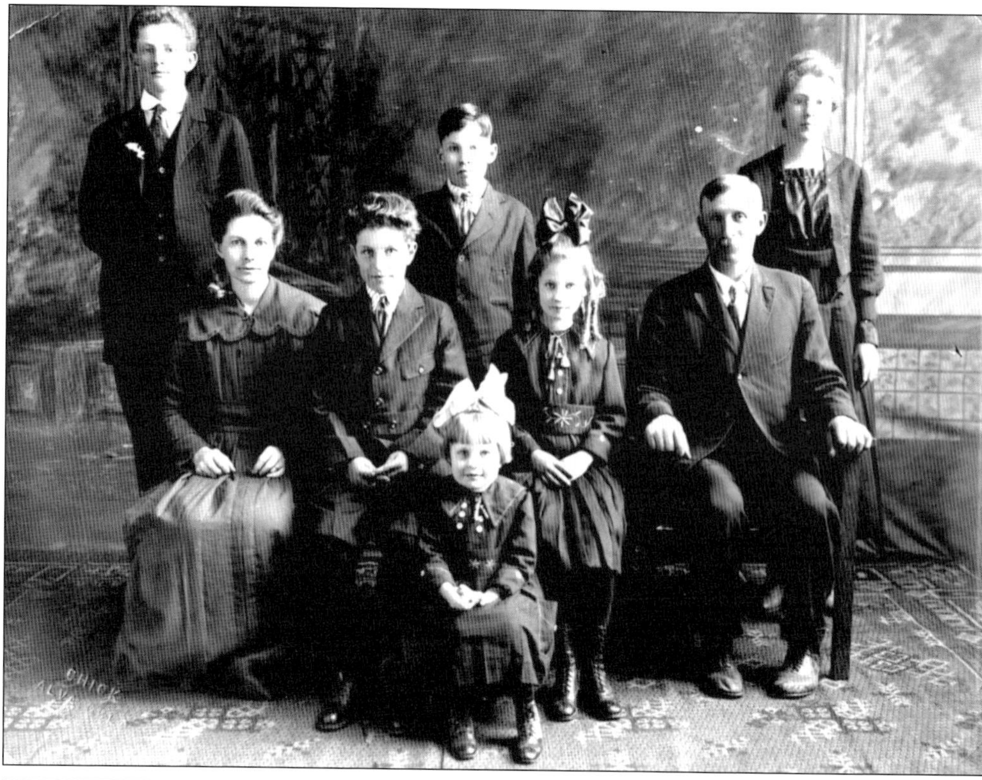

The family of Johannas and Matilda Nelson (the name was changed from Nielson when the family arrived in the United States from Denmark) is shown in this image. From left to right are (first row) Gladys; (second row) Matilda, Anthon, Mary, and Johannas; (third row) Nels, Tom, and Dorthea. (Courtesy of Lorraine (Nelson) Malzahn.)

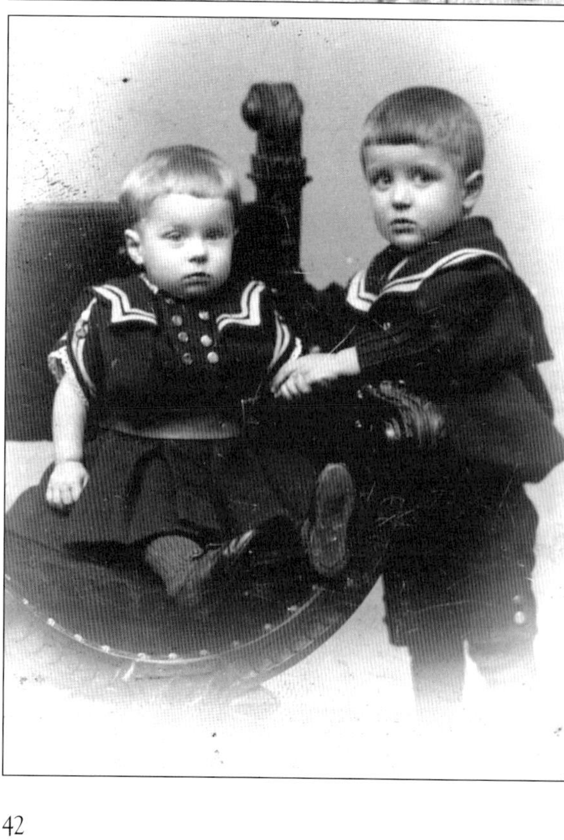

Chris (standing) and Willie Nielson were born in Denmark and settled in the United States with their parents. The family lived in a dugout on their homestead, 35 miles west-northwest of Alva. At ages nine and ten, Chris (born in 1896) and Willie (born in 1897) went after the cows and were swept away and drowned by the swift currents of a rain-swollen creek. (Courtesy of Lorraine (Nelson) Malzahn.)

Peter and Anna Marie Pederson, great-grandparents of Lorraine (Nelson) Malzahn, lived in Thisted, Denmark. Johannas ("John") and Matilda, accompanied by their three children, set sail for the United States and didn't see their parents again until years later when part of the family went to Denmark for a visit. If was not uncommon for immigrants to see their relatives for the last time when boarding ships bound for America. (Courtesy of Lorraine (Nelson) Malzahn.)

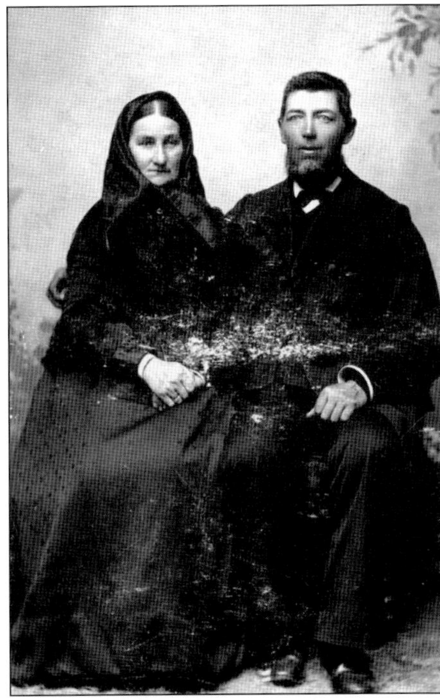

Chris (front row, right) and Martine (front row, left) Jenson and family are posed in this formal photograph. Martine was John Nelson's sister. In 1901, the Jensons sent $203.50 to Martine's brother so that he, Matilda, Chris, Willie, and baby Dorothea could immigrate. Even though the Jenson homestead was in the Manchester area, they are included in this history because all of the Nelson descendents who have lived in this county stem from the Jensons' original financial assistance. (Courtesy of Lorraine (Nelson) Malzahn.)

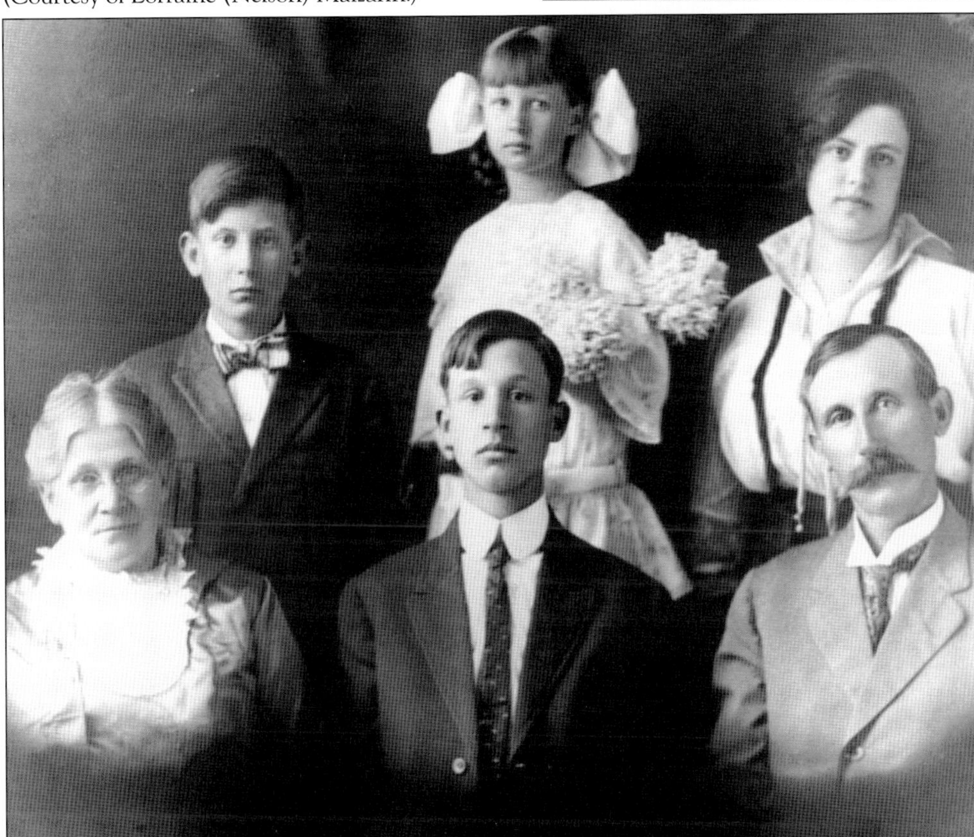

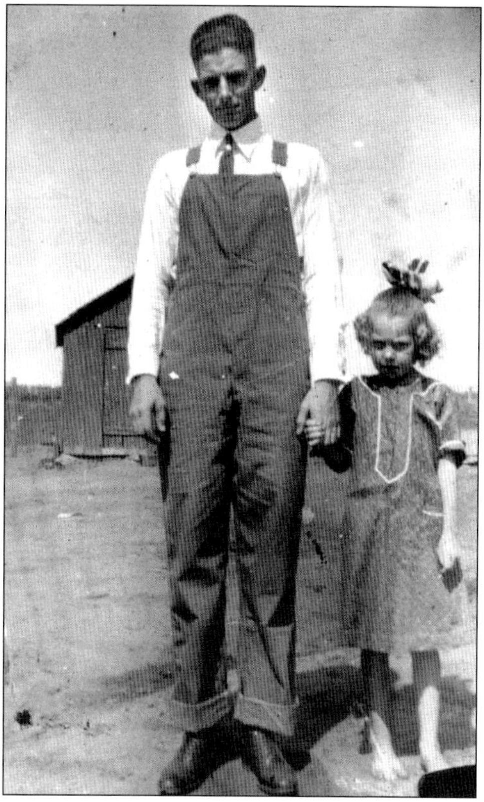

Nels Nelson and Gladys (Nelson) Bennett on their homestead northwest of Alva. Nels Nelson was a farmer, schoolteacher, and deputy sheriff in Woods County all of his life. (Courtesy of Lorraine (Nelson) Malzahn.)

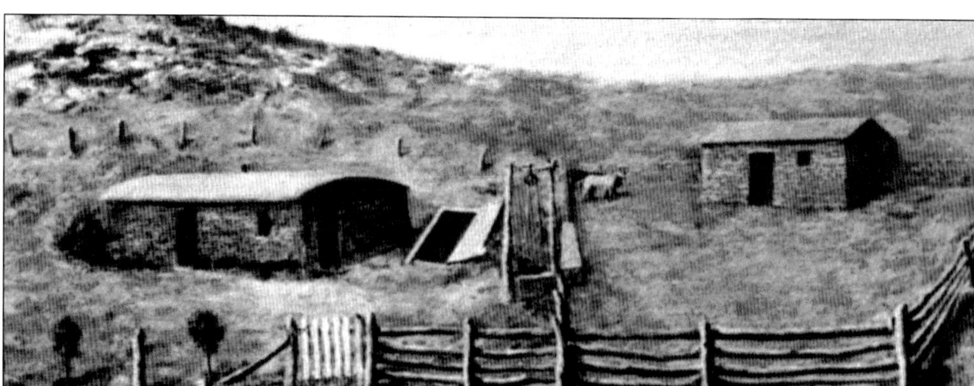

Matilda Nelson, in writing her history, told how cottonwood trees were used as flooring in the soddie. Plaster on the walls and a shingle roof replaced dirt and sod. After time, the cottonwood floor began to warp, allowing bugs and snakes to get into the house. Matilda became tired of the invasion and the wood floor was ripped out, leaving the Nelsons to once again live on a dirt floor.

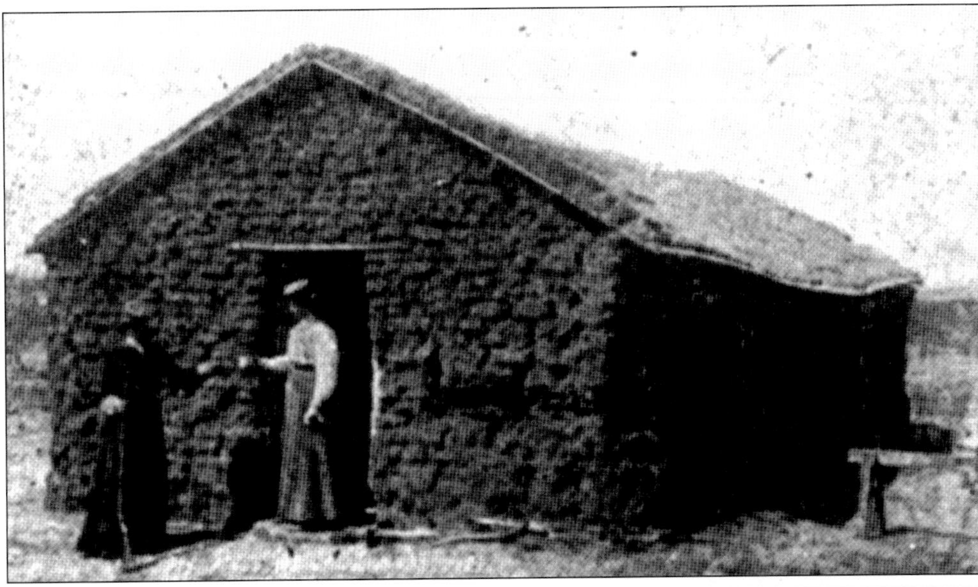

At this soddie on the prairie, ladies gather to visit, sew, and exchange gossip. (Courtesy of the Oklahoma Historical Society.)

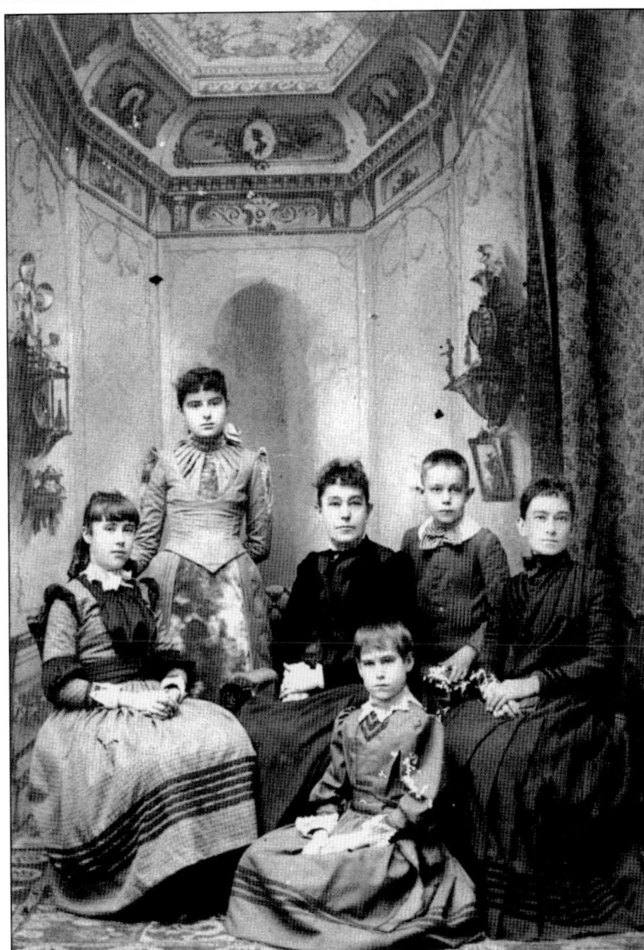

L.A. Little, great-grandfather to Warren Little, came with his family from Iowa around 1906 and settled in northwest "M" (Woods) County on 3,000 acres situated on the Yellowstone Creek. This property became known as the Little Ranch. (Courtesy of Warren Little.)

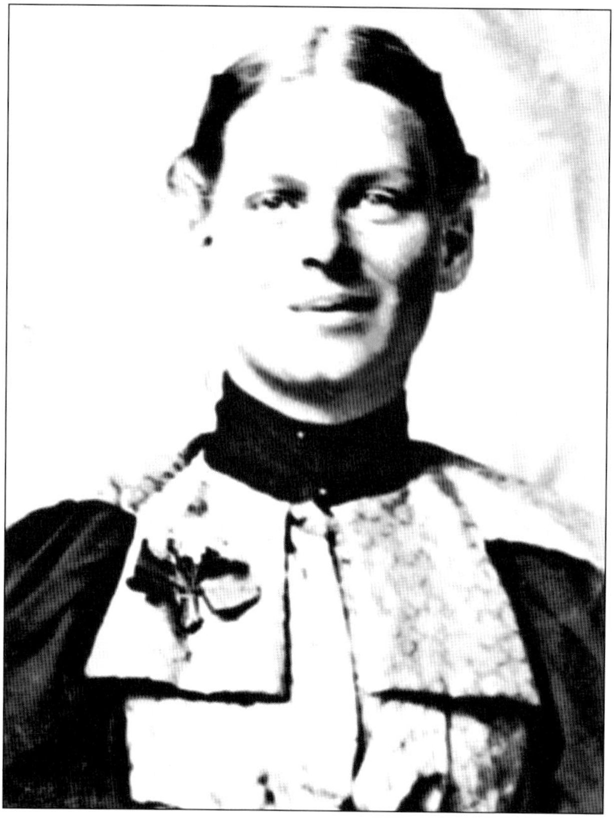

Lizzie Bush was the sister of Roger Bush Sr. She was a large lady in stature and worked with her father and brothers on the threshing crew they ran. The Bush family came from the Texas Panhandle and settled 30 miles northwest of Alva in Woods County on what would be named the Bush Ranch. (Courtesy of Warren Little.)

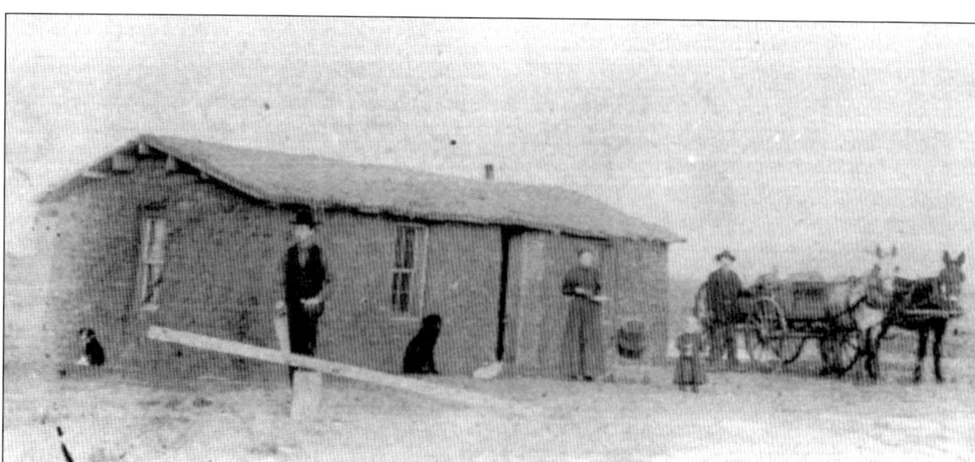

It was recorded that this was the first soddie built after the land run. It was close to Helena, which was originally in "M" (Woods) County. (Courtesy of Oklahoma Historical Society.)

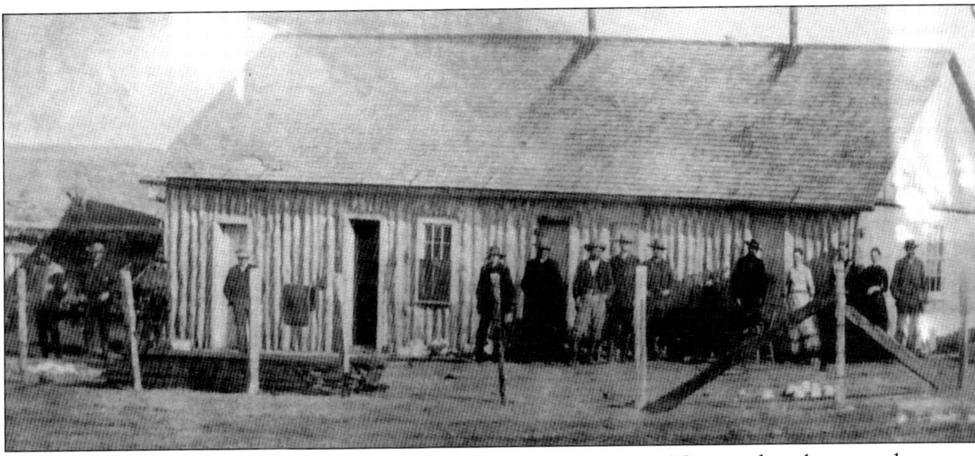

This house, built in 1885, is constructed with logs and stucco. Notice the glass windows and fencing. This home was located northwest of Alva on the Kansas state line. (Courtesy of Alva Cherokee Strip Museum.)

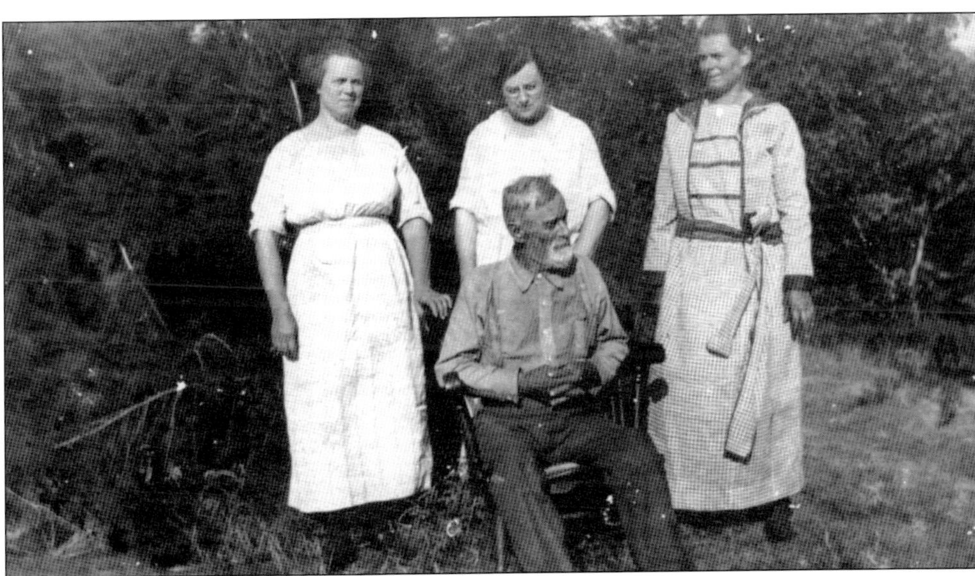

In this photograph are Croizer Bush's grandfather and, standing to the far right, Lizzie Bush. The other women are unidentified. (Courtesy of Warren Little.)

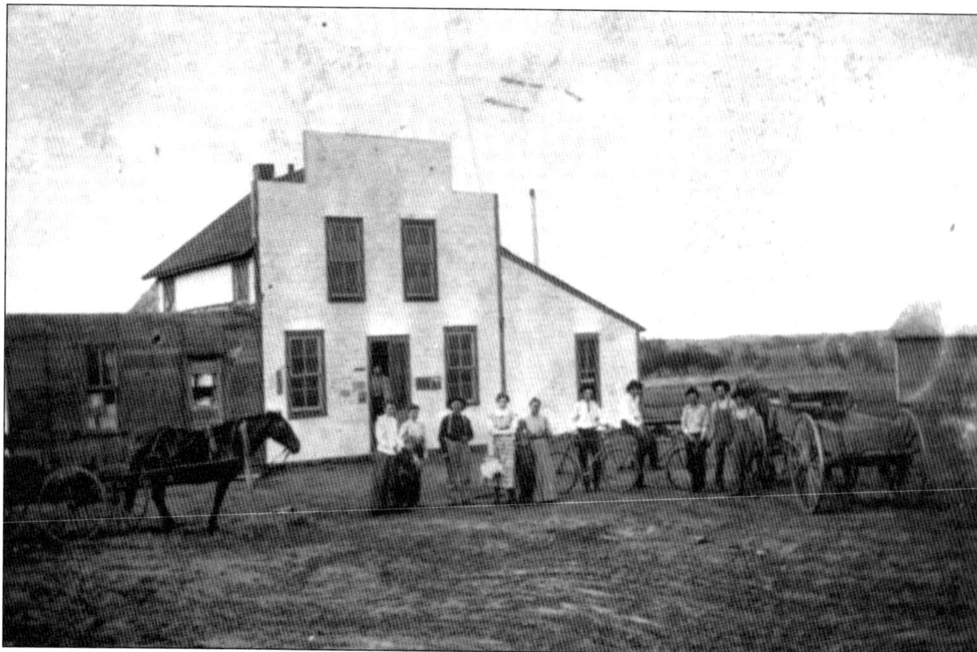

This is a typical general store of the early 1900s. General stores sold a little bit of everything, meeting the homesteaders' needs.

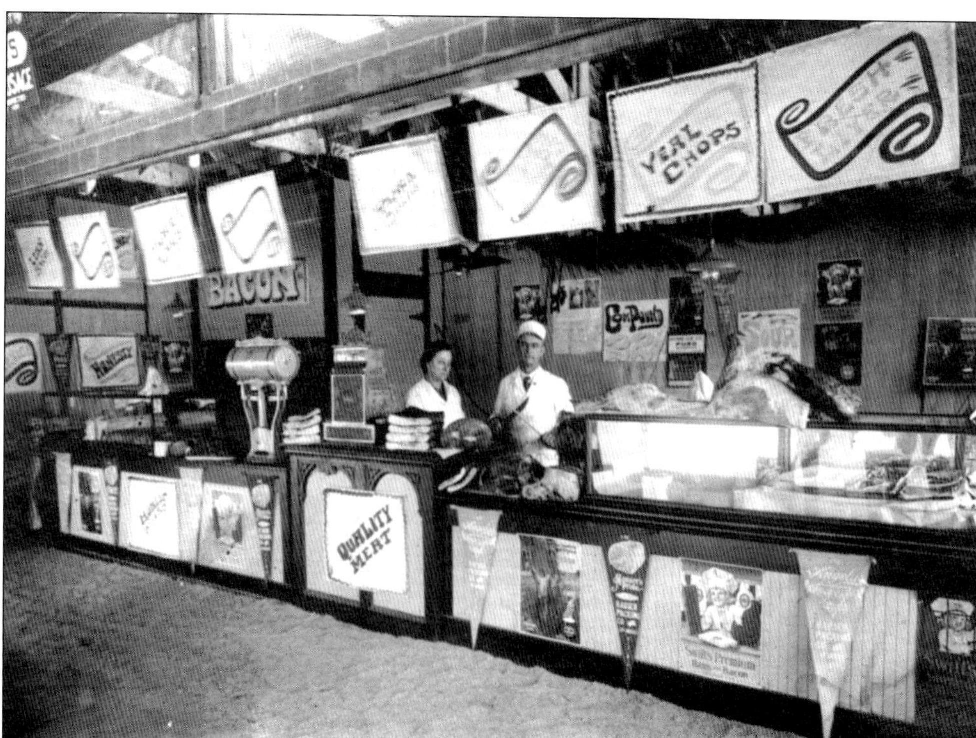

This general store, most likely photographed sometime in the early 1900s, was located somewhere in "M" (Woods) County. (Courtesy of Warren Little.)

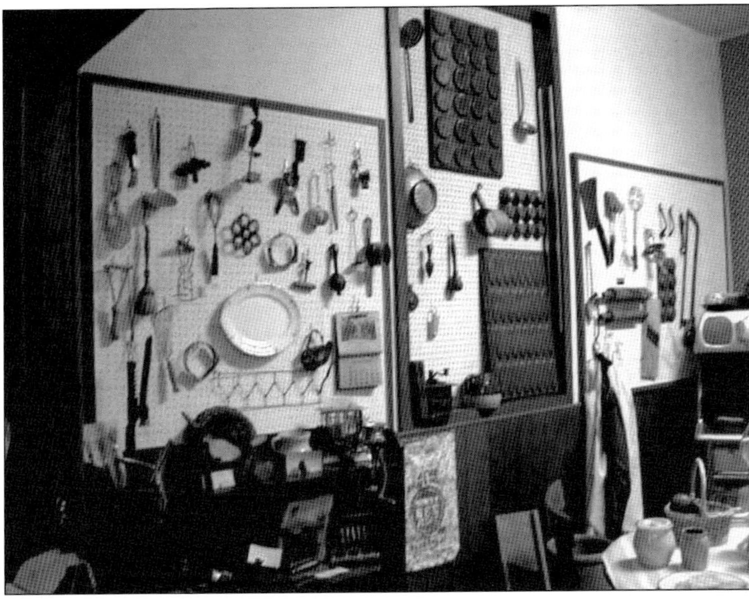

In this photograph, taken at the Alva Cherokee Strip Museum, some kitchen items used by pioneers are on display. (Courtesy of the Alva Cherokee Strip Museum.)

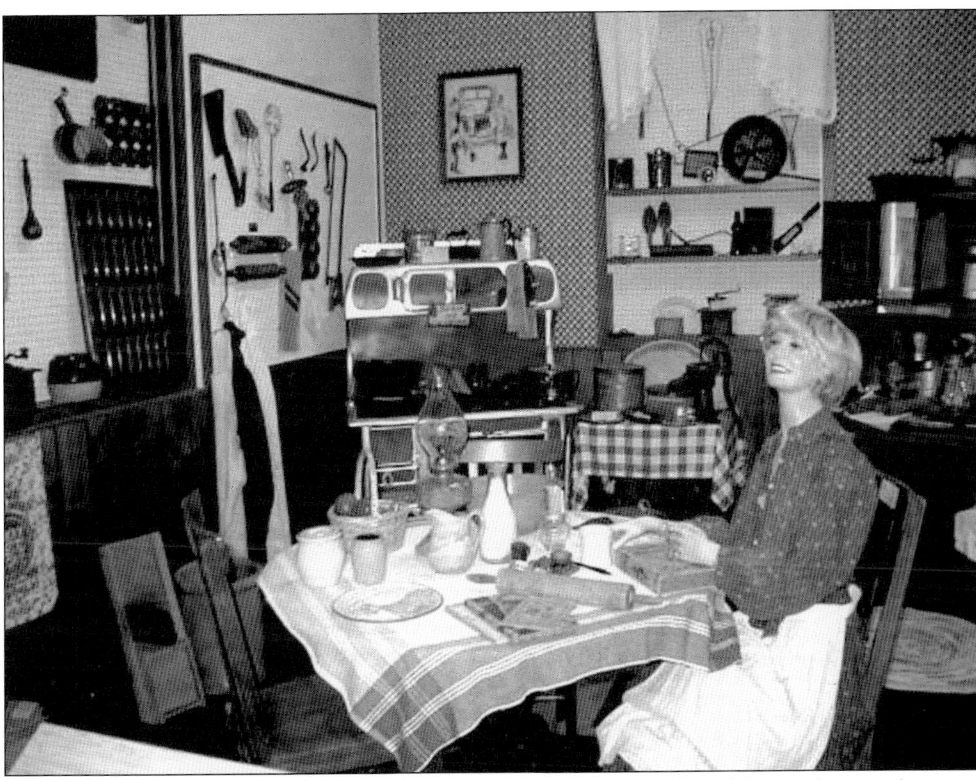

This Alva Cherokee Strip Museum exhibit displays a pioneer kitchen. Notice the woodstove in the back of. A woodstove was often kept burning all day through the whole year, generally with a pot of beans on the back burner and a pan of corn bread for the family, the hired help, or a traveler who might stop by. (Courtesy of the Alva Cherokee Strip Museum.)

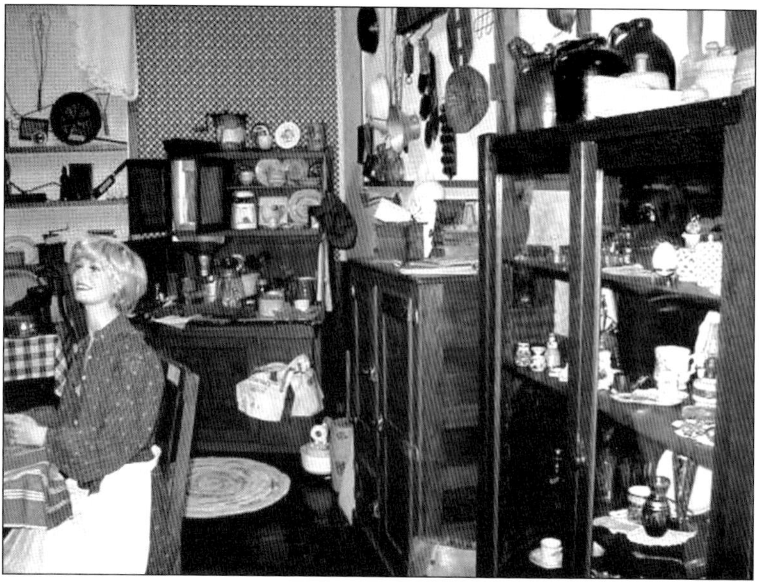

On the wall to the right, in the center of this photograph, is an old oak icebox. When available (mostly to people who lived in towns and had access to ice), they were a great help preserving food. Without an icebox, fruit and other foods were generally stored in cellars where it was cool. (Courtesy of the Alva Cherokee Strip Museum.)

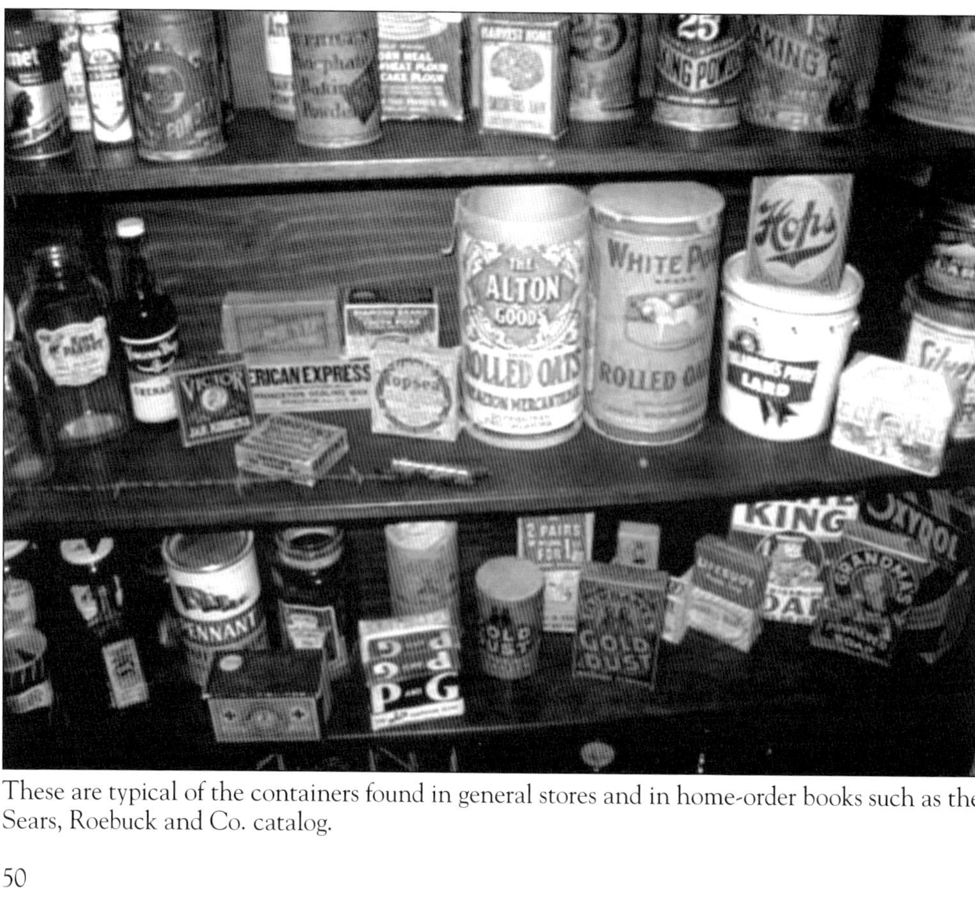

These are typical of the containers found in general stores and in home-order books such as the Sears, Roebuck and Co. catalog.

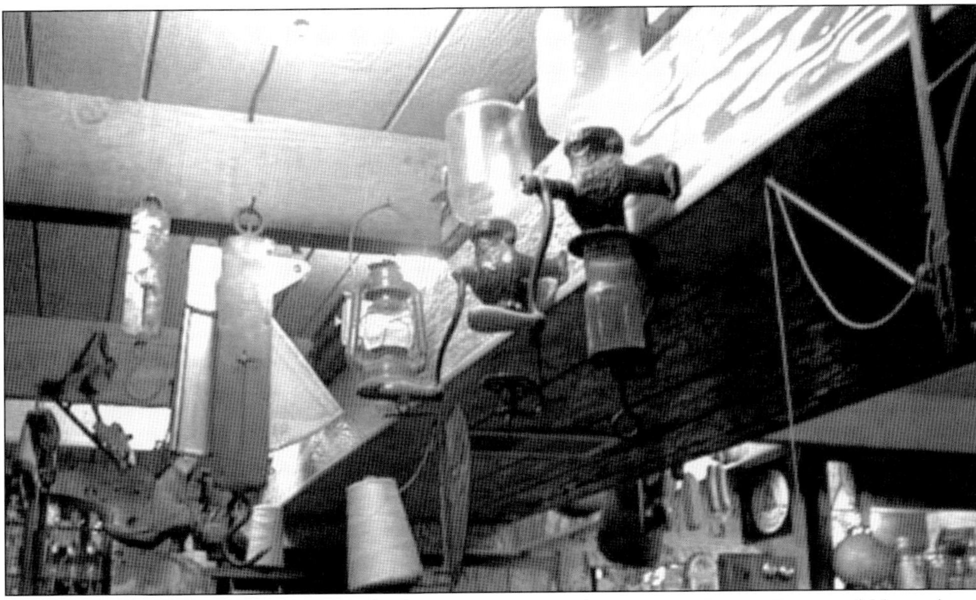

A coffee grinder, lanterns, and a scale for use in a general store were items that would have been for sale to the homesteaders.

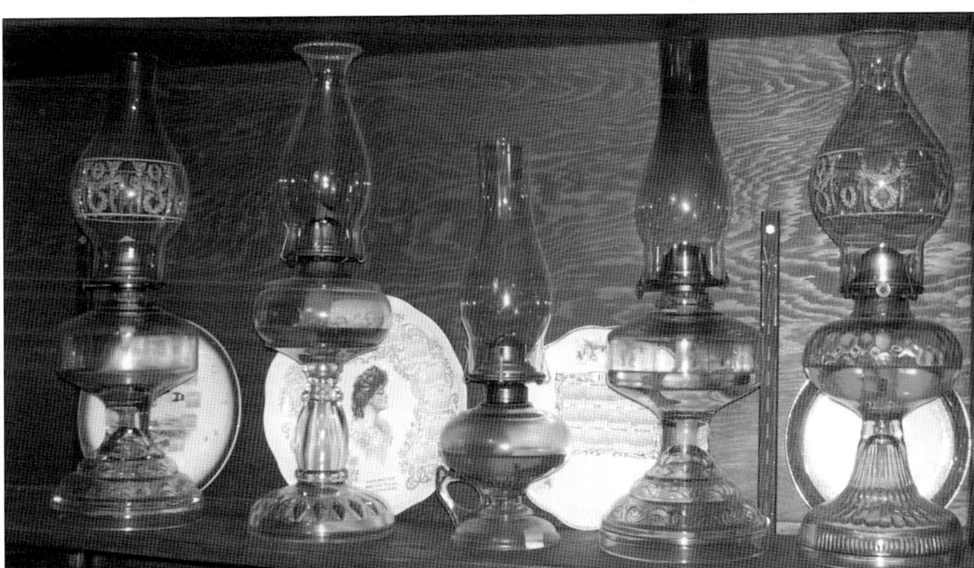

In this photograph are oil lamps like those used by pioneers in the Oklahoma Territory.

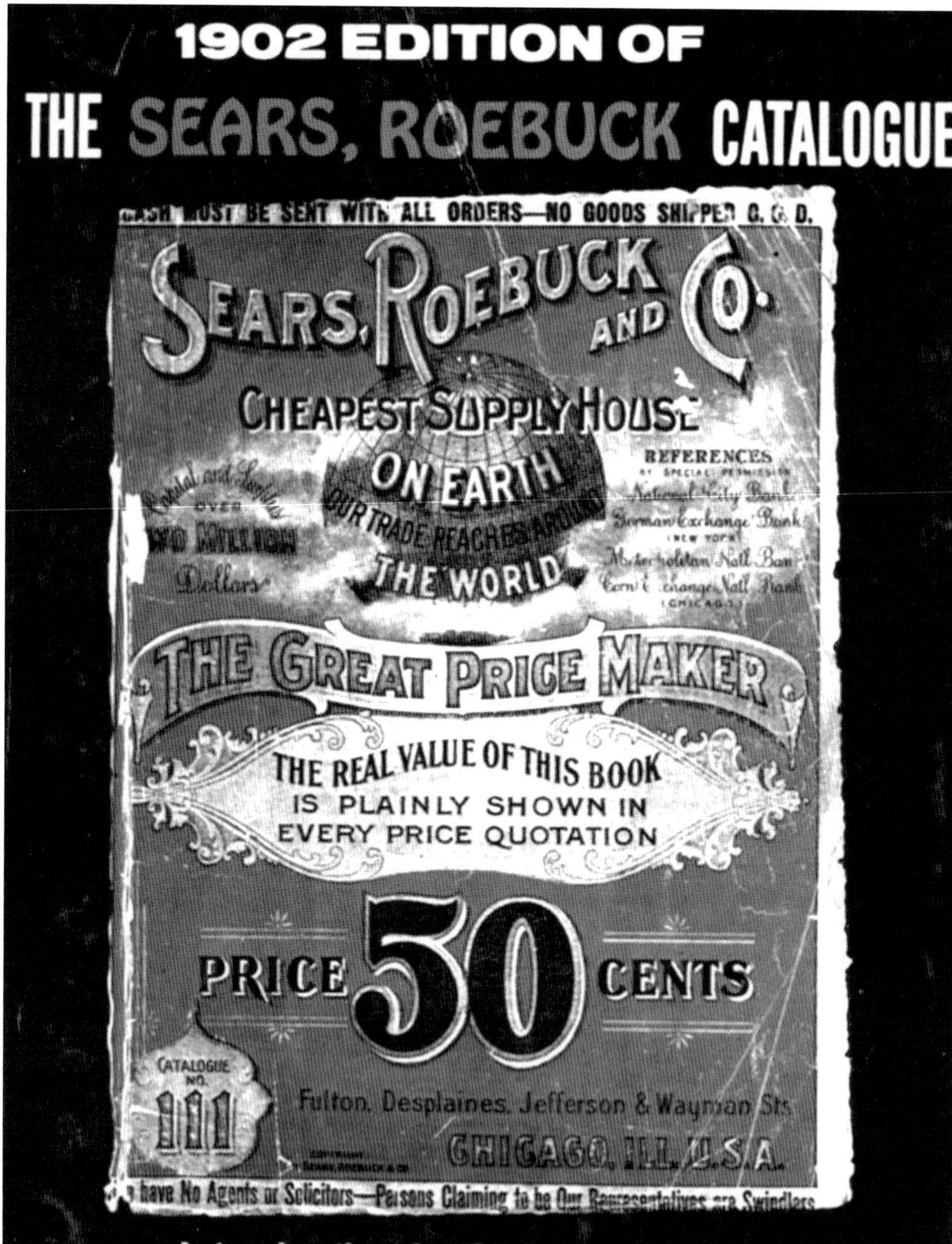

Anything that the homesteader might need could be found in this 1902 catalog from Sears, Roebuck and Co. Everything from food to plows and clothing to farm machinery was available. These catalogs were a couple of inches thick and would have been pored over by everyone in the family.

Four

Cattle and Crops

On March 7, 1883, the Cherokee Strip Live Stock Association was incorporated under the laws of the state of Kansas. Four months later, its directors leased from the Cherokee Nation over six million acres of the Cherokee Outlet. Members of the association grazed their cattle in the outlet until the federal government purchased it in 1890. Prior to the coming of the railroads, it was necessary to drive the cattle to market from Texas to the railheads in Kansas.

With the land run of 1893 and the arrival of the homesteaders, the open range of the cattlemen began to change. Fences went up and homesteaders began plowing the prairie in preparation for planting their crops. The homesteaders tried to raise broomcorn without much luck, but their crops improved when they planted wheat.

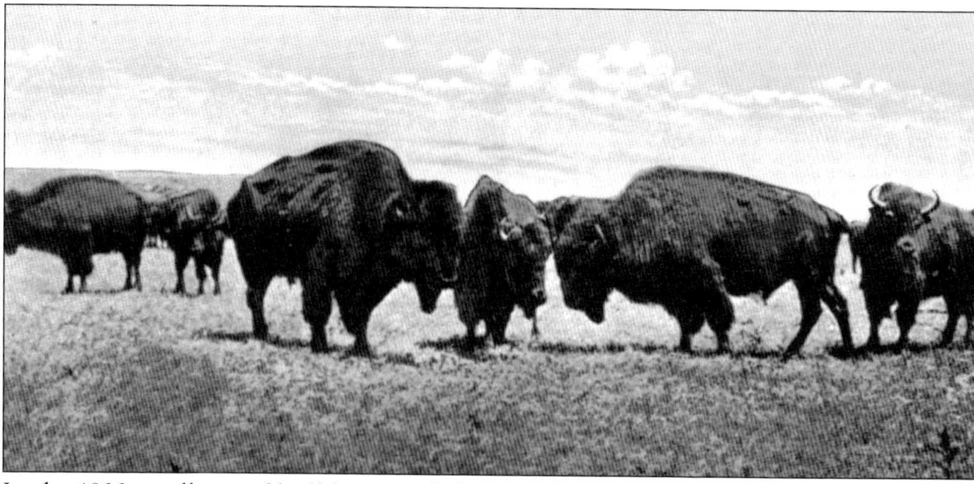

In the 1800s, millions of buffalo roamed through the Cherokee Strip. The fur traders were primarily responsible for the depletion of the buffalo herds. In Avard and the northwest area of "M" (Woods) County, buffalo wallows are still visible. The natural springs in those areas made a good place for buffalo and other wildlife to gather.

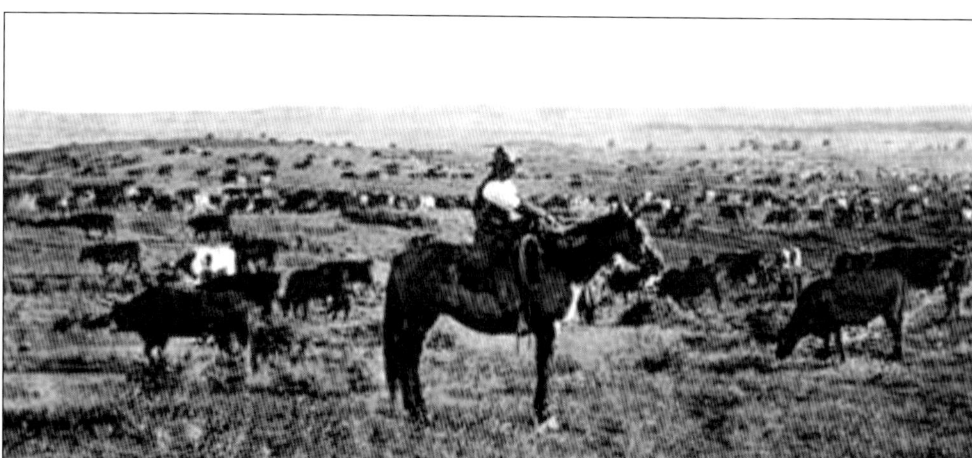

In this photograph, the terrain and view appear to be in western "M" (Woods) County. The cattle are not longhorns. They are of other various breeds that were brought in to breed with the longhorn in order to produce a better grade of cattle. (Courtesy of the Alva Cherokee Strip Museum.)

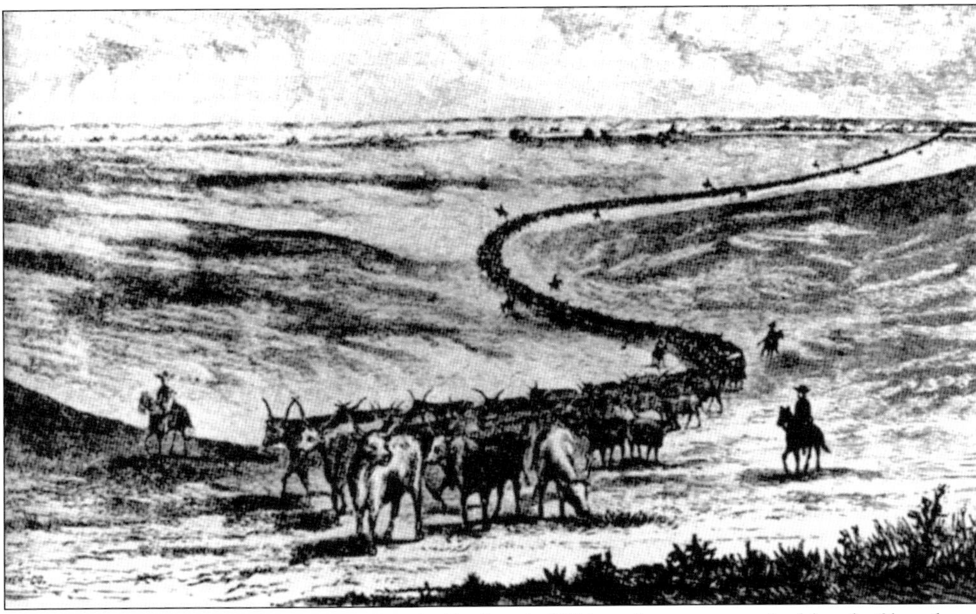

In this illustration from the Kansas Pacific Railway's 1874 guide map, a typical herd of longhorn is driven on the Chisholm Trail. Feeder trails went all over Texas and Oklahoma. One of those feeder trails went through "M" (Woods) County. There were ample outlets to a feeder trail, before homesteads came, to join up with the main Chisholm Trail to go to the Kansas railheads.

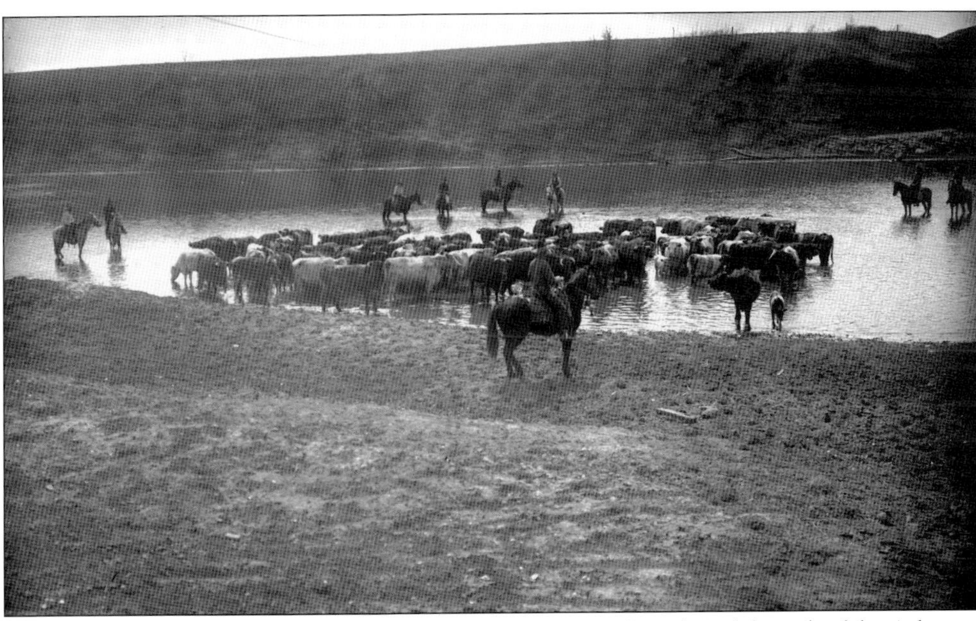

In this photograph from the 1880s, a small herd is watering in the Salt Fork branch of the Arkansas River. (Courtesy of Western History Collection, University of Oklahoma Press.)

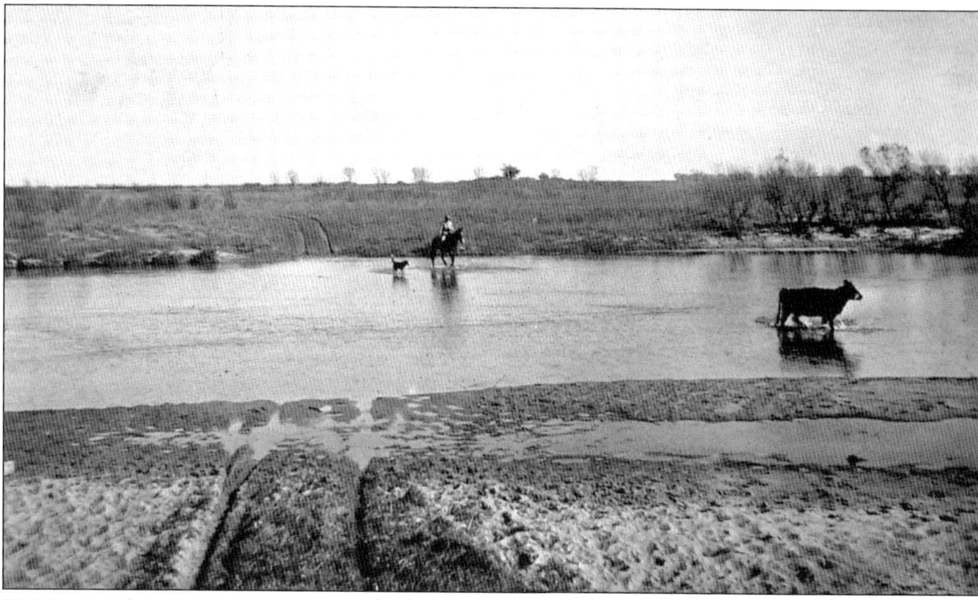

Driving cattle across a river was a tricky business. It was always dangerous because of the potential for quicksand and swift currents. (Courtesy of Alva Cherokee Strip Museum.)

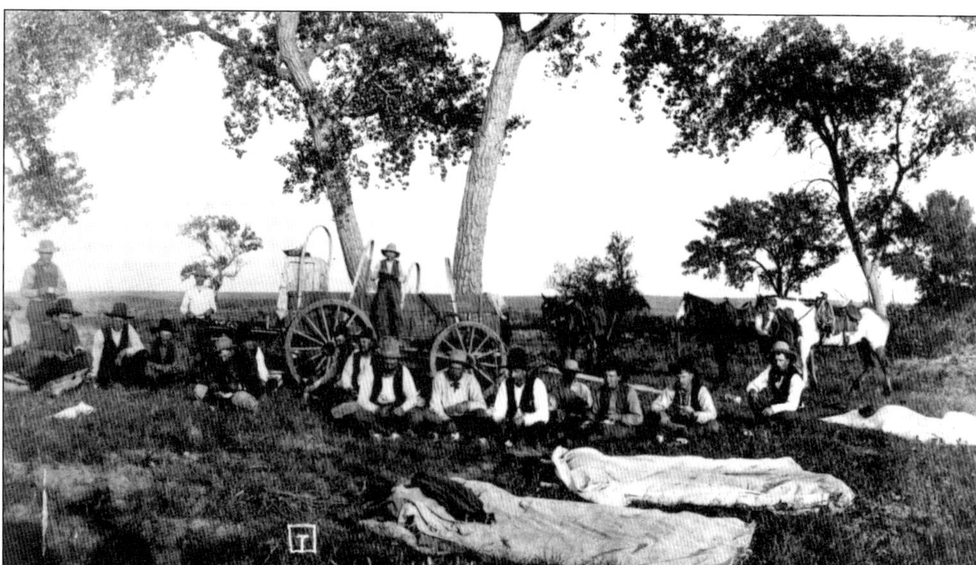

Cowhands are resting around the chuck wagon in this photograph. This was their living, sleeping, and dining area when on the trail. (Courtesy of Western History Collection, University of Oklahoma Press.)

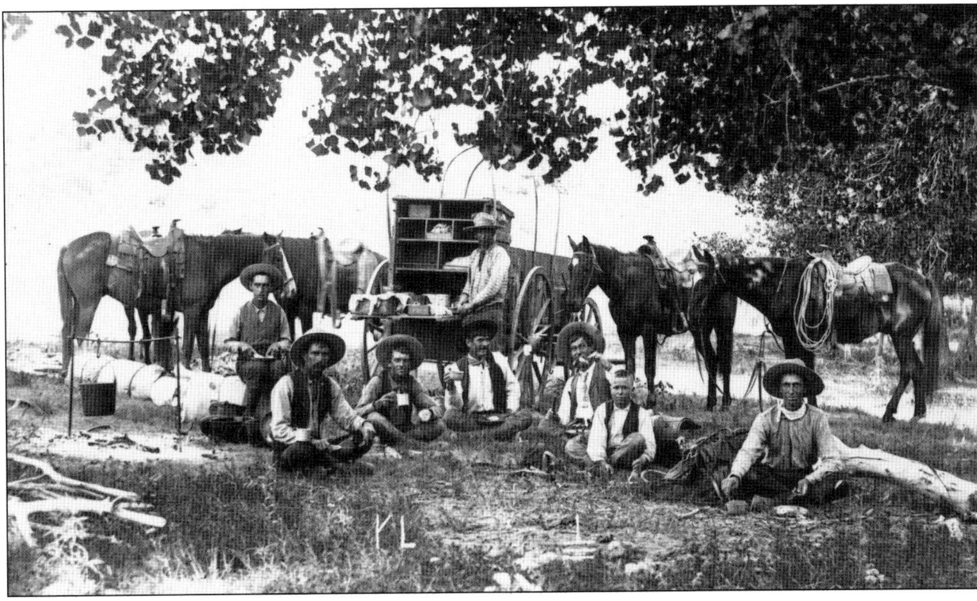

Cowboys sit around the chuck wagon at mealtime during a roundup in the Cherokee Outlet. (Courtesy of Western History Collection, University of Oklahoma Press.)

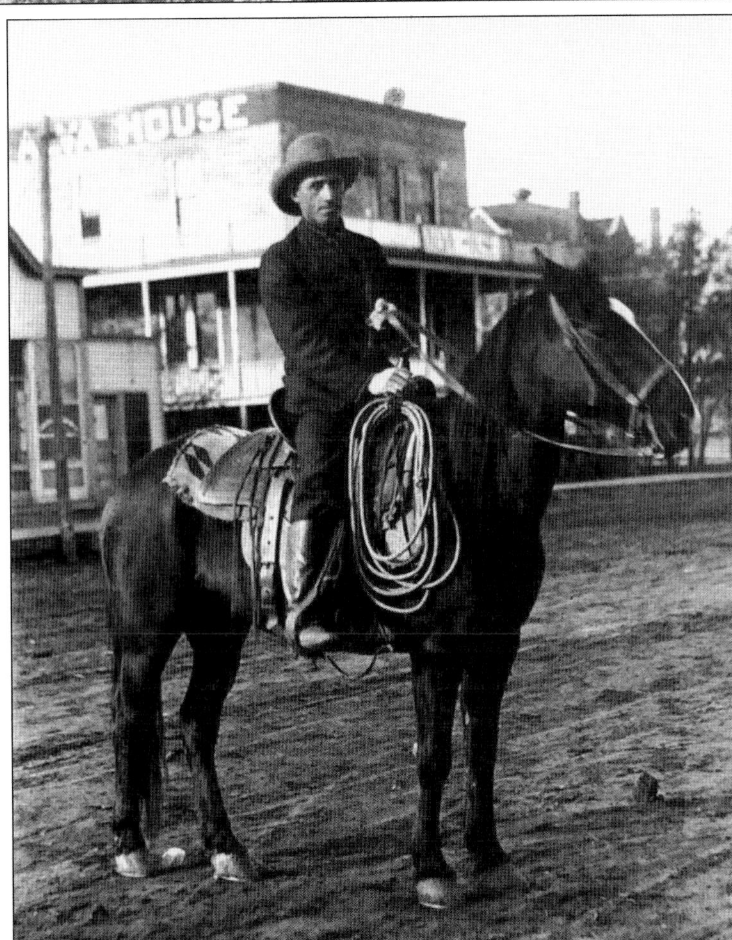

A cowboy's life was adventurous, but it was also dirty, lonely, and often brutally hard. Owing to the nomadic lifestyle of most cowboys, they generally owned only their horses and what could be carried. Cowboys didn't just herd cattle; plenty of grueling chores were also required of them. Riding and repairing fences, digging stock tanks, branding, and loading and shipping cattle added to their herding duties.

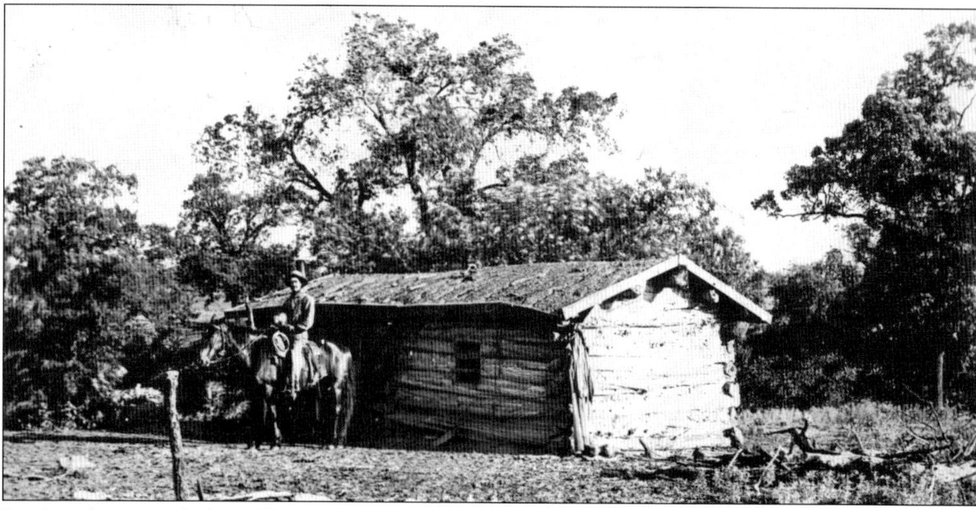

In this photograph from the 1880s, a cowboy is seated on his mount beside a typical line shack. These shacks were used in the outlet to accommodate cowhands. (Courtesy of Western History Collection, University of Oklahoma Press.)

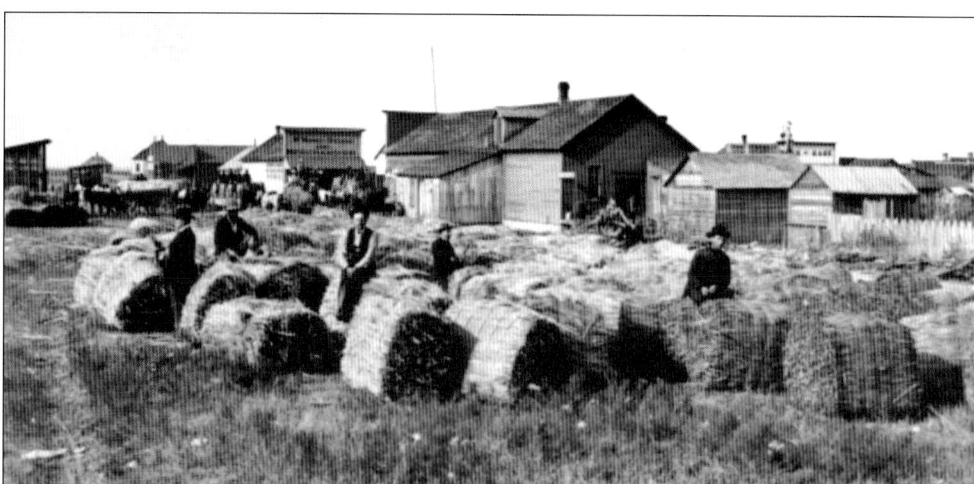

In 1903, broomcorn could be raised for $20 per ton. Corn was pulled in the morning, threshed and put on slats to dry in the afternoon, and then stored in corn sheds. When dried properly, broomcorn retains its color and weight. Proper drying also prevents the fiber from becoming harsh and brittle. Broomcorn cured in the sun loses all vitality as it dries and shrivels up and loses half its value.

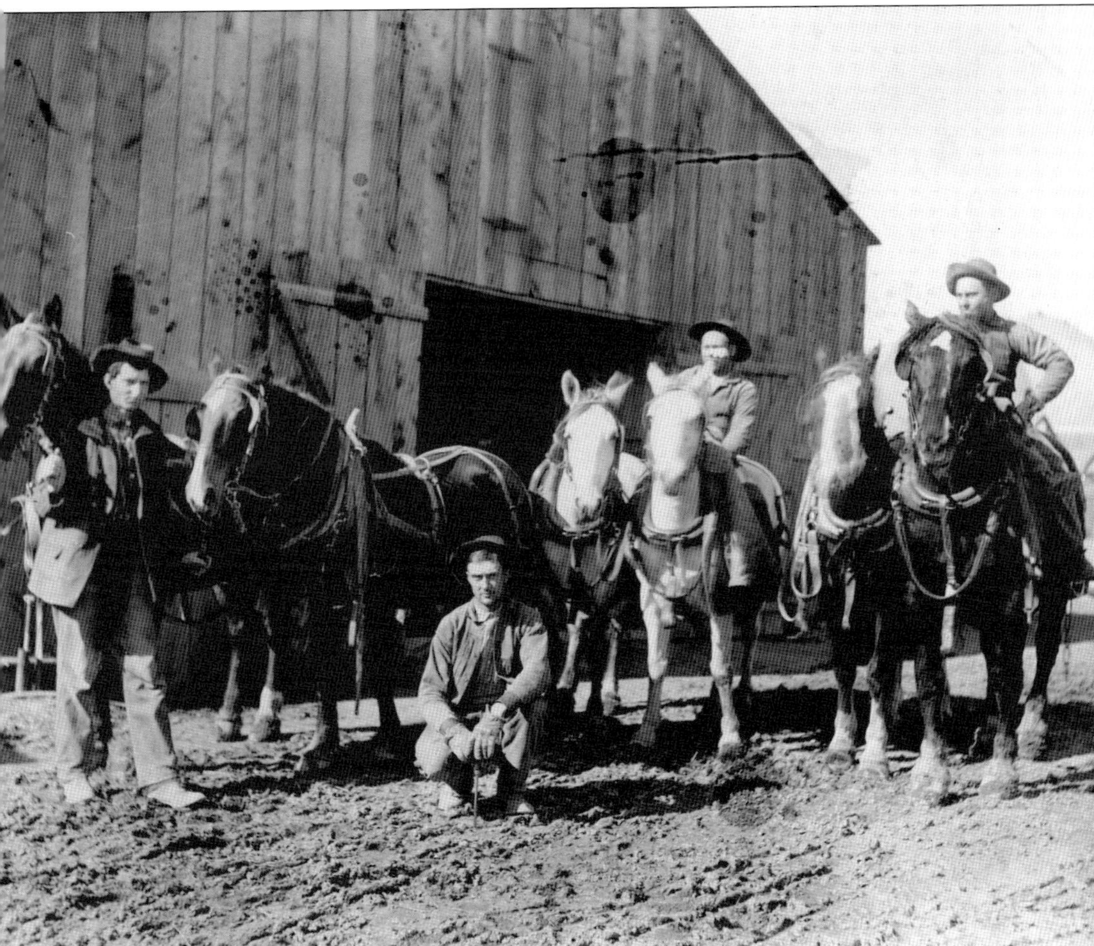

From the looks of this scene, taken about 1905, the men have come in from a day of plowing, or harvesting. The only one known in this image is on the far right, Guy Kinzie. According to his journal, a wage for a full day farming was $2.40; board and room for a single man per month averaged about $31.25.

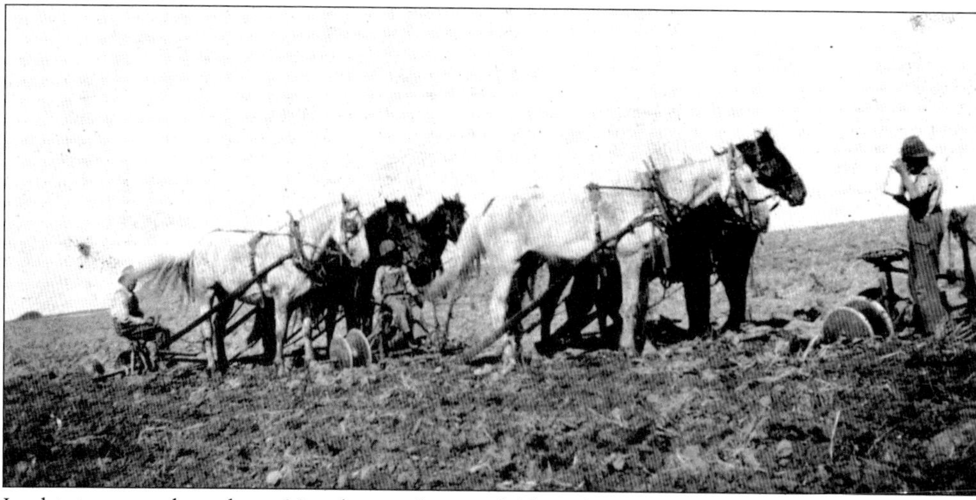

In this image, taken about 30 miles northwest of Alva, three teams of horses pull disks to break up the ground. The boys appear to be taking a break, enjoying a drink of water from a stone jug. (Courtesy of Warren Little.)

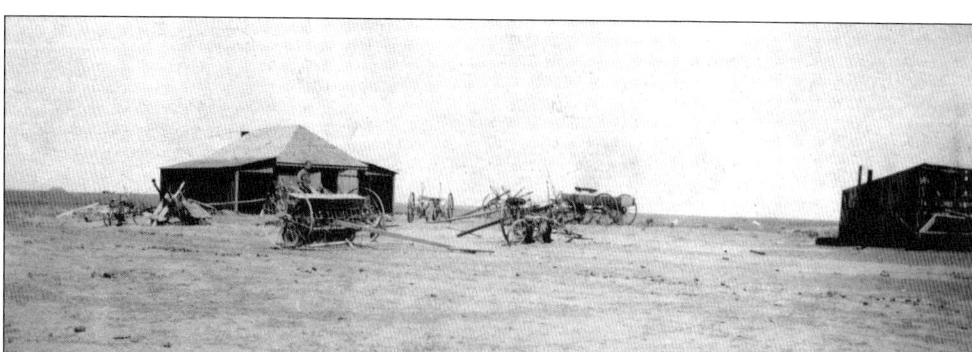

This is the original house built by Aaron and Mary May on the May Ranch. The Mays and their sons were traveling from Wann in the Cherokee Nation on their way to Montana when a windstorm blew the canvas off their covered wagon. They learned of a homestead on the Kansas line that was for sale and purchased 160 acres. The family lived in a dugout for many years until a house could be built. (Courtesy of Warren Little.)

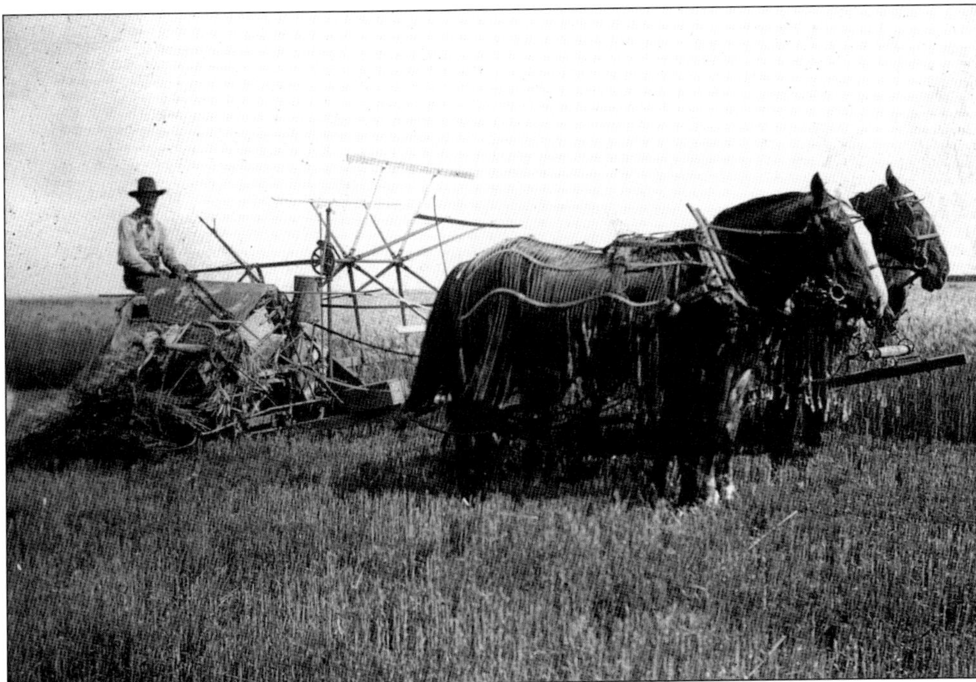

Charlie Nelson was photographed with a wheat binder on the Nelson family's land. (Courtesy of Joy (Cameron) Sherman.)

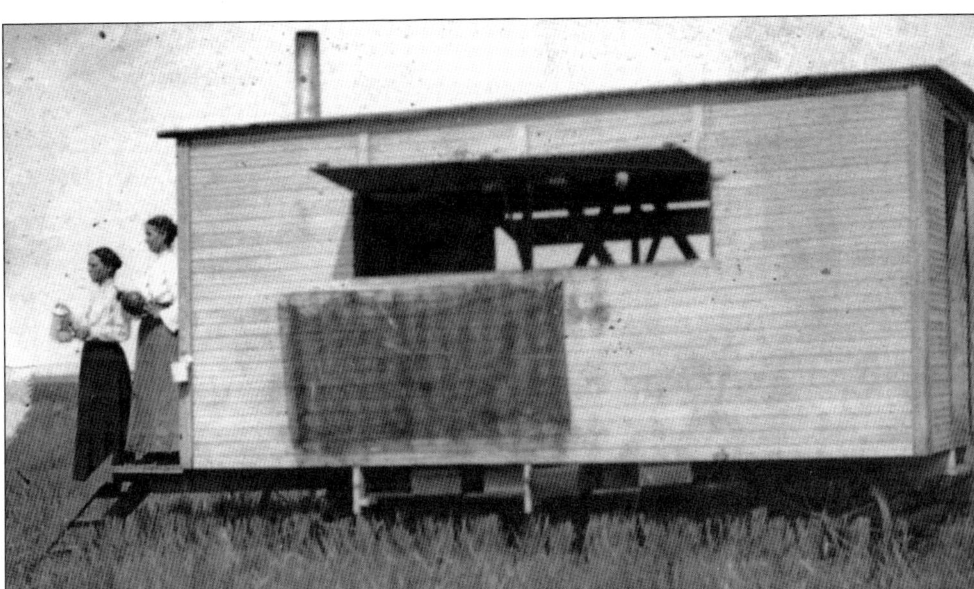

During the wheat harvest, Dora Cline and her helper would have the "cook shack" parked near the wheat fields in order to feed her husband and his harvesting crew. A hired hand looked after the shack, moving it and doing errands for the cook.

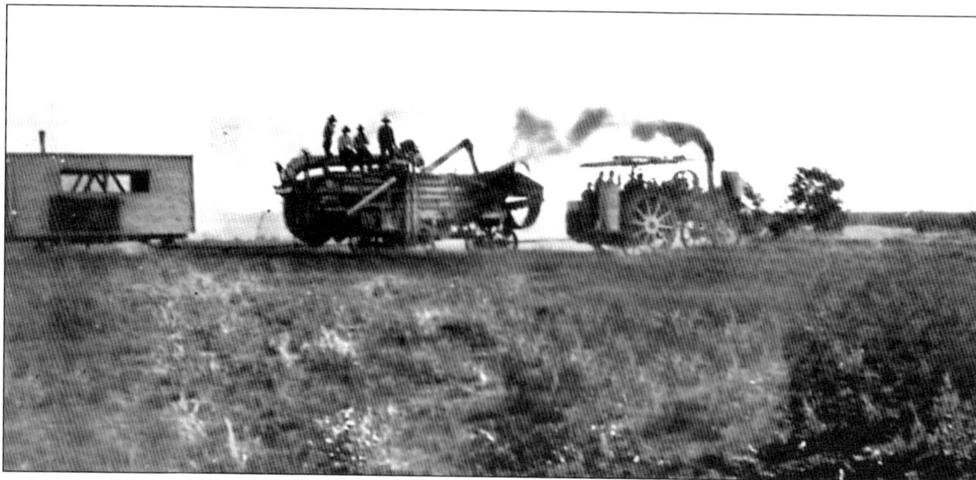

In this photograph from around 1900, an early steam thresher, followed by a cook shack, move along together. (Courtesy of Alva Cherokee Strip Museum.)

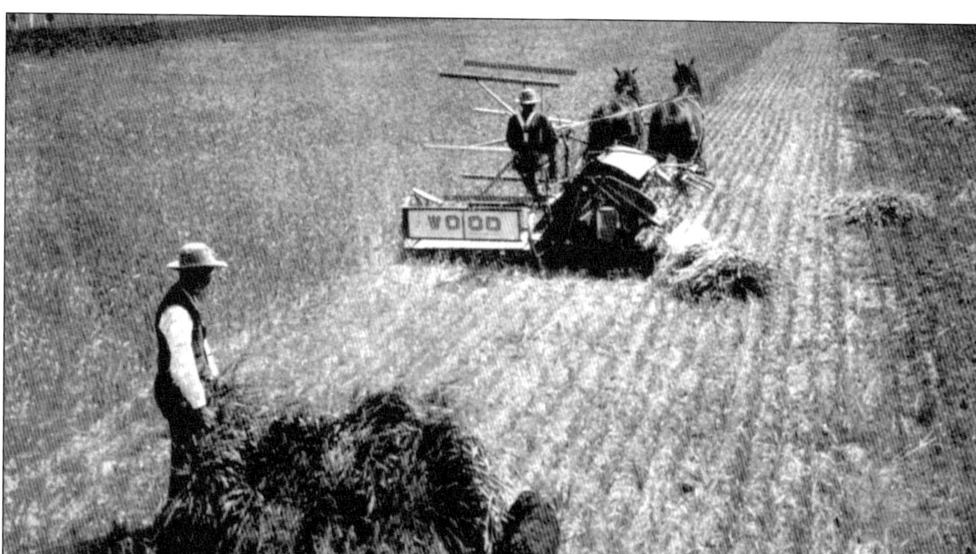

This type of binder was in existence prior to the 1850s and was used to bind the wheat in bundles. One man could operate the machine driving two or three horses, but it was a slow process. Settlers could look out over an expanse of prairie that was dotted with small teepee-like shocks of golden grain. Several bundles would be stacked on end by hand, forming a shock.

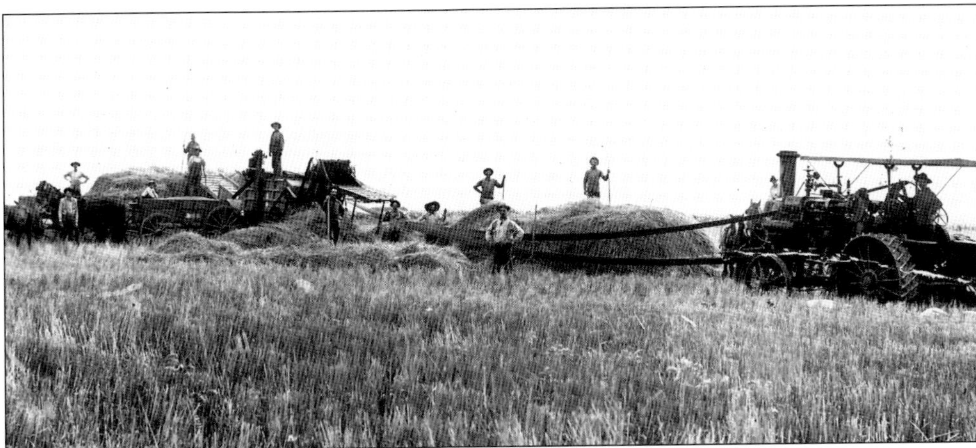

During harvest and threshing, work lasted from early in the morning until late in the day. Crews consisted primarily of men and boys who were away from home. They returned year after year to the same crews, no matter how far away they lived. If the Fourth of July caught them unfinished in the field, time was taken out in the evening for ice cream on the lawn and a general good time. Boys who left the farm to work in towns came home during harvest until they had families of their own. (Courtesy of Alva Cherokee Strip Museum.)

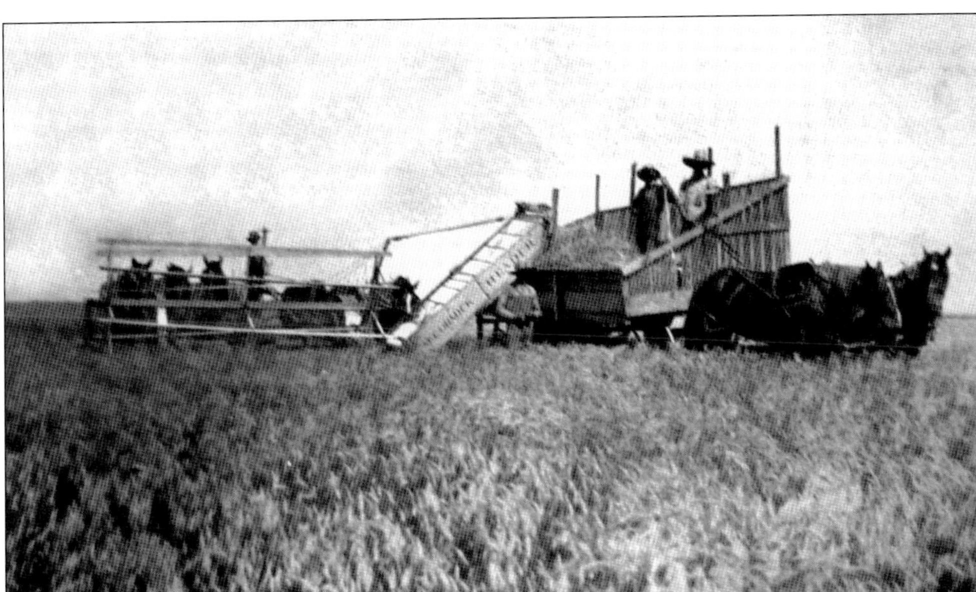

A header and header barge start on a wheat field that is ready for harvesting. This method was an improvement over the binder method. (Courtesy Alva Cherokee Strip Museum.)

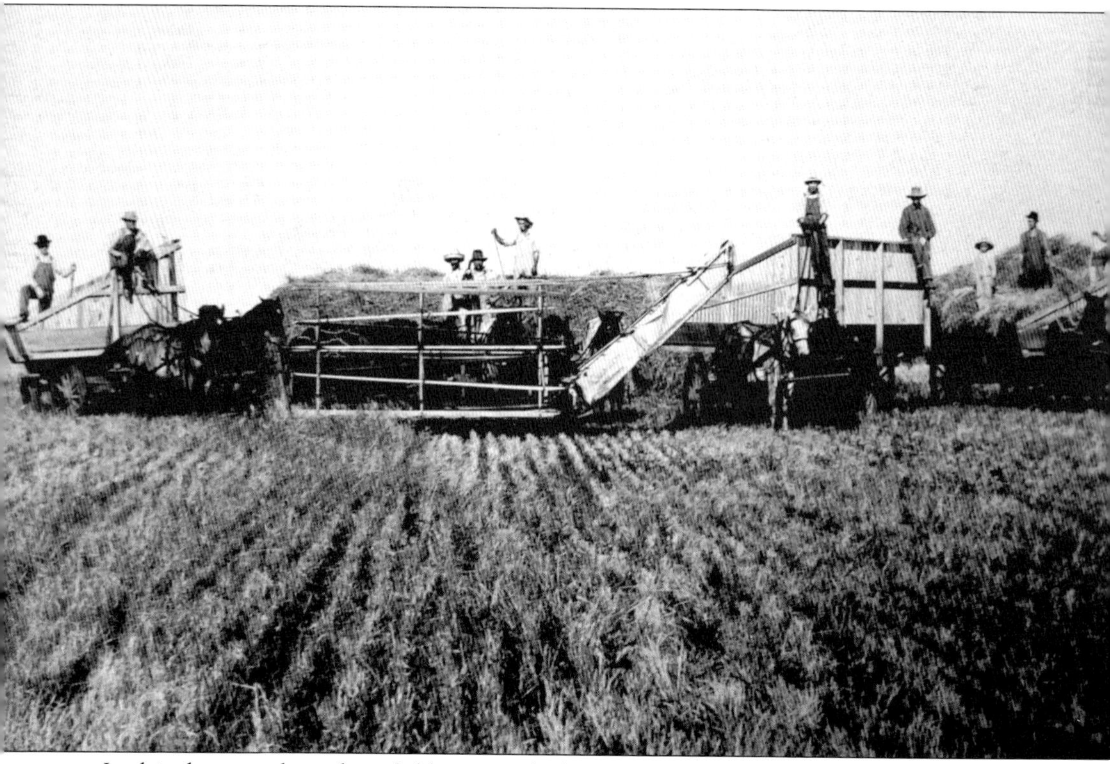

In this photograph, a wheat field is cut and wheat straw stacked using a header and header barge. The season lasted through the hottest part of the summer until every field was cleared in the fall. In 1897, the price of wheat shot up to $1 per bushel, making everyone anxious to cash in. (Courtesy of Alva Cherokee Strip Museum.)

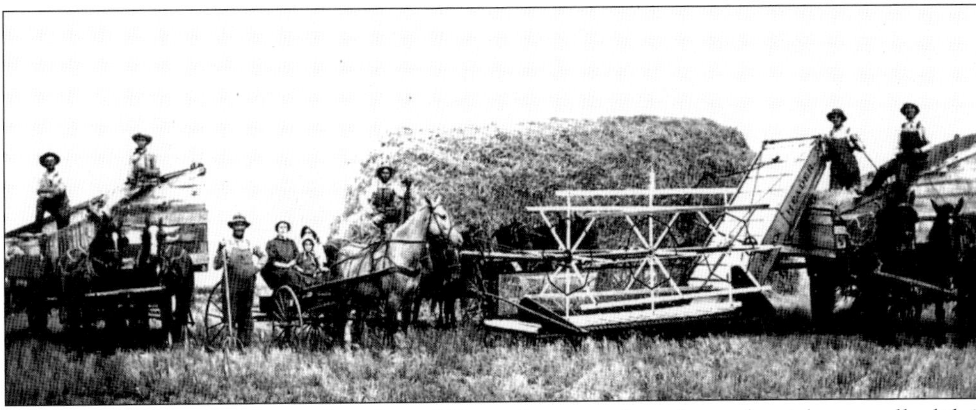

Families turned out to harvest the wheat. Where there were large boys, the girls generally didn't need to work outside. Rare indeed, however, was the home where the women of the family were not glad to lend a hand in a pinch. During free hours, eager children pounced on any stray heads of grain they could find or played hide-and-seek among the shocks. (Courtesy of Alva Cherokee Strip Museum.)

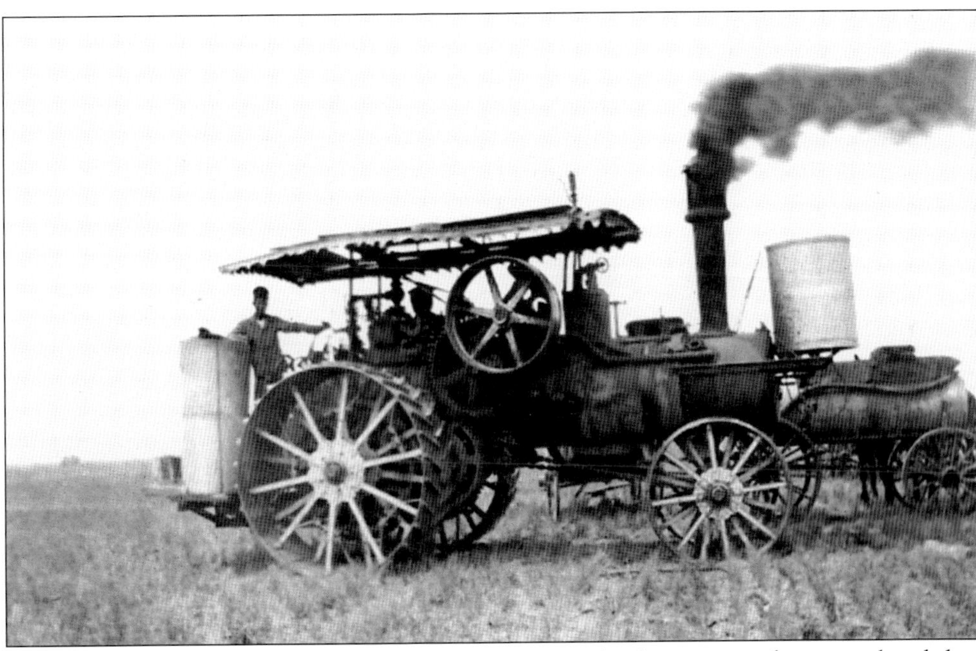

Steam engines replaced horses in threshing. The steam whistle announced its arrival and then gave orders to the crew. A water hauler was necessary to keep the engine going. He would drive a horse-drawn wagon that hauled a water tank. The tank had a pump with a long handle that would be worked back and forth to suck water out of a pond and then again to pump it into the steam engine. (Courtesy of Alva Cherokee Strip Museum.)

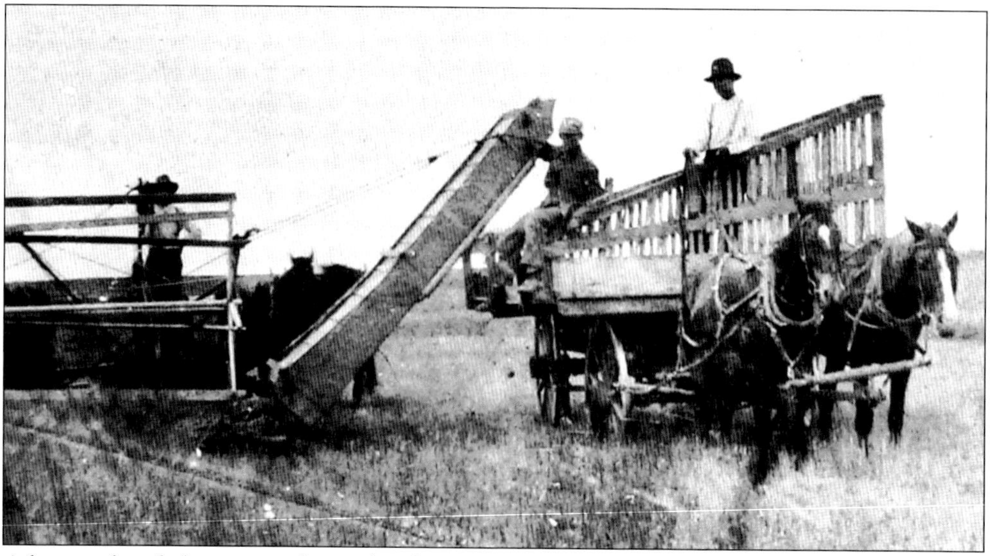

A harvest hand clears straw from a header as another drives a header barge alongside. A header crew usually consisted of eight to ten men who followed the season as did the threshers. (Courtesy of Alva Cherokee Strip Museum.)

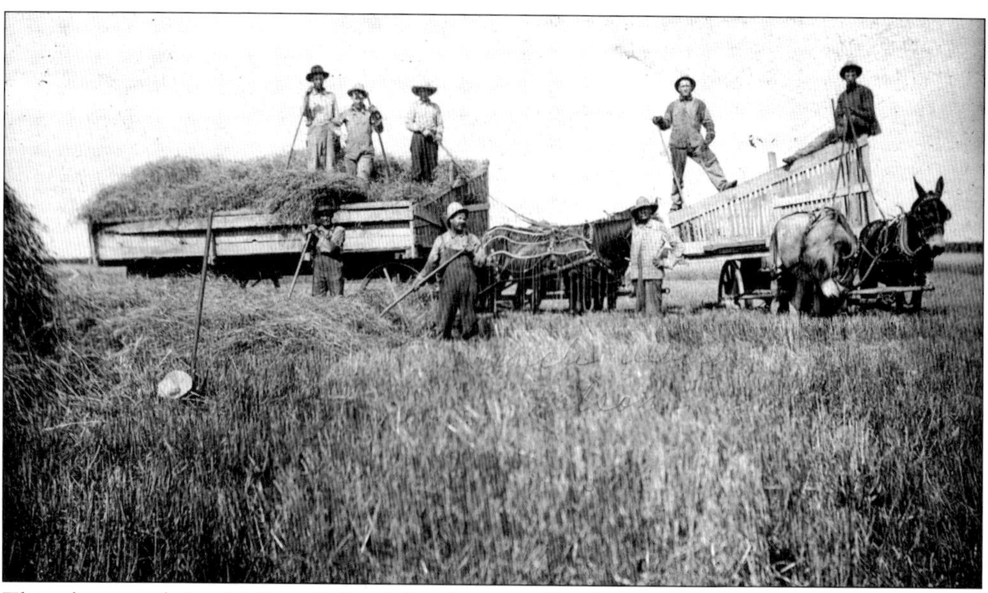

This photograph is of Albert Nelson's header crew. Headers cut the grain and elevated it to a wagon. Six horses were hitched immediately in front of the driver and pushed the header. The cutting blades were in front of the horses. On a good day, 25 to 35 acres could be cut. (Courtesy of Joy (Cameron) Sherman.)

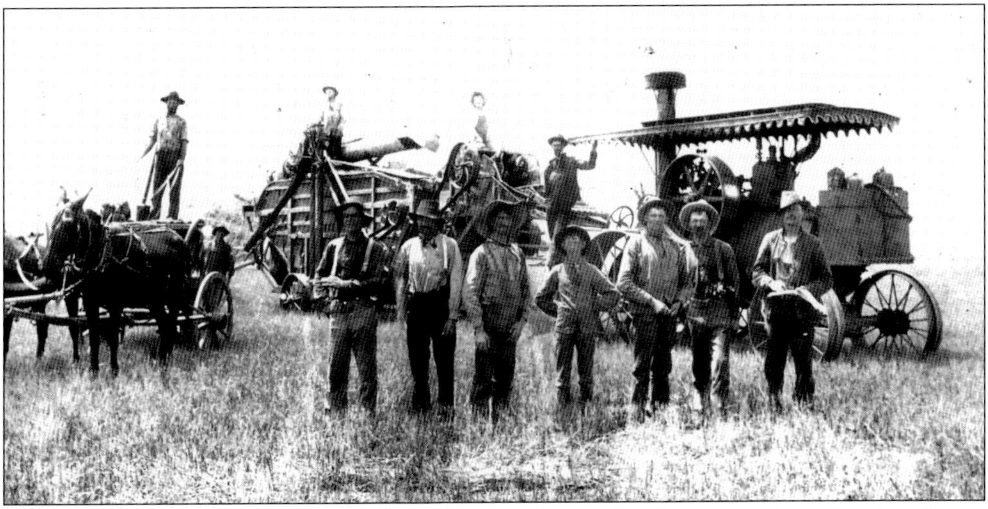

In this photograph, taken by a traveling photographer, a threshing crew from the Avard area stands in front of their equipment. (Courtesy of Alva Cherokee Strip Museum.)

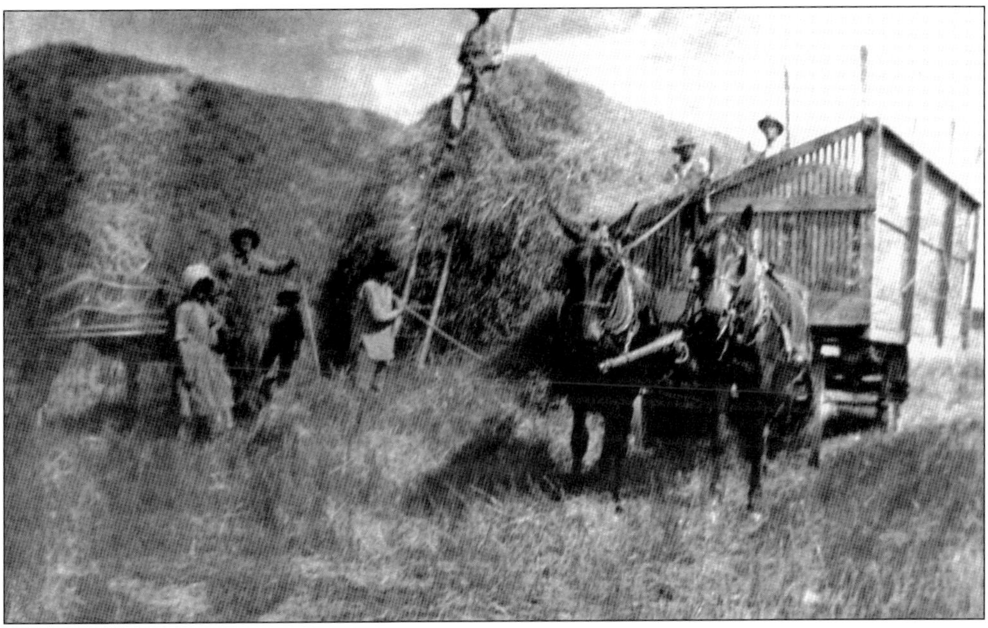

This wheat is stacked for the threshing crew. If the wheat became wet it would be torn apart to dry. If left in stacks of headed wheat, there might be considerable spoilage. (Courtesy of Alva Cherokee Strip Museum.)

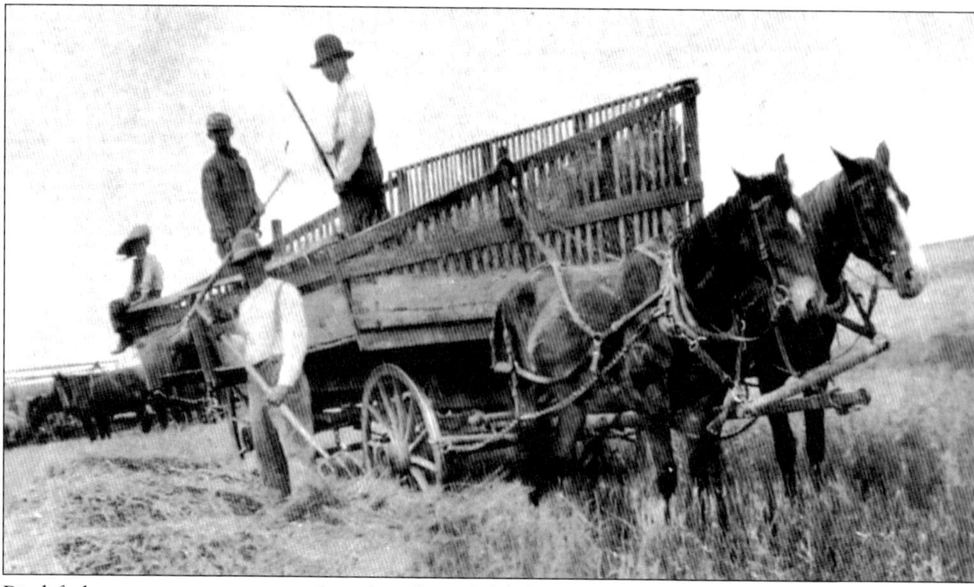

Pitchforks were a necessary tool in the wheat field. (Courtesy of Alva Cherokee Strip Museum.)

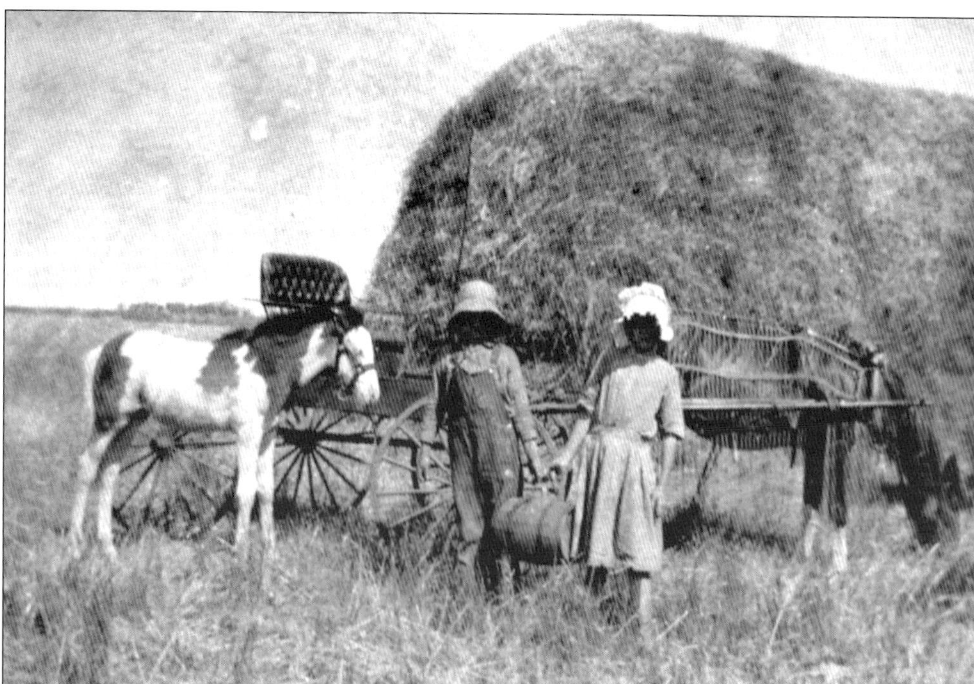

Children often carried drinking water to the field. A jug of cool well water was often taken to the field and set inside a shock or some other available shade. A well-soaked gunnysack securely fastened about the jug helped to keep the water cool throughout the day. (Courtesy of Alva Cherokee Strip Museum.)

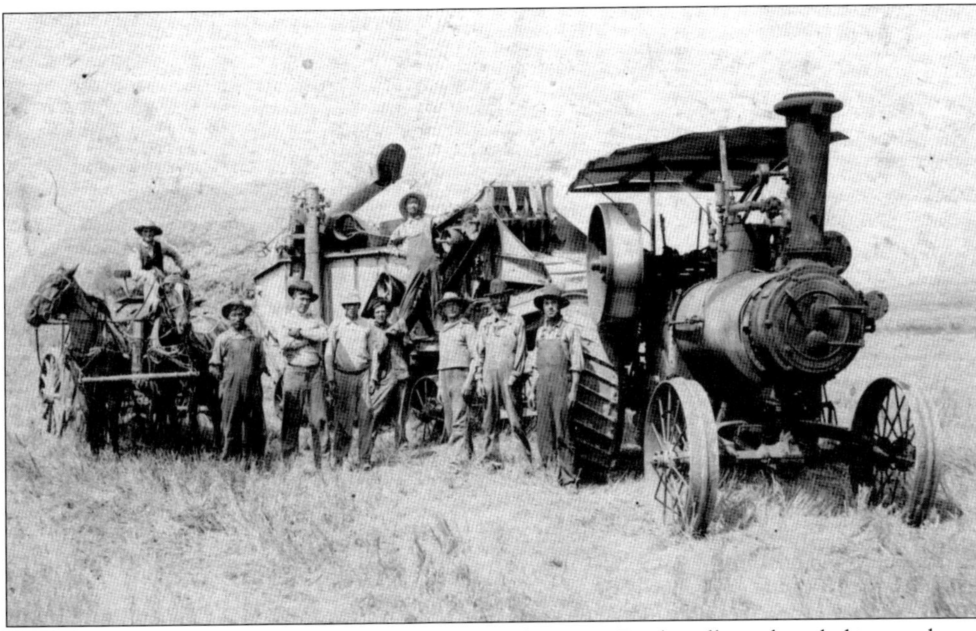

The Bush harvest crew that originally came from the Texas Panhandle and settled in northwest "M" (Woods) County poses in this photograph. (Courtesy of Warren Little.)

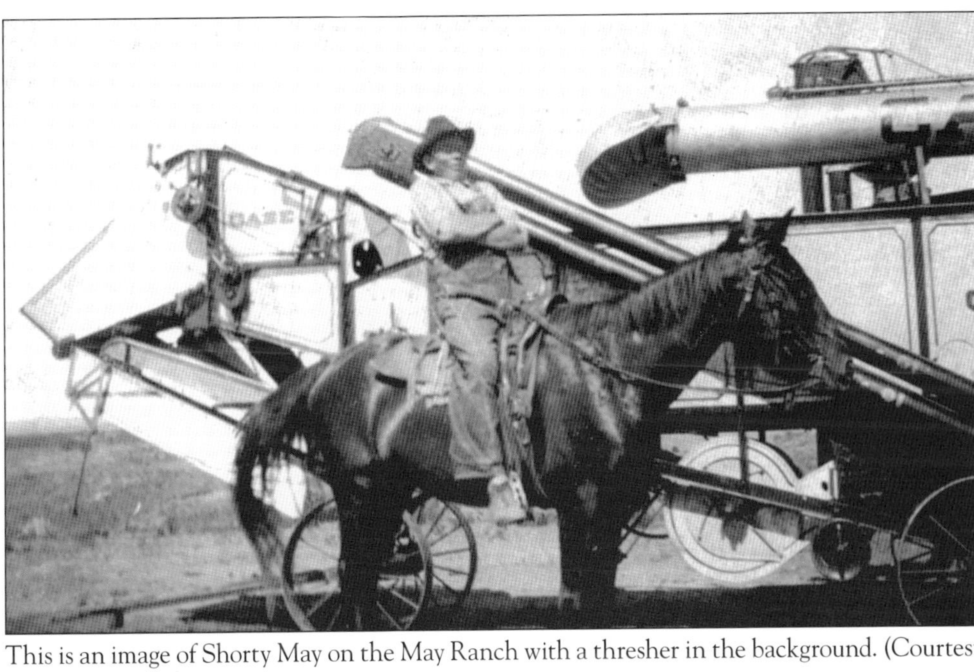

This is an image of Shorty May on the May Ranch with a thresher in the background. (Courtesy of Warren Little.)

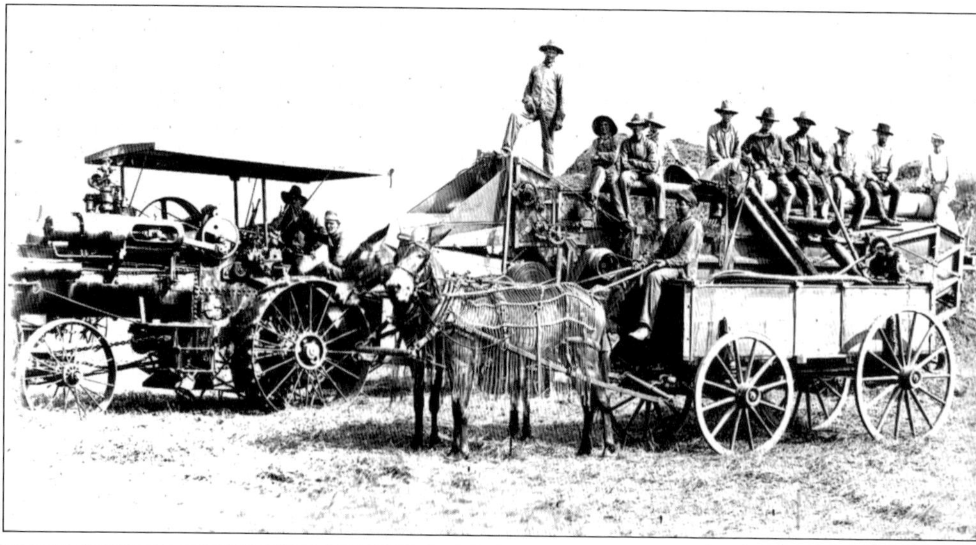

In this harvested field, the traditional end-of-harvest photograph was taken. (Courtesy of Alva Cherokee Strip Museum.)

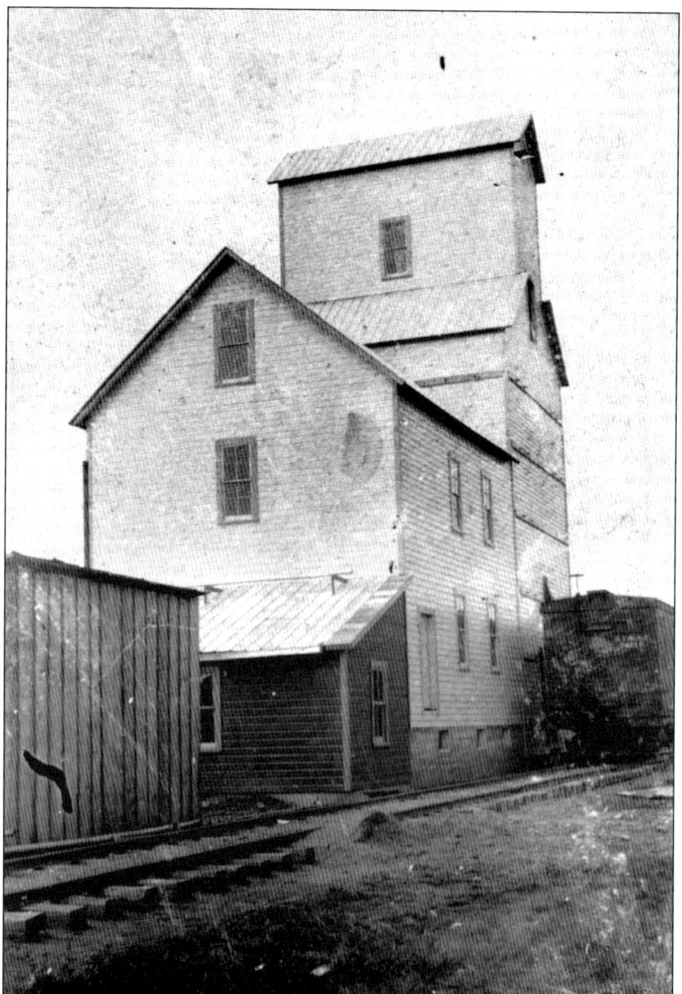

William Cameron built and ran this grain elevator next to the Santa Fe Railroad tracks in Capron, Oklahoma. Part of this elevator still stands today. (Courtesy of Joy (Cameron) Sherman.)

Five

Early Schools

For the benefit of public schools, Congress set aside sections 16 and 36 in each congressional township to be used for schools; the president had the discretion to set aside other lands. President Cleveland decided to withhold sections 13 and 33 in each congressional township. The former section was to be used for universities, agricultural colleges, and normal schools. The latter was to be used for public buildings. Because of these acts, the Cherokee Strip had plenty of schools. The territorial governor was besieged with inquires from people who were interested in these lands for other purposes. The question was referred to the secretary of the interior, who recommended that Congress take action. It did, and their policy allowing the lands to be leased still holds. The leased lands continue to provide funds for the support of schools.

Typical of most of the school districts in "M" (Woods) County in the early days, things such as the lack of money and people's thoughts of survival hindered education at first. The first winter passed without thought of school. By the autumn of 1894, all of the women and children had come to the county and were eager to get things started. In some places, a teacher was hired immediately. This was usually someone qualified who already lived in the district. A short term of three or four months would be taught in a local home if no other space was available. The pay for each month of a three-month session was $40. Pay was gathered with warrants that were cashed at a discount unless held for a year. Until the drought was broken and things in the area improved, the shorter school session prevailed. Textbooks were any that could be found in the neighborhood. Even old newspapers were used to teach the students. The ingenuity of the residents at making needed items out of things available allowed homemade blackboards and other necessities to be acquired. By 1899, there were 223 one-room school districts in "M" (Woods) County meeting an average of 70 days a year.

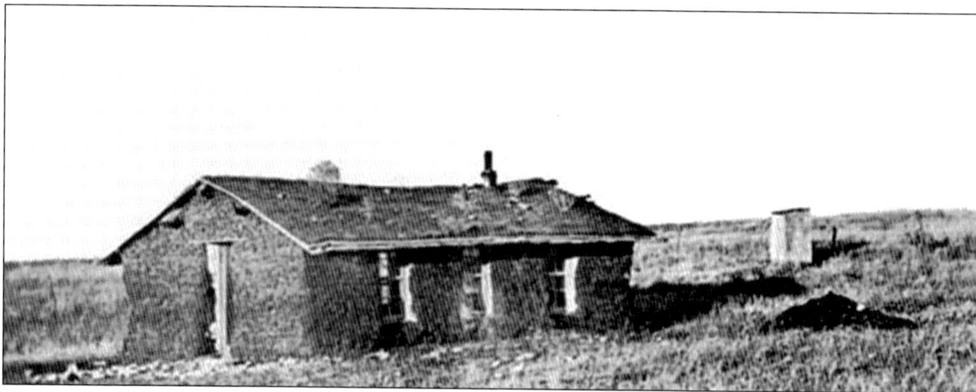

A generous farmer in the center of the district donated an acre of land. The local men lost no time erecting a sod and dirt building with a dirt floor. This schoolhouse was soon bursting at the seams with children, so a new wood-frame building was put up as soon as possible.

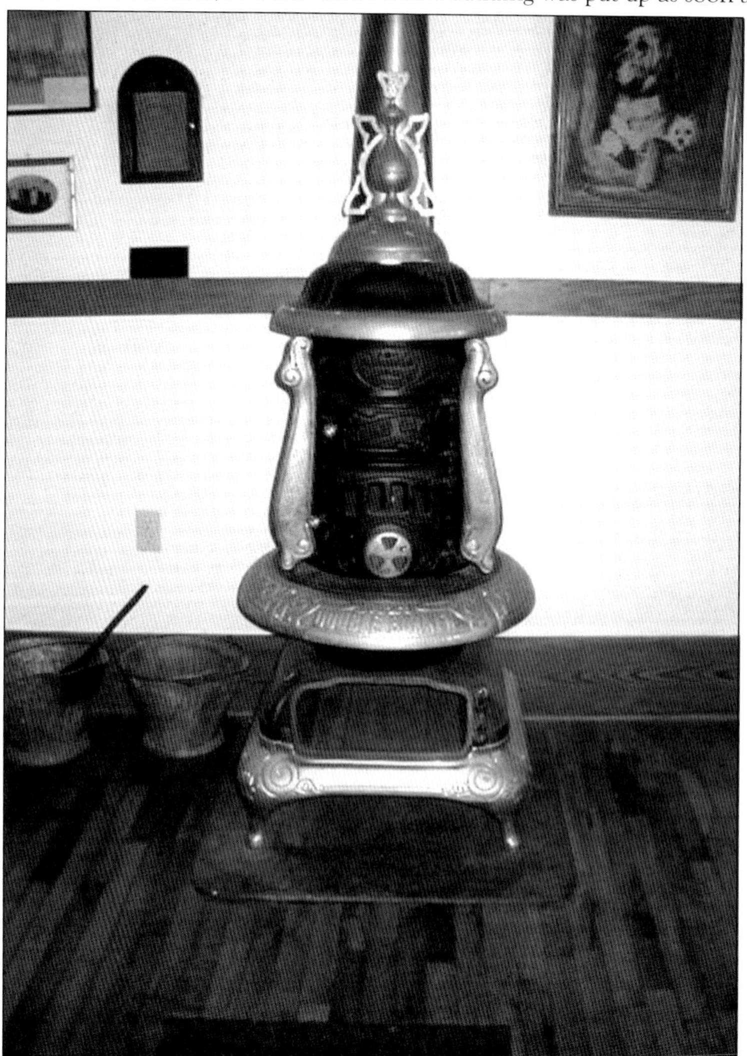

This was a typical white schoolhouse of the period, complete with a big potbellied stove set in the center to keep everyone warm. Students toasted their fronts while their backs chilled and then turned around and reversed matters. (Courtesy of the Alva Cherokee Strip Museum.)

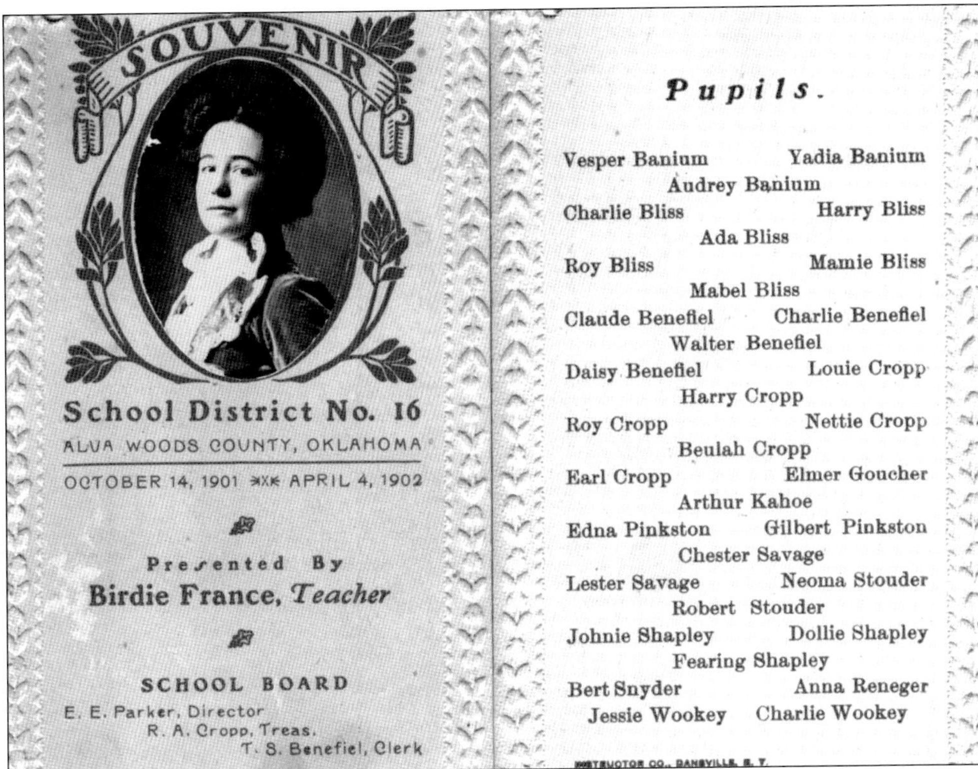

SOUVENIR

School District No. 16

ALVA WOODS COUNTY, OKLAHOMA

OCTOBER 14, 1901 — APRIL 4, 1902

Presented By

Birdie France, *Teacher*

SCHOOL BOARD

E. E. Parker, Director

R. A. Cropp, Treas.

T. S. Benefiel, Clerk

Pupils.

Vesper Banium — Yadia Banium
Audrey Banium
Charlie Bliss — Harry Bliss
Ada Bliss
Roy Bliss — Mamie Bliss
Mabel Bliss
Claude Benefiel — Charlie Benefiel
Walter Benefiel
Daisy Benefiel — Louie Cropp
Harry Cropp
Roy Cropp — Nettie Cropp
Beulah Cropp
Earl Cropp — Elmer Goucher
Arthur Kahoe
Edna Pinkston — Gilbert Pinkston
Chester Savage
Lester Savage — Neoma Stouder
Robert Stouder
Johnie Shapley — Dollie Shapley
Fearing Shapley
Bert Snyder — Anna Reneger
Jessie Wookey — Charlie Wookey

INSTRUCTOR CO., DANSVILLE, N. Y.

Social life in the early 1900s centered on the school and school programs. Spelling bees and ciphering matches could occupy an entire evening and were enjoyed by all. With a schoolhouse every three miles, contests naturally arose. Another entertainment available was the literary society that would meet in the schoolhouses. People came from miles away by whatever means available, including walking (often while carrying a younger child). Instruments of different types would often appear to entertain the residents of an evening.

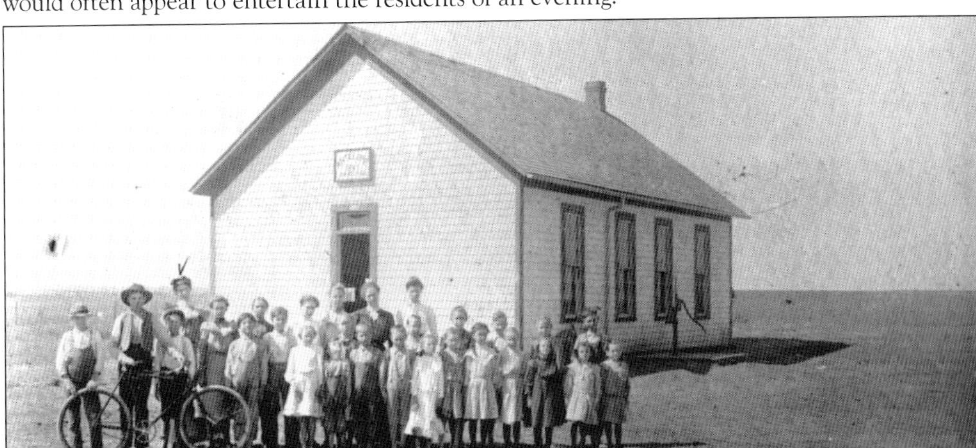

This school in Antelope (east of Avard) finely got a water well and pump in 1903 and the children no longer had to carry water to the school from a neighboring house. Before the pump, each pupil hoped to be called on by the teacher to go to the nearest house with the water bucket. Somehow, carrying it between them, the students managed to get back with enough water to quench the thirst of all.

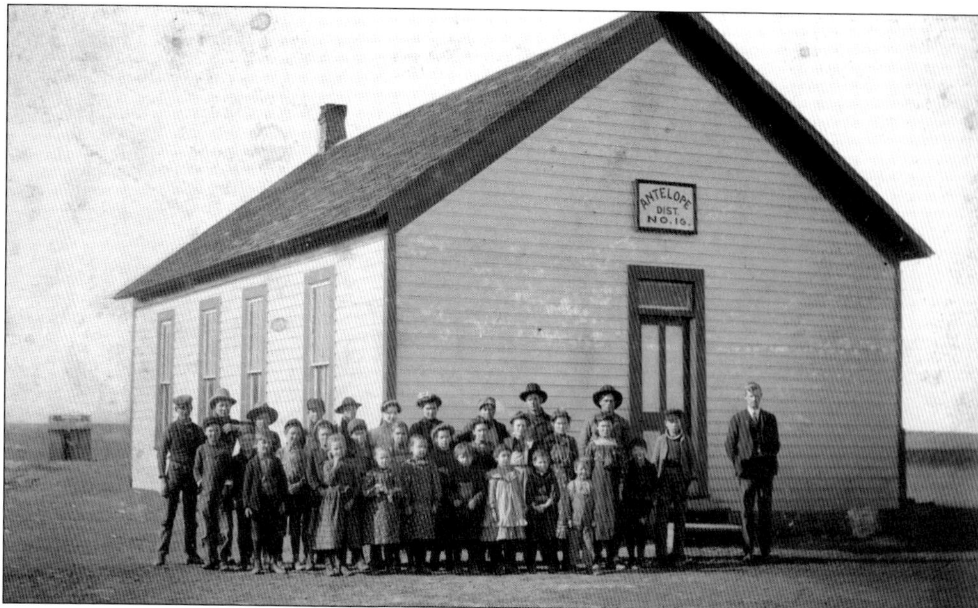

In 1903, the teacher and students of school district No. 16 in Antelope posed for their class photograph. They are, from left to right (first row) Earl Cropp, ? Adkins, Lera Bainum, Audrey Bainum, unidentified, Mae Andre, Irene Goucher, and Real Cropp; (second row) Ed Tetren, Lester Savage, Chester Savage, Fearing Shapley, Bob Stouder, Mabel Bliss, Daisy Benefiel, Dolly Shapley, Nettie Cropp, Mary Link, Anna Link, unidentified, and Fred Teten; (third row) John Shapley, Roy Bliss, Walter Benefiel, Harry Cropp, Henry Tetren, Zaida Bainum, Ada Bliss, Charley Wookey, Harry Bliss, and Claude Benefiel. Their teacher, Mr. Terbush, is standing apart from the group to the right.

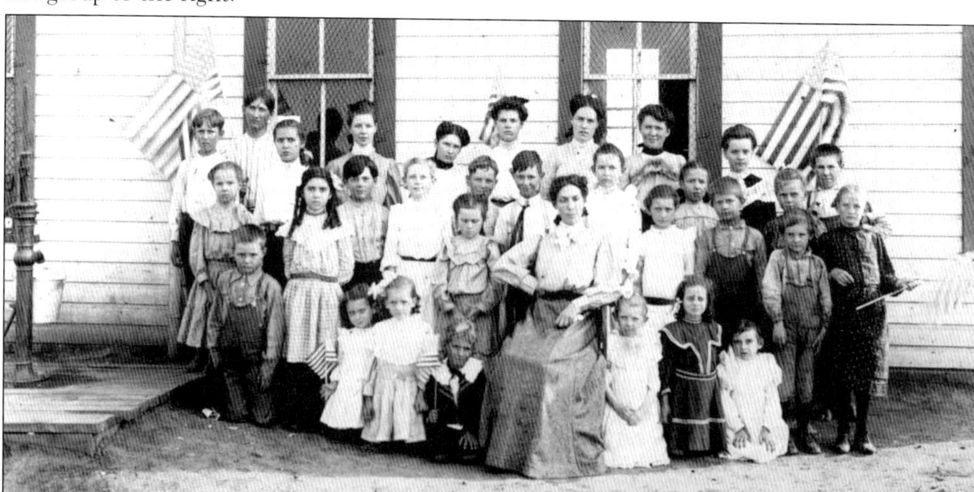

This photograph is of school district No. 16 in 1905. The students and teacher posed in front of their school are, from left to right (seated) teacher Mabel Jackson; (first row) Velma Andre, Irene Goucher, Gail Salvage, Myrtle Eld, Irene Watson, and Goldie Barnes; (second row) Lera Bainum, Dick Teten, Mae Andre, Frank ?, Myrtle Eld, Mary Link, Chester Savage, Florence Eld, Vivian Savage, Audrey Bainum, Floyd Bliss, Albert Foucher, and Dessie Goucher; (third row) Fearing Sharpley, John Shapley, Mabel Bliss, Zaida Bainum, Dolly Shapley, Mamie Bliss, Naomi Stouder, Anna Link, Daisy Benefiel, and Robert Stouder.

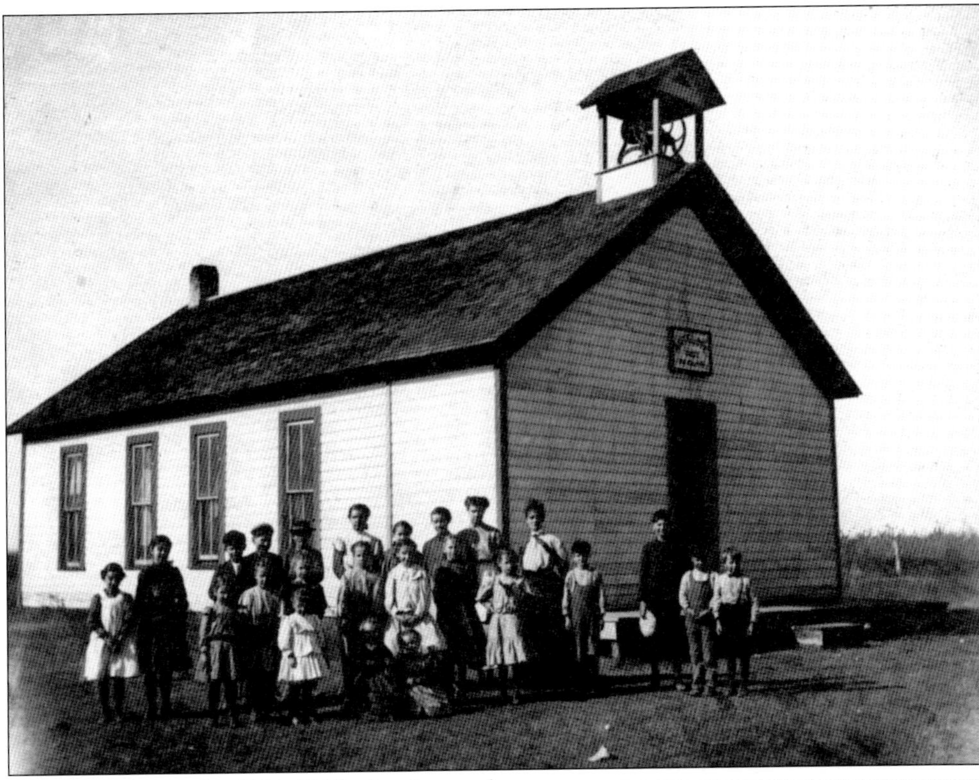

Sometime during the 1906–1907 school year, the Antelope school acquired a bell tower and bell. The students and teacher during that school year were, from left to right (first row) Velma Andre, Lorena Bainum, unidentified, Lera Bainum, Vivian Savage, Dessie Goucher, Stillman Goucher, Chester Savage, Glenn Goucher, and Garnett Savere; (second row) Goldia Barnes, Mae Anre, Floyd Bliss, Lester Savage, Fearing Shapely, Mabel Bliss, Audrey Bainum, Daisy Benefiel, Mamie Bliss, and Clara Howard, their teacher.

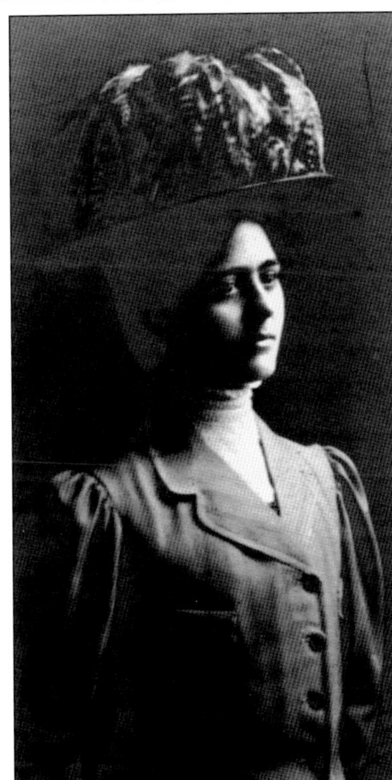

Clara Howard was the teacher at Antelope School District No. 16 in 1907. She later married Judge Bickel from Alva.

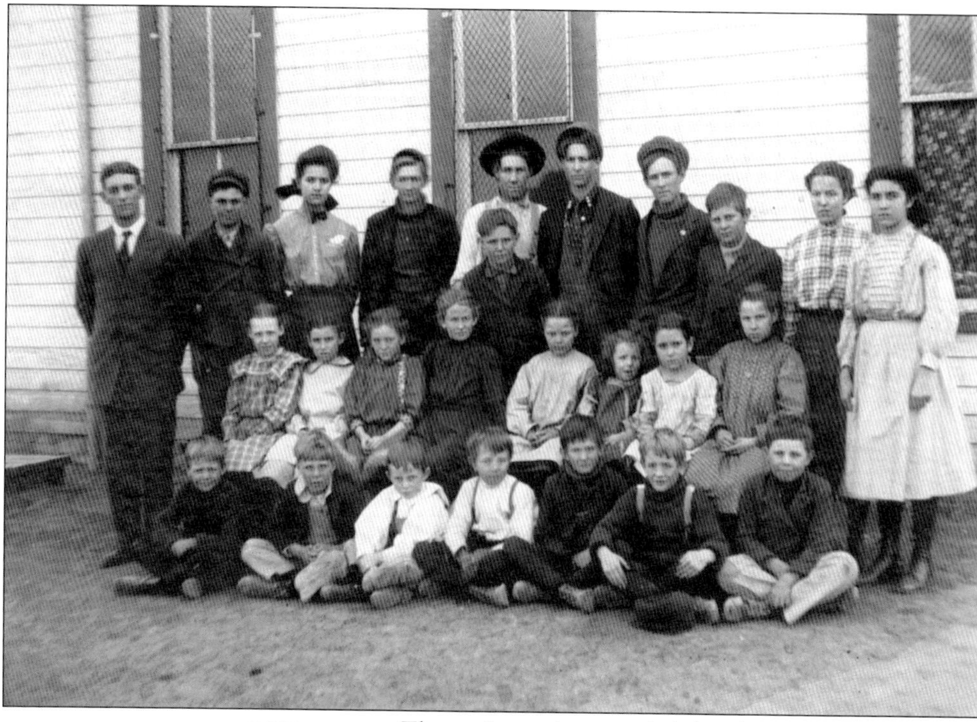

The students who attended Antelope School District No. 16 during the 1908–1909 school year were, from left to right (first row) Glenn Goucher, Dick Teton, Bariman Barnes, Garnett Savere, Albert Goucher, Stillman Goucher, and Ralph Bliss; (second row) Hildreth Gray, Goldia Barnes, Irene Goucher, Dessie Goucher, Ralph Teton, Lorena Bainum, Letha Savere, Velma Anders, and Lera Bainum; (third row) teacher T.V. (Tom) Terbush, Ed Teton, Mabel Bliss, Elmer Goucher, Bob Stander, unknown, Fearing Shapley, Floyd Bliss, Audrey Bainum, and May Andre.

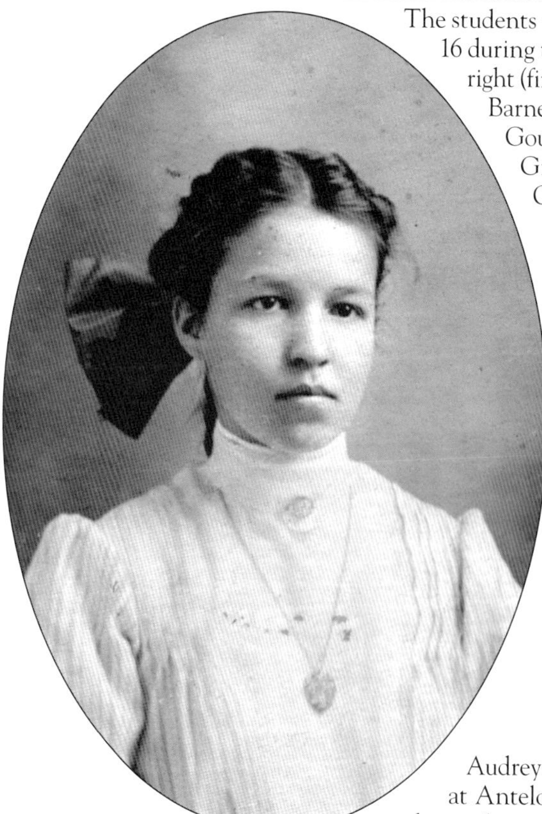

Audrey (Bainum) Kinzie's school picture was taken at Antelope School District No. 16. The dress and hairstyle were typical at that time.

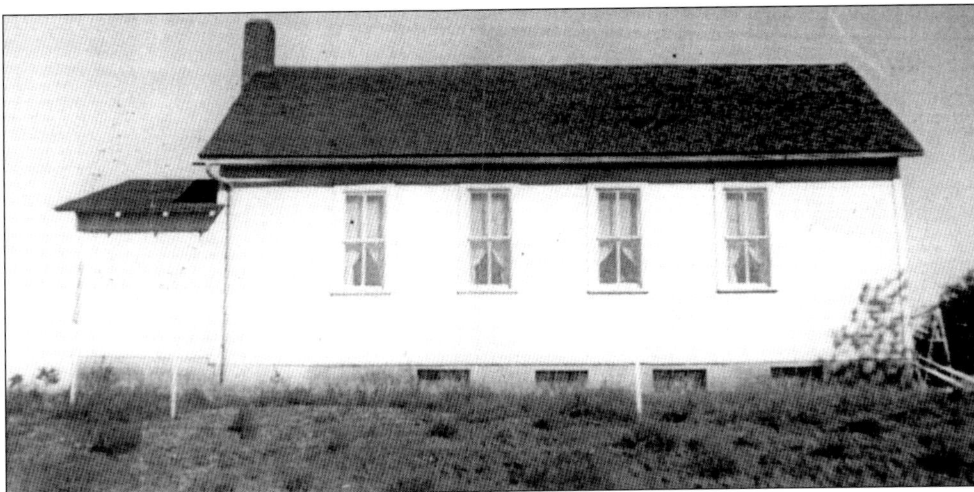

The McKeever schoolhouse, west of Alva, is typical of the one-room schoolhouses found in early "M" (Woods) County. In 2001, this building was moved to the campus of Northwestern Oklahoma State University and restored to its original condition. (Courtesy of Alva Cherokee Strip Museum.)

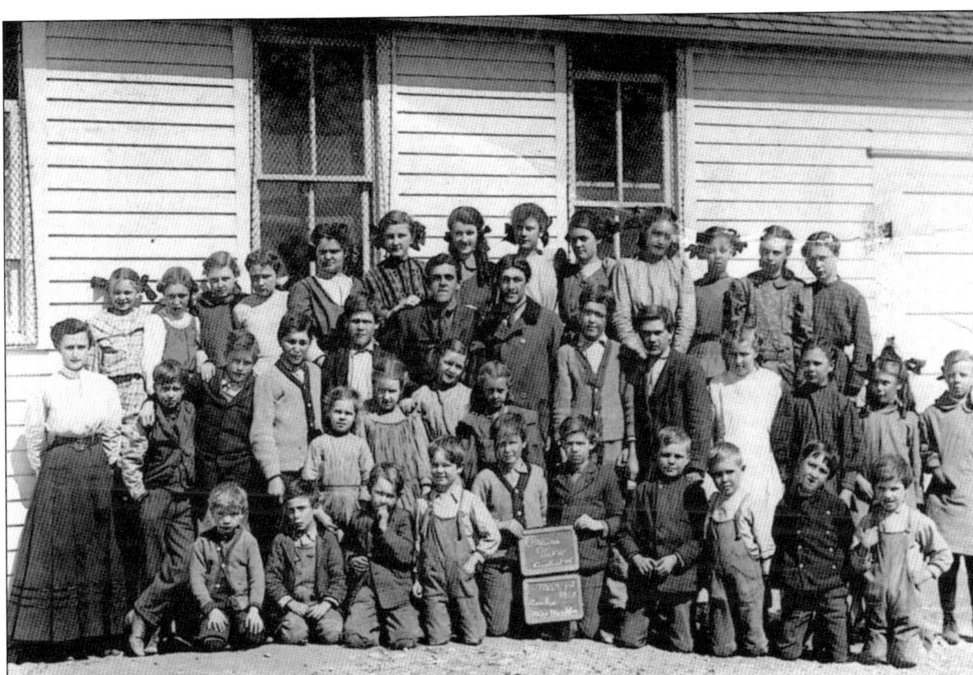

The teacher and students from Prairie View School are not identified, but they represent the many students who attended this one-room school from its beginnings in 1894 until it closed in 1948. Until this building was constructed, classes were held in local dugout homes. (Courtesy of Alva Cherokee Strip Museum.)

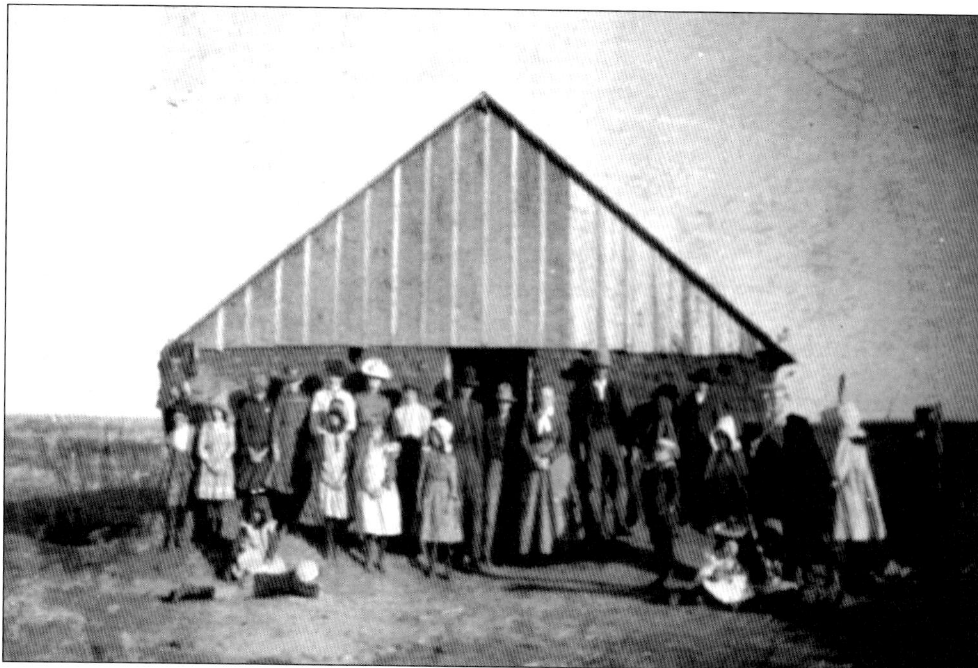

A teacher and students from Hankins School, northwest of Alva, were photographed by their sod schoolhouse. (Courtesy of Alva Cherokee Strip Museum.)

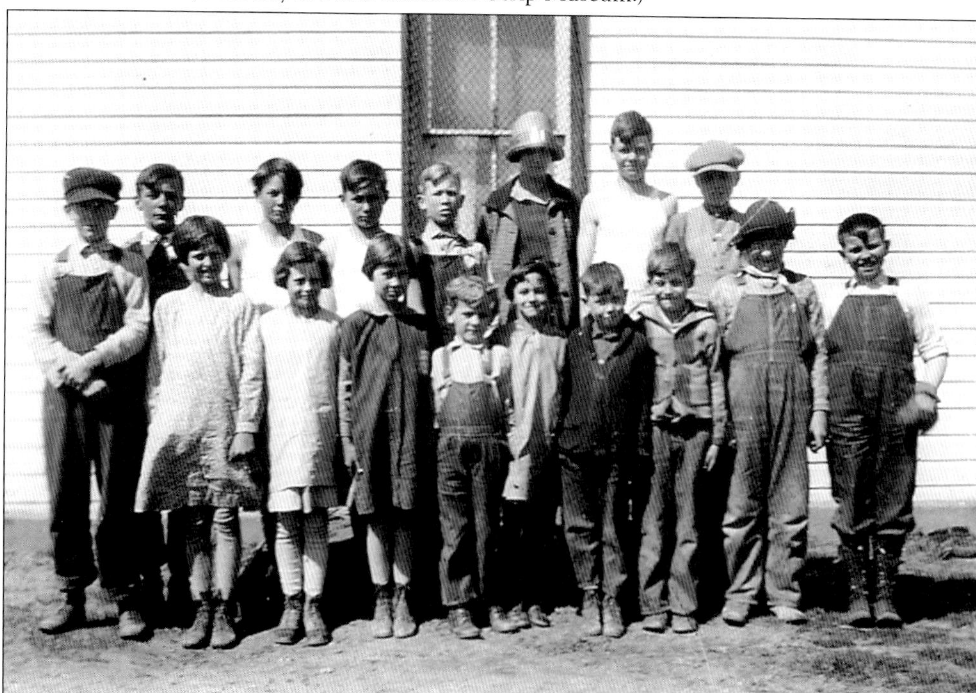

Union Center School District No. 67 was located north of Dacoma. At one time, the teachers at this school were Dora (Nelson) Hickman and Nels Nelson. In the late 1970s, the school was moved to the grounds of the Cherokee Strip Museum and restored. (Courtesy of Lorraine (Nelson) Malzahn.)

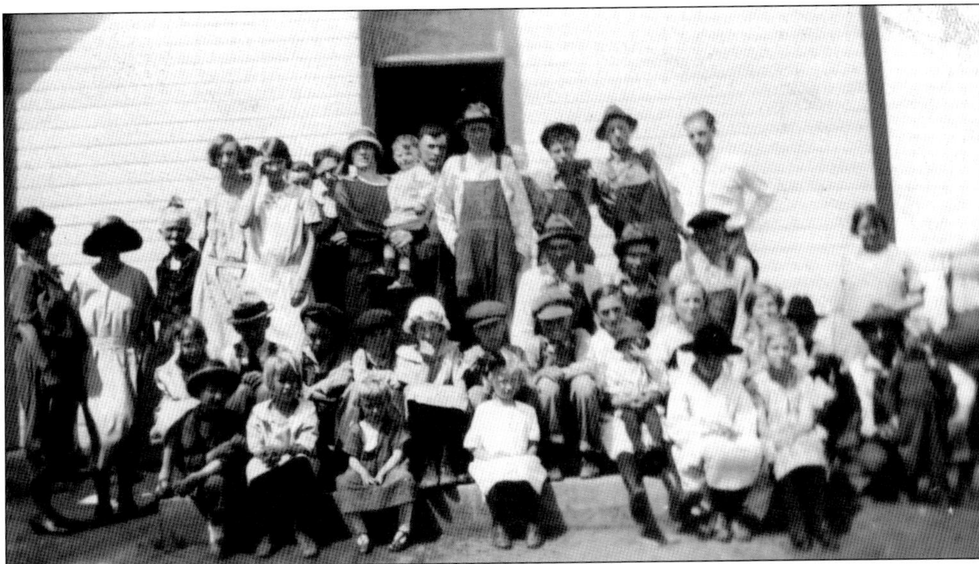

Nels Nelson was a teacher at Highland School, located northwest of Alva. (Courtesy of Lorraine (Nelson) Malzahn.)

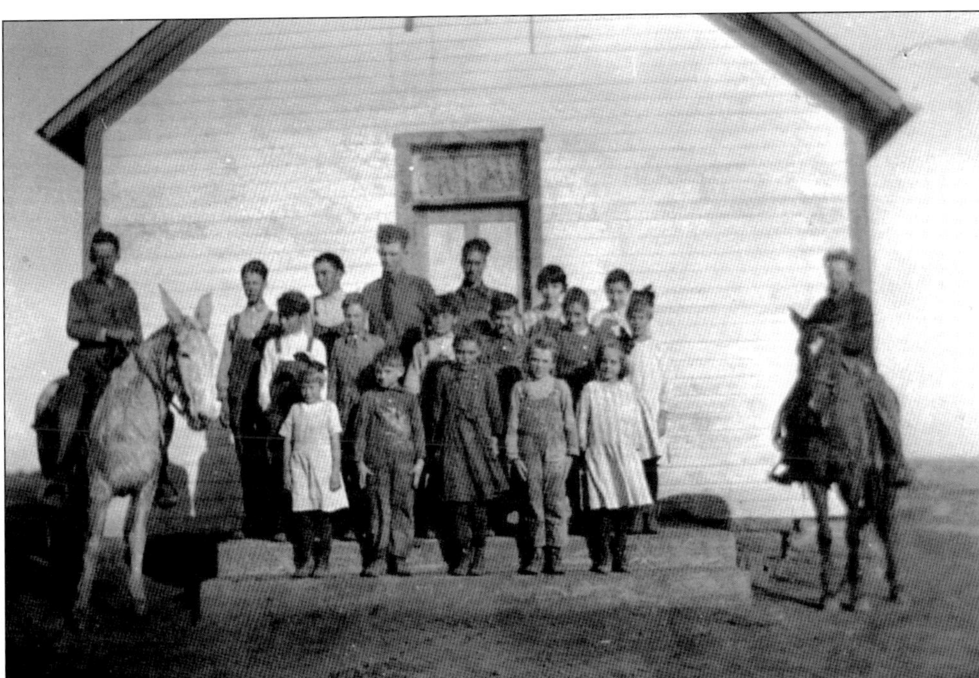

Nels Nelson, teacher at Highland School northwest of Alva in the Isenbart and Murley District, was photographed with a couple of boys showing off a horse and a mule. (Courtesy of Lorraine (Nelson) Malzahn.)

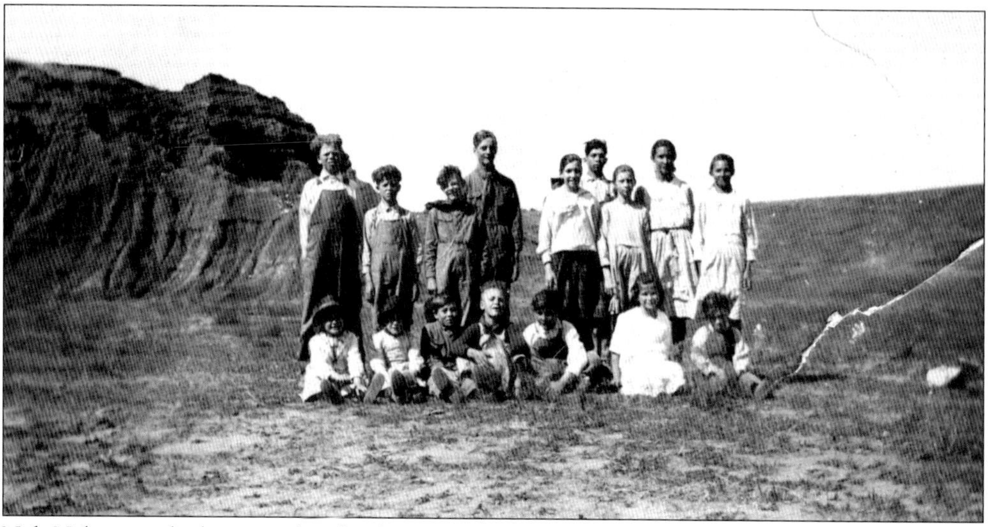

Nels Nelson worked as a teacher for the Lone Star School District, northwest of Alva. Notice the rough terrain behind the students. (Courtesy of Lorraine (Nelson) Malzahn.)

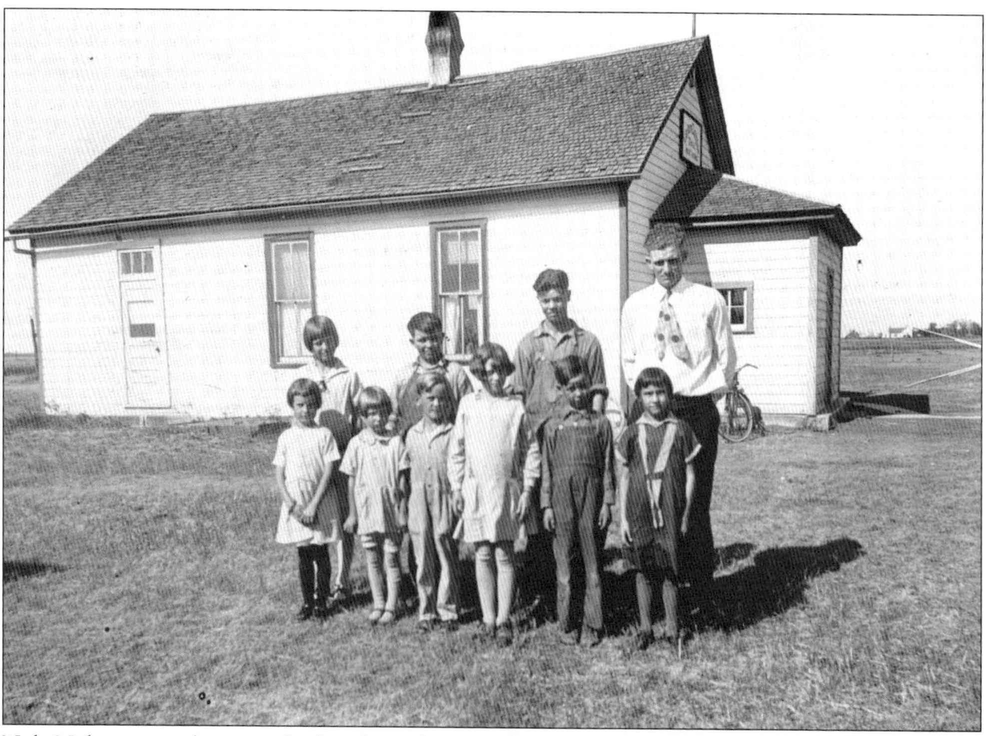

Nels Nelson was photographed with students in front of this typical one-room schoolhouse on the prairie. (Courtesy of Lorraine (Nelson) Malzahn.)

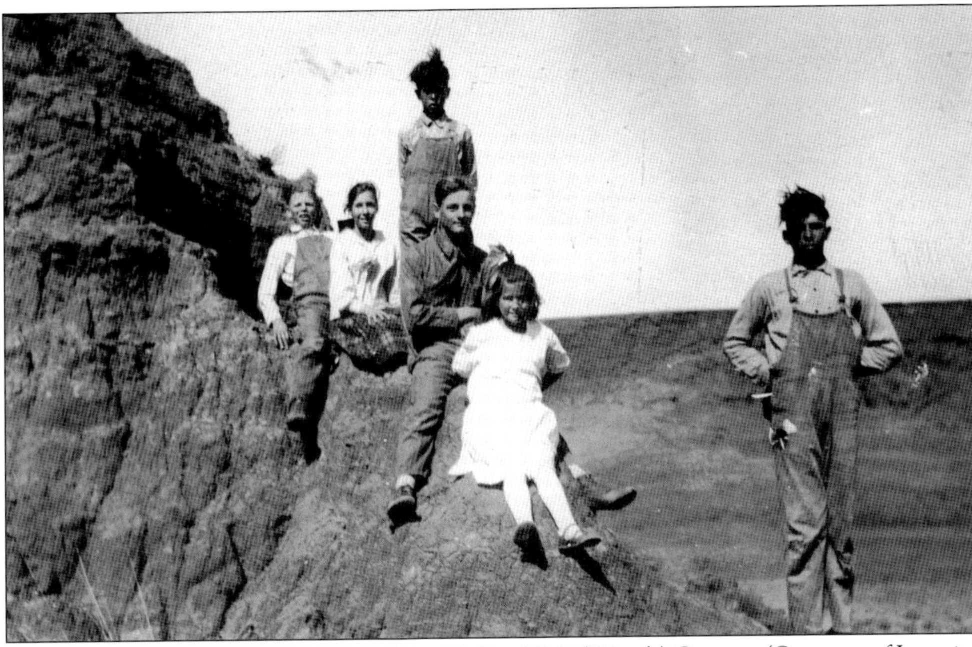

Northwest of Alva, students pose on the red hills of "M" (Woods) County. (Courtesy of Lorraine (Nelson) Malzahn.)

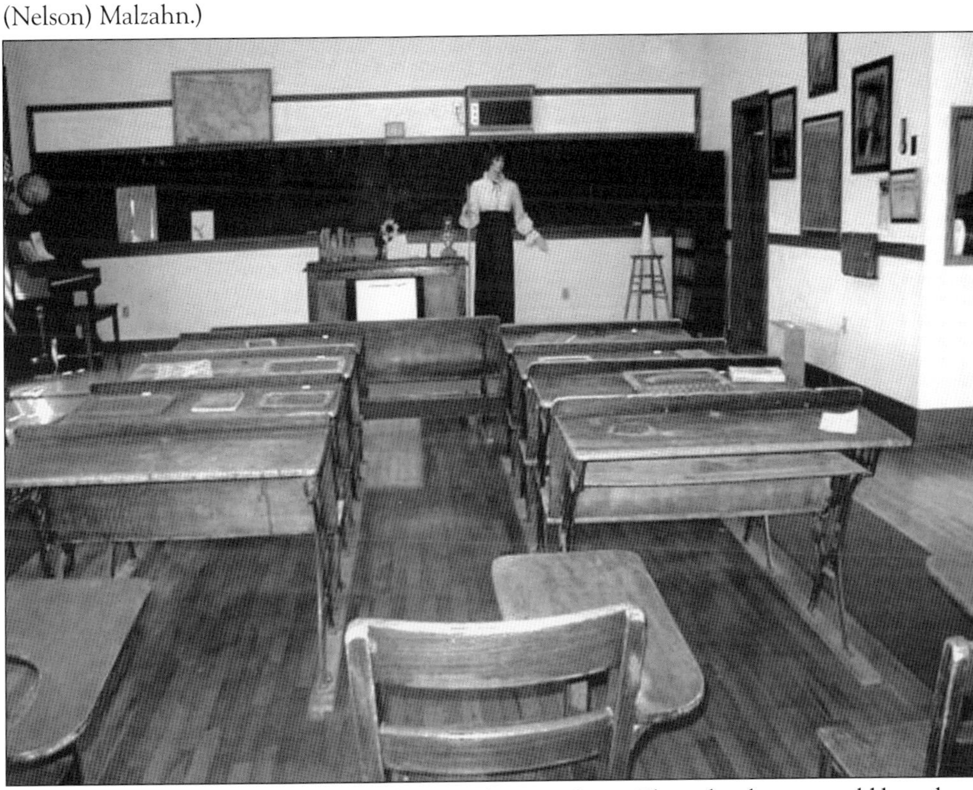

Desks in schoolhouses generally seated two to three students. This schoolroom would have been constructed after the sod schoolhouse that was first erected for the children. (Courtesy of Alva Cherokee Strip Museum.)

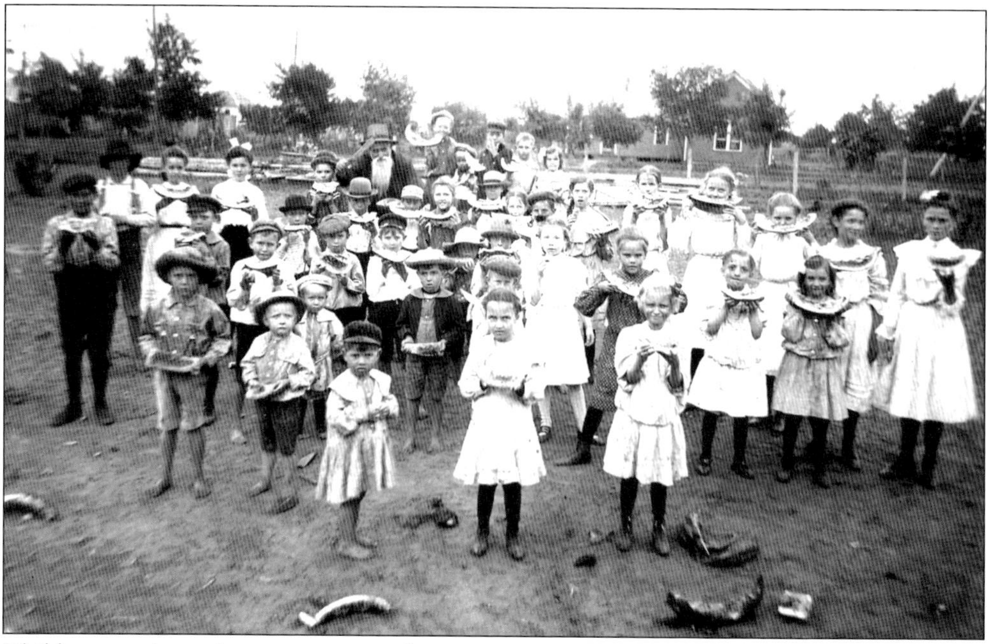

Children are shown here in a watermelon-eating contest. Watermelons were sometimes stored in straw stacks to be eaten later with ice cream made with ice from the water tanks. There was also a medium-size yellowish melon called "pie melon." It was raised easily and made a very good sauce. (Courtesy of Alva Cherokee Strip Museum.)

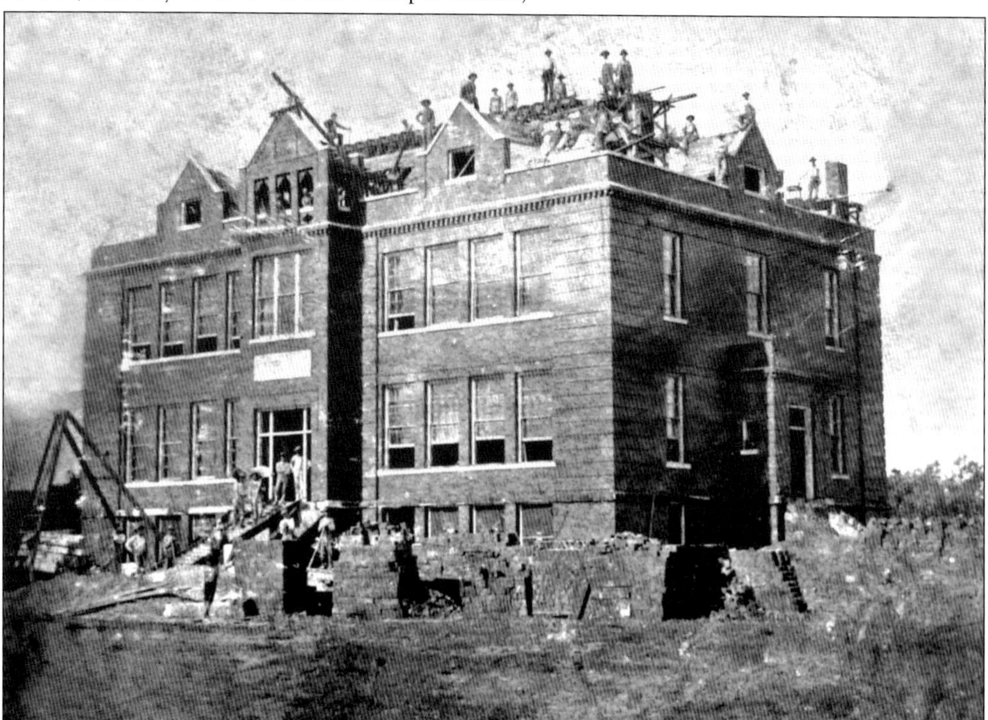

In Alva the West Side School (Washington School) built this large brick structure in 1904. It replaced the first school built in 1895 after it burned. (Courtesy of Alva Cherokee Strip Museum.)

Six

Higher Education

Four years after the Cherokee Outlet opening in 1893, aggressive businessmen in Alva induced the Oklahoma Territorial Legislature to approve the establishment of a northwestern territorial normal school. The cost of the school was to be approximately $130,000 and it was to be the largest educational structure in the state, measuring 155 feet in length by 125 feet in depth and more than 100 feet in height.

On March 10, 1897, the fifth territorial legislature assembly passed a bill establishing a normal school at Alva. The people of northwestern Oklahoma had presented a similar bill two years previously but it met with too much opposition. However, pioneers in this area were not easily sidetracked and their children's education was at stake. Perseverance paid off and the bill was eventually passed. Controversy over the school's establishment led to litigation, but the Supreme Court sustained it as regular and legal. James Fryre, a homesteader who had arrived during the land run, generously gave the land for the school. In his book *The Cherokee Strip*, Mr. Rainey remarks on the structure that was erected. The building at Alva presents the most imposing architecture and is one of the most appreciated state institutions to this day.

The school's original function was to train teachers by providing two years of college-level classes. The demand for teachers and better teacher training became critical as one-room schoolhouses proliferated. As a result, in 1919 Northwestern evolved into a four-year, degree-granting institution known as Northwestern State Teacher College.

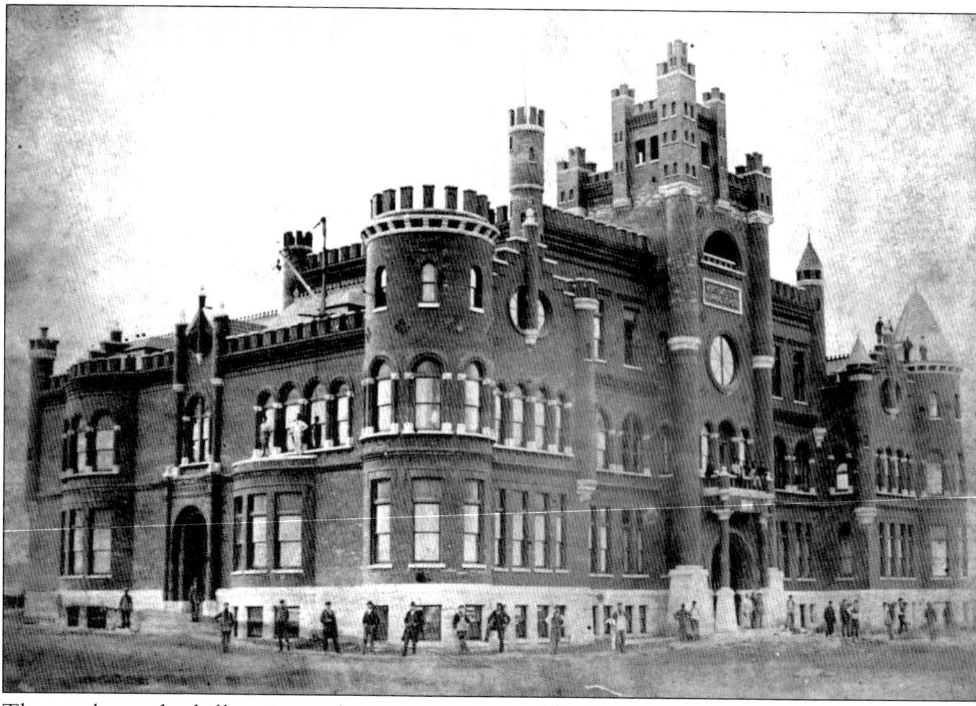

The castle on the hill, as it was known, was inspired by Dr. James E. Ament, a widely traveled Alva pioneer. He had visited a Norman castle in France and was greatly impressed by its grandeur. He and the architect Joseph Foucart, a native Frenchman, drew up the plans for the edifice. It was first condemned as a folly and later hailed as a masterpiece of architectural beauty. (Courtesy of Alva Cherokee Strip Museum.)

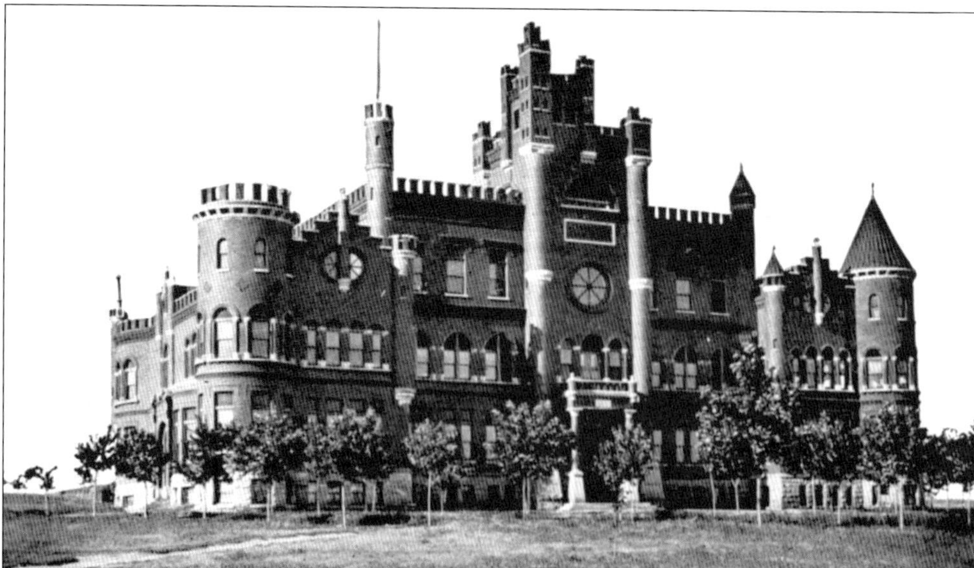

The dream of more to come at the castle never developed. The original castle was intended to be one wing of a larger castle, which was to be built as Northwestern Normal School grew over the years, but chances for the building to be enlarged disappeared when fire broke out on March 1, 1935, causing its total destruction. (Courtesy of Alva Cherokee Strip Museum.)

The first president of Northwestern was Dr. Ament. His faculty consisted of two teachers, Sarah Bosworth and Mrs. Delisle. The school opened before the building was completed and the first classes were held in the Congregational church. The initial enrollment totaled 68, but it increased steadily over the years. This image depicts an advertisement that was in the *Alva Pioneer.* (Courtesy of Alva Cherokee Strip Museum.)

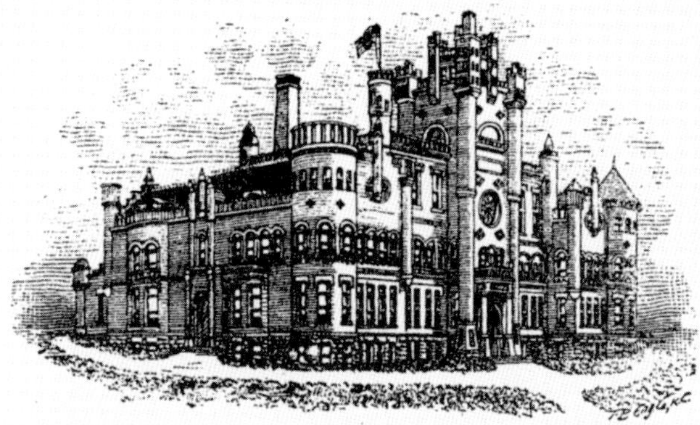

NORTHWESTERN TERRITORIAL NORMAL SCHOOL

OPENS ITS WINTER TERM JANUARY 15, 1900.

ENROLLMENT FOR TERM JUST CLOSED 327.

DIPLOMA—A Territorial Certificate. TUITION—Free, including music and elocution. Expenses less than at any other school in the Southwest.

"THE YOUNG LADIES' HALL"

just opened gives furnace heated sitting room and bed room, both furnished, and good board, for $2.75 PER WEEK.

FOUR COURSES:—Preparatory, Special and Two Normal.

For further information address the President,

JAMES E. AMENT, Alva, Okla.

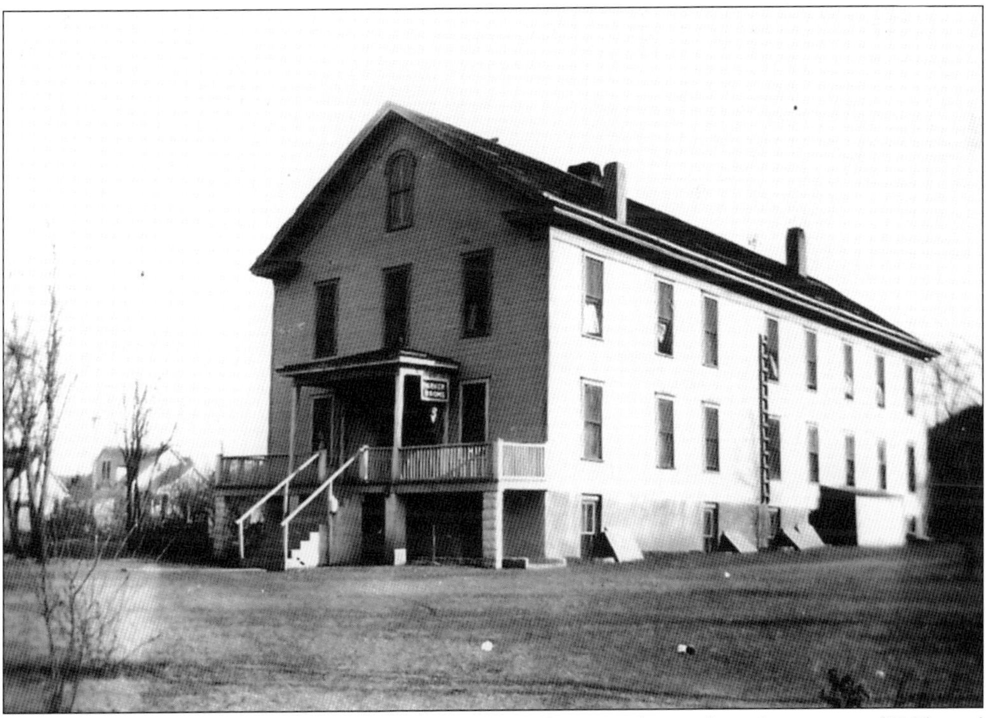

Northwestern Normal School had a dormitory for girls. It was located on the corner of Fifth and Maple Streets where the present Assembly of God Church stands. It was very nicely furnished for the time and had a large dining hall in the basement. (Courtesy of Alva Cherokee Strip Museum.)

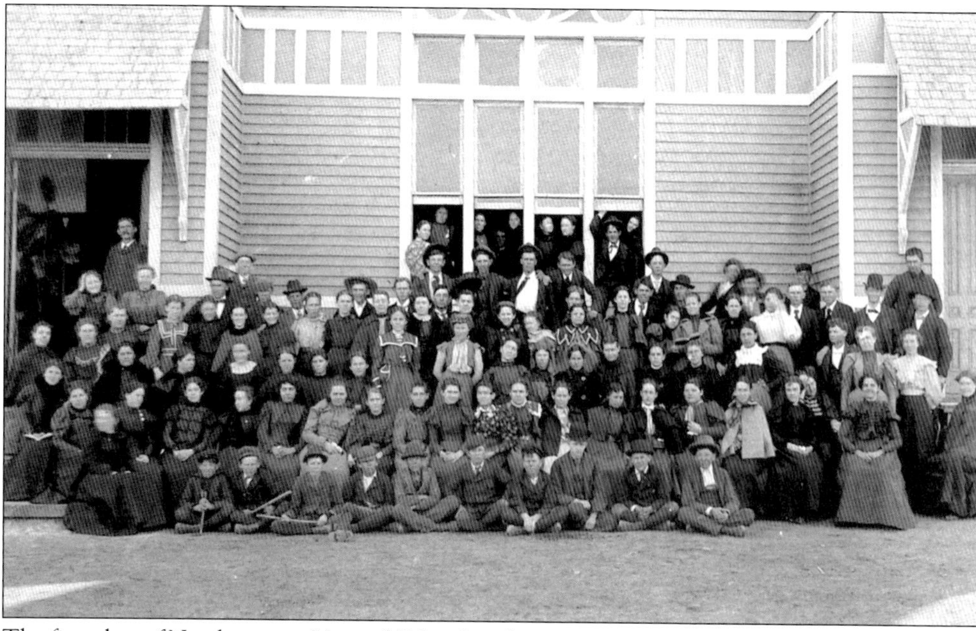

The first class of Northwestern Normal School students met at the Congregational church building until the castle was completed. This photograph was taken on September 23, 1897. (Courtesy of Alva Cherokee Strip Museum.)

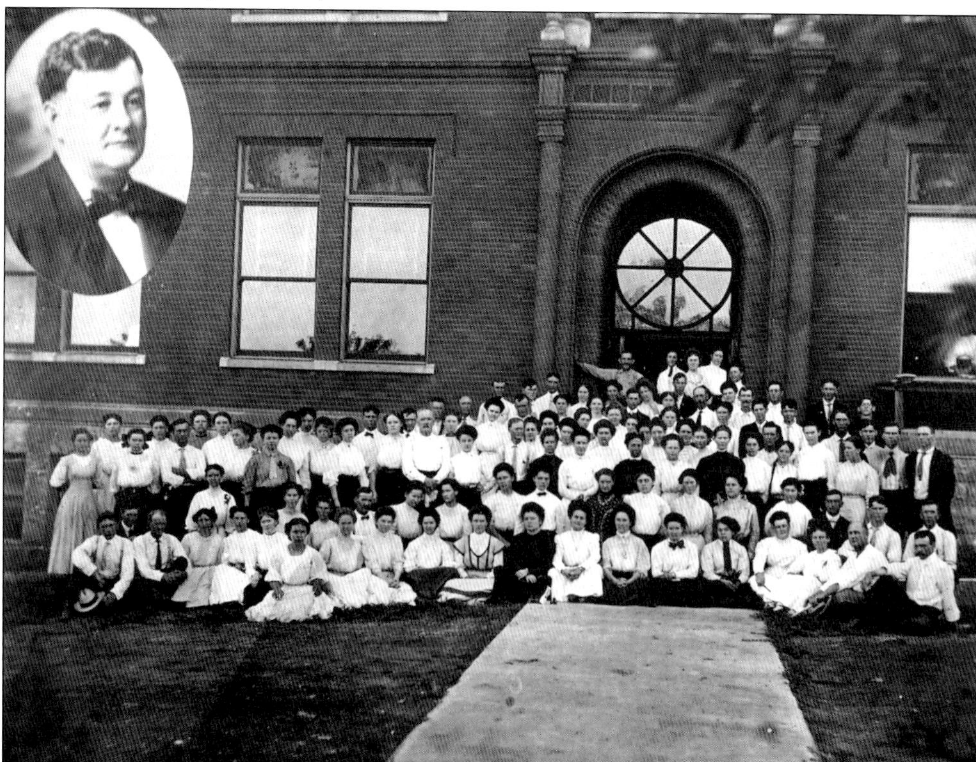

The first class of Northwestern Normal School to graduate from the castle gathered for this photograph. (Courtesy of Alva Cherokee Strip Museum.)

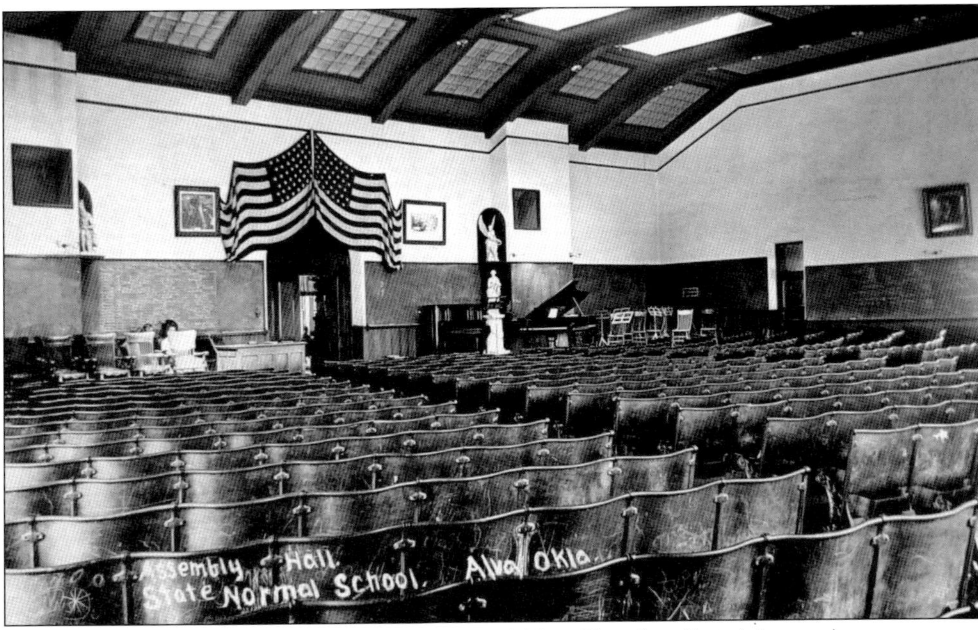

This is Assembly Hall, in the castle. (Courtesy of Alva Cherokee Strip Museum.)

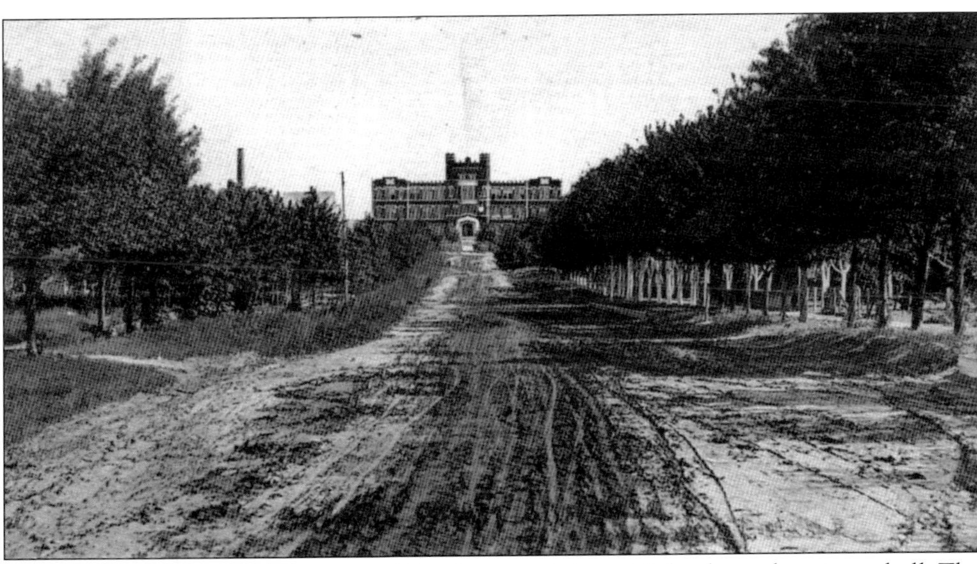
The second building on the campus of Northwestern Normal School was the science hall. This photograph was taken looking south along College Avenue. Notice the unpaved street.

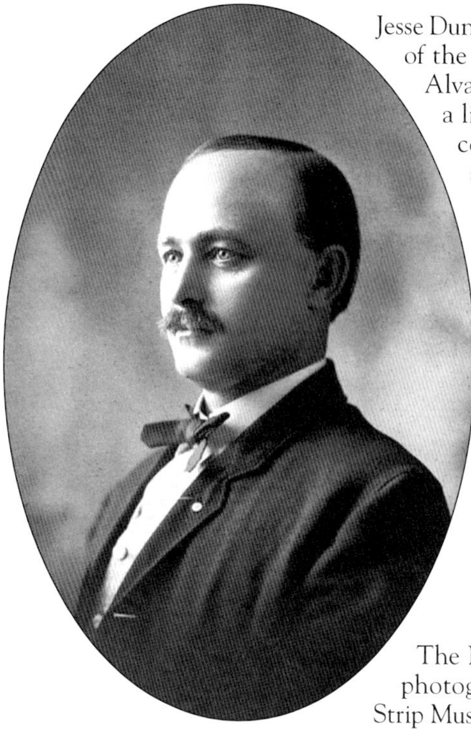

Jesse Dunn was a former Alva attorney who became a justice of the Oklahoma Supreme Court. Dunn, who came to Alva on September 16, 1893, was always ready to give a liberal share of his time and assistance in city and county affairs of public interest. Jesse Dunn Hall at Northwestern Oklahoma State University is named after him. (Courtesy of Alva Cherokee Strip Museum.)

The Northwestern Normal School baseball team was photographed in 1904. (Courtesy of Alva Cherokee Strip Museum.)

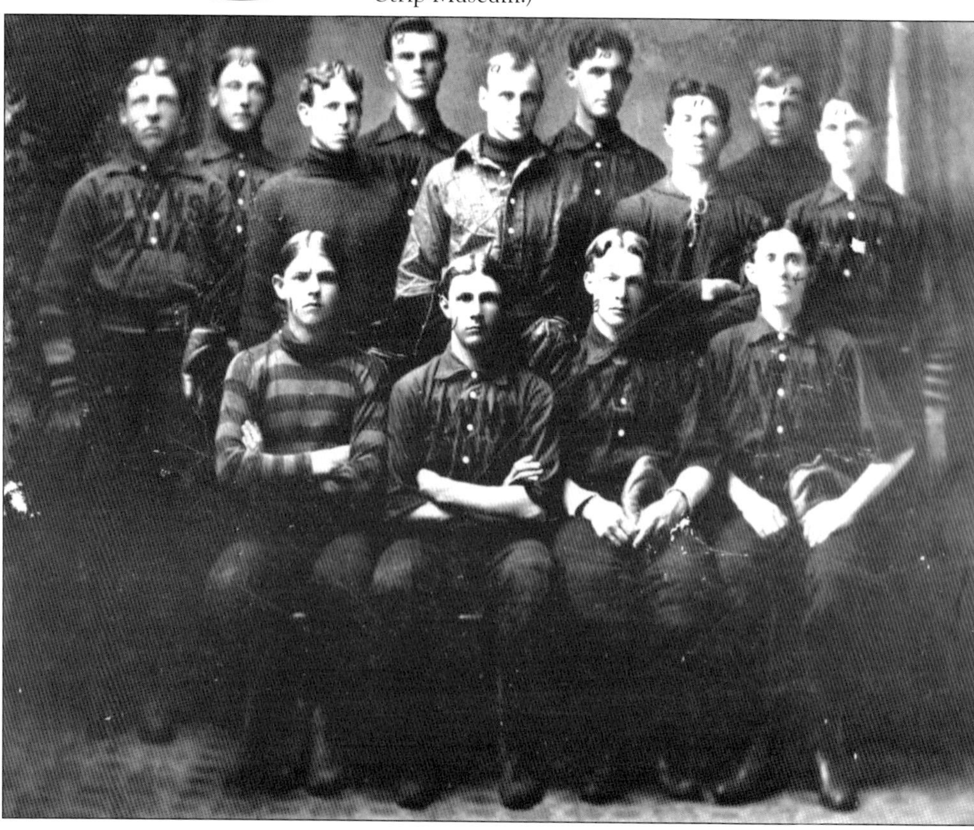

Seven
Early Trains

In 1885, it was announced that the Southern Kansas Railway, a subsidiary of the Santa Fe, would build south from Kiowa, Kansas, into the Cherokee Outlet in order to load cattle from the ranches there. The line was worked on throughout 1886. In 1887, the first train went all the way to the Texas Panhandle at Higgins. At that time, Alva contained only some loading pens and a section house to shelter the railroad men. This is almost all that existed there until the run of 1893.

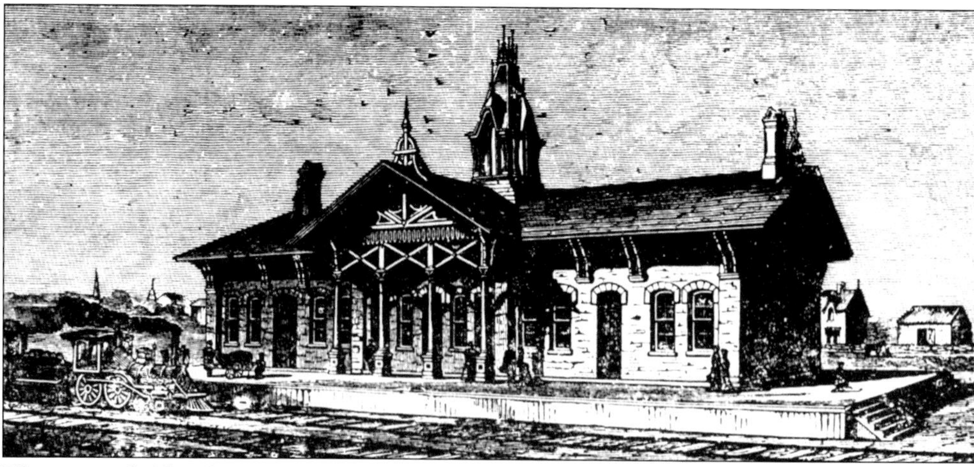

The original Alva Santa Fe train station, built in 1896, is shown here before the cupola and chimney were blown off. (Courtesy of Alva Pioneer Newspaper.)

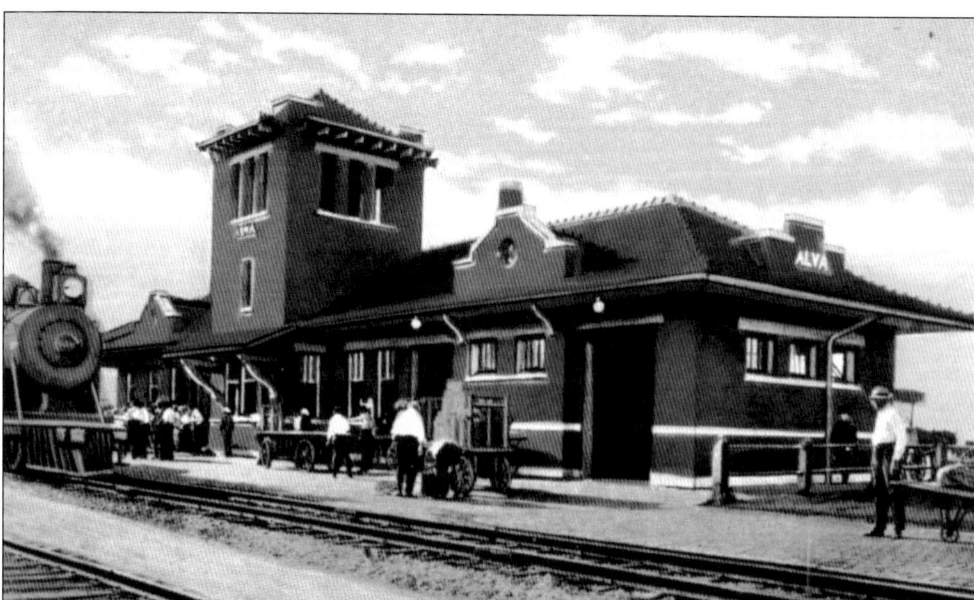

In 1904 this brick Santa Fe station was built. It served until the 1960s when it was torn down and removed.

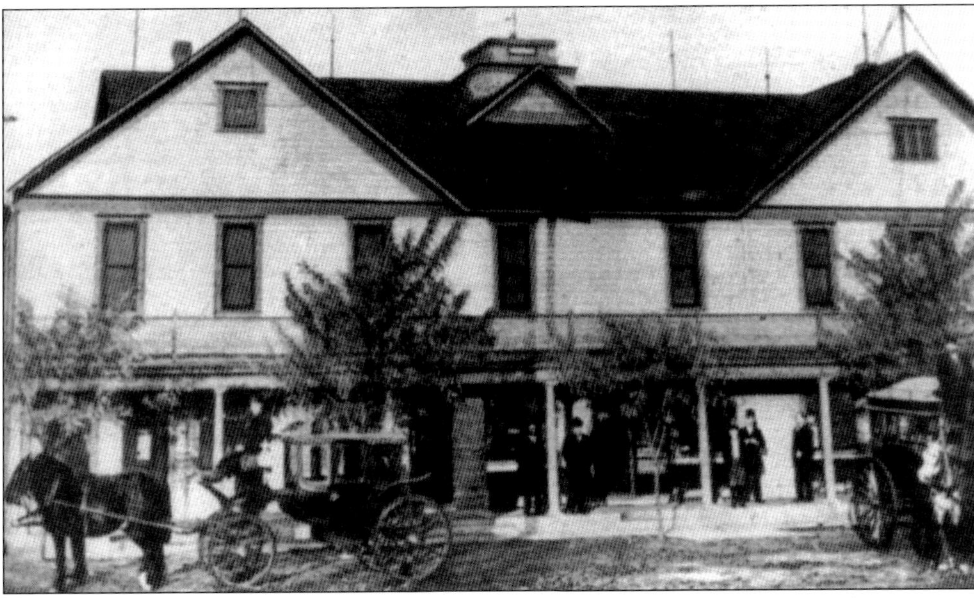

The St. Nichols Hotel was two blocks south of the train station. It provided rooms for the passengers and the crews of the Santa Fe Railroad. (Courtesy of the Alva Cherokee Strip Museum.)

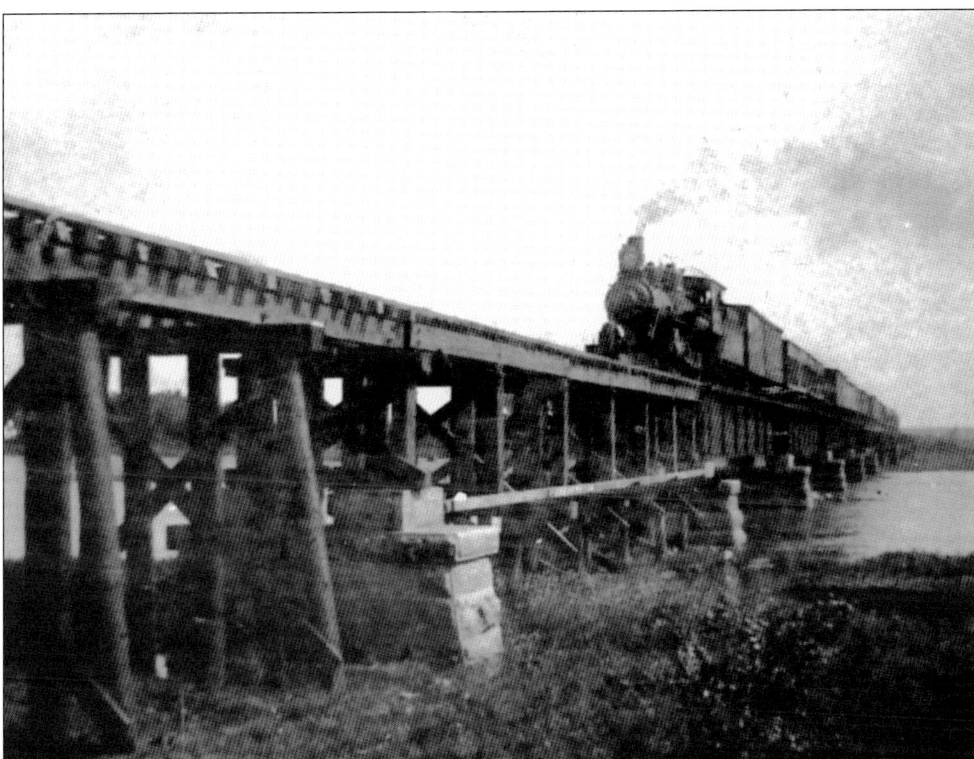

The railroad bridge into Alva was built in the mid-1880s. (Courtesy of the Alva Cherokee Strip Museum.)

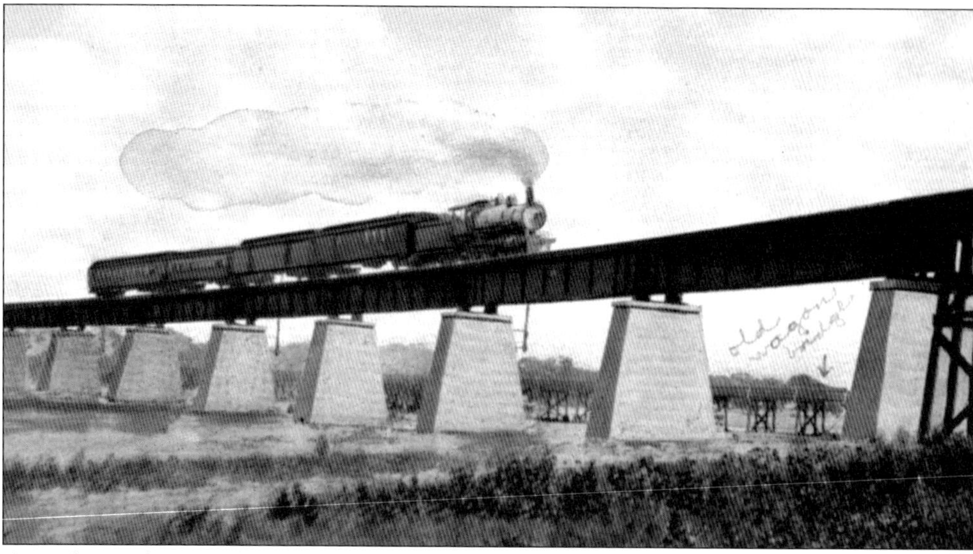

According to history, the railroad bridge into Alva was the first bridge in "M" (Woods) County. It was across the Salt Fork of the Arkansas River on the north side of Alva. The framework was torn away and the bridge rebuilt in 1903. Notice the wagon bridge in the background.

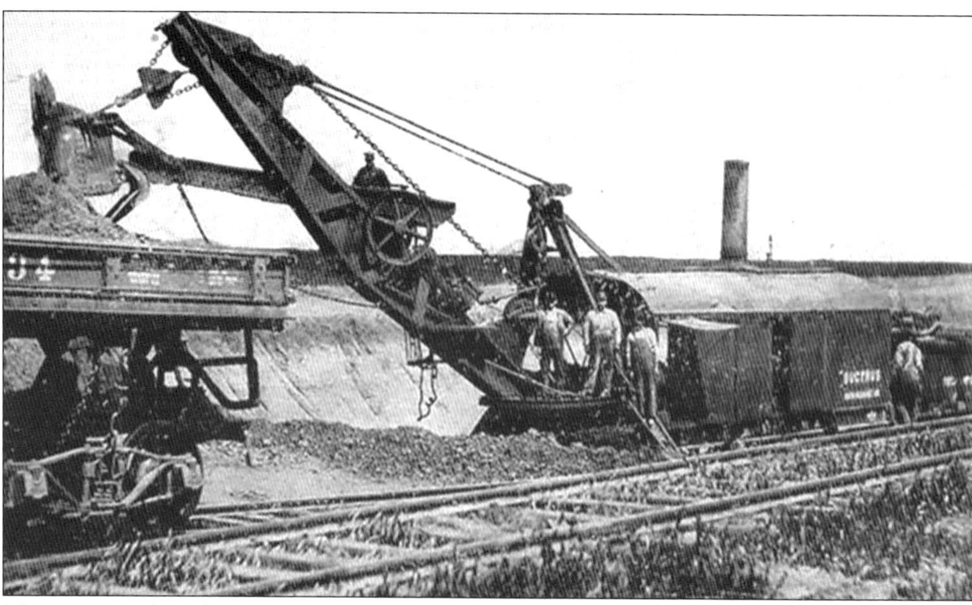

These steams shovels are cleaning out terrain southwest of Alva for the train tracks. The dirt was used as fill for the original Alva train station. (Courtesy of the Alva Cherokee Strip Museum.)

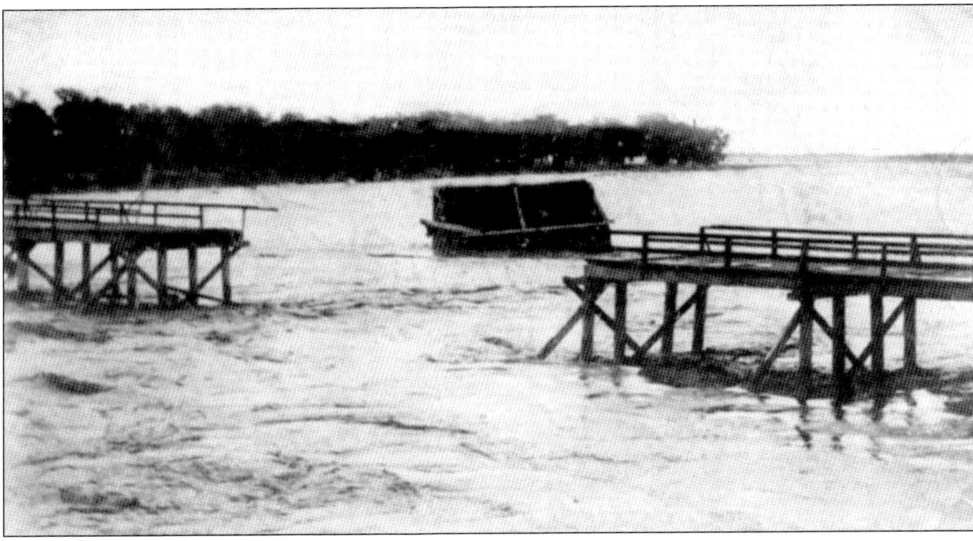

A large structure floated down the flood-swollen Salt Fork and wiped out a few of the spans of the wagon bridge. It had to pass under the Santa Fe Bridge before this point. There is no record to show if there was damage to the railroad. (Courtesy of the Alva Cherokee Strip Museum.)

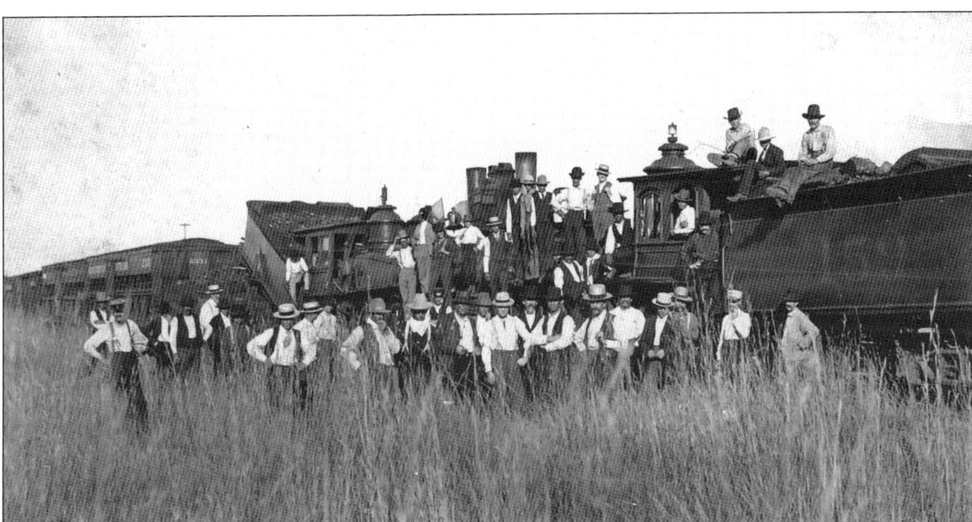

This wreck on the Santa Fe happened just northeast of Capron. It is unclear what caused the accident. (Courtesy of the Alva Cherokee Strip Museum.)

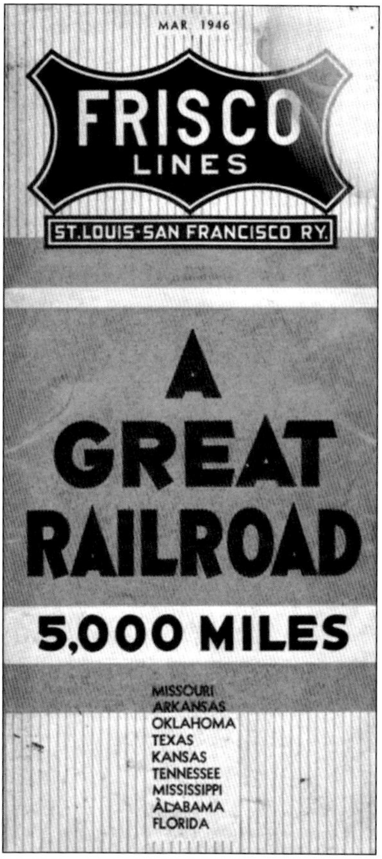

Frisco Railroad ran from St. Louis to San Francisco, going thru Avard. As a result, early pioneers thought that Avard would become a center for commerce.

At Avard, the Frisco and Santa Fe Rail Railroads intersect. In the early 1900s, most of the broomcorn, livestock, and other commodities were hauled to Avard, often from as far as 40 miles away, for shipment.

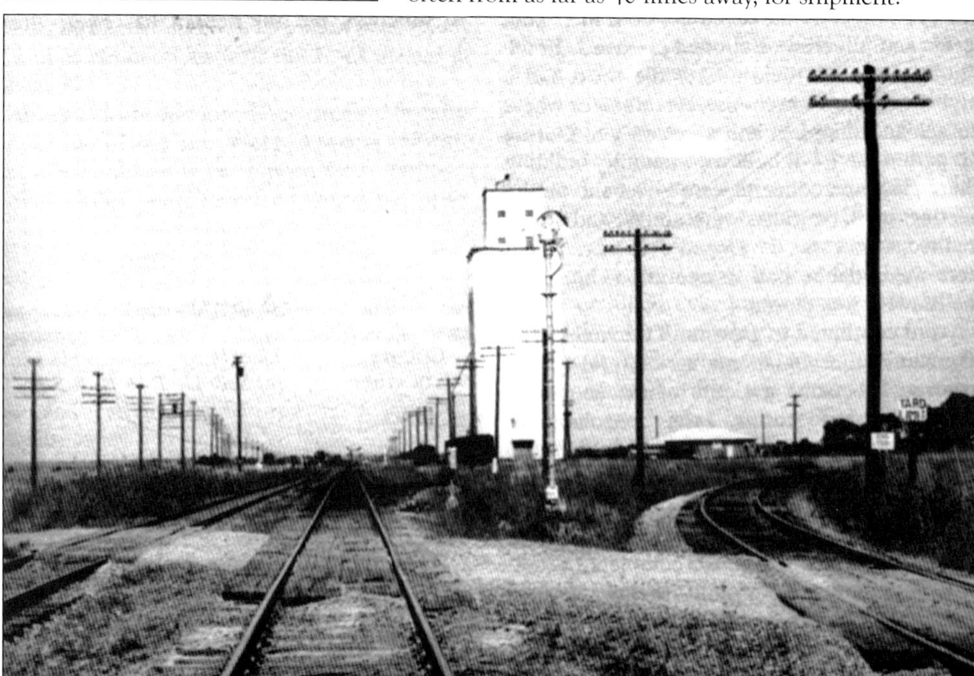

Eight

FIRST CHURCHES

The first congregations in Alva were organized in 1893, but many did not have buildings of their own for a number of years. The different churches shared buildings or met in the homes of their members. The congregations that have images in this chapter are those that acquired buildings before 1907. However, there were two churches that were organized before statehood for which images cannot be found. These were the United Brethren, organized in 1905, and the Zion Lutheran Church, organized on May 21, 1899.

In the country, church and Sunday school were established at the same time as the schools. In Antelope and other country school districts, meetings were regularly held in school buildings. Most pastors had a circuit of two or three "charges" to look after, so services were held less often. However, since there were three resident ministers in the Antelope district, regular services were easily managed.

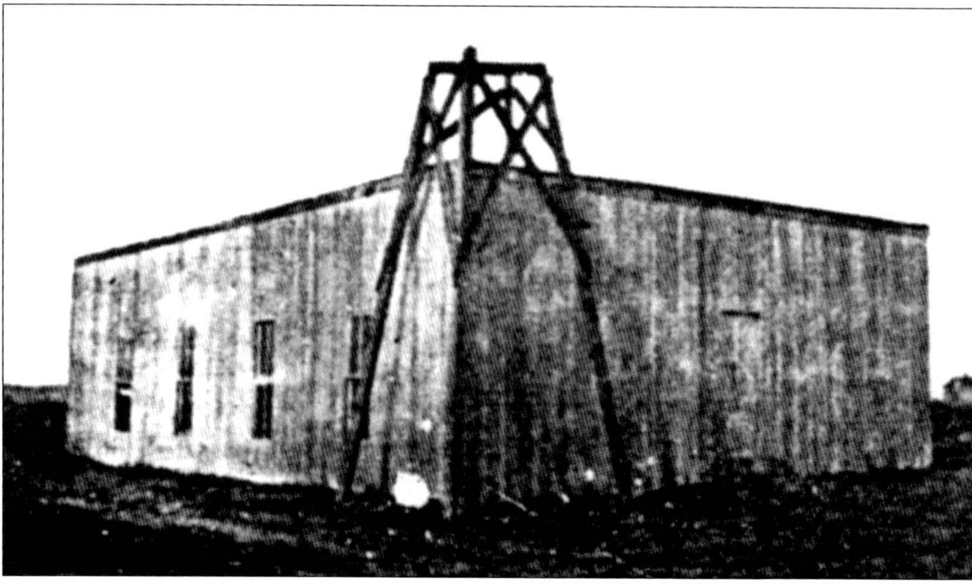

The first church building in Alva, the Union Church, was located where the old armory stands today. The church was finished in November 1893, just in time for Thanksgiving services. It was used alternately by the Congregationalist, Christian, Baptist, and Methodist congregations. (Courtesy of the First United Methodist Church.)

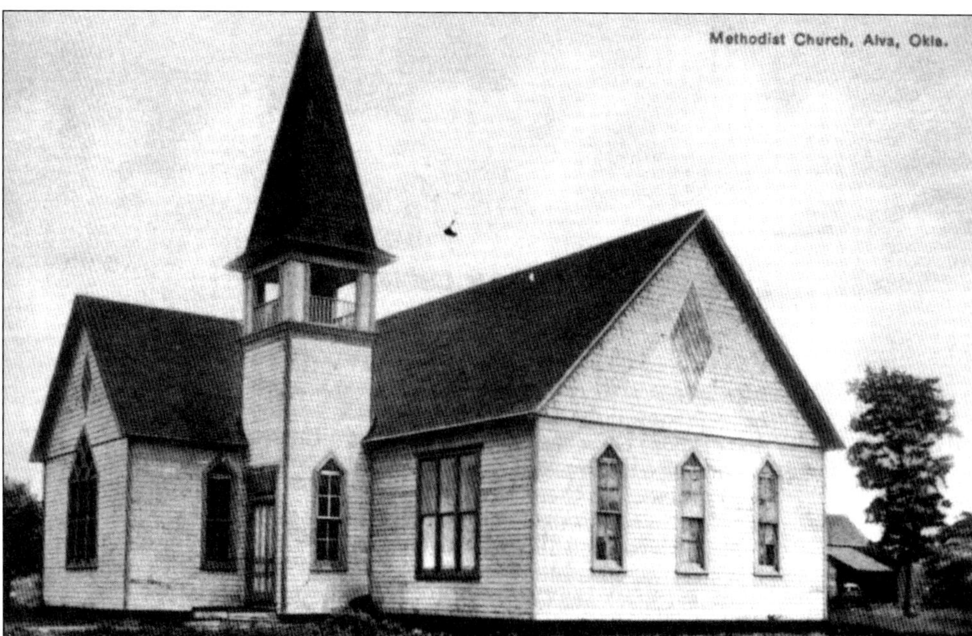

Before the Methodists had their own church, they would sometimes meet in Andy Beegle's cafe on the south side of the square. When Beegle wanted to communicate with the congregation, he stood in front of his cafe and blew his bugle and they would come. In 1897, First Methodist Church was built at 317 Barnes Avenue. The building was sold, and it was vacated on February 1, 1910. (Courtesy of the First United Methodist Church.)

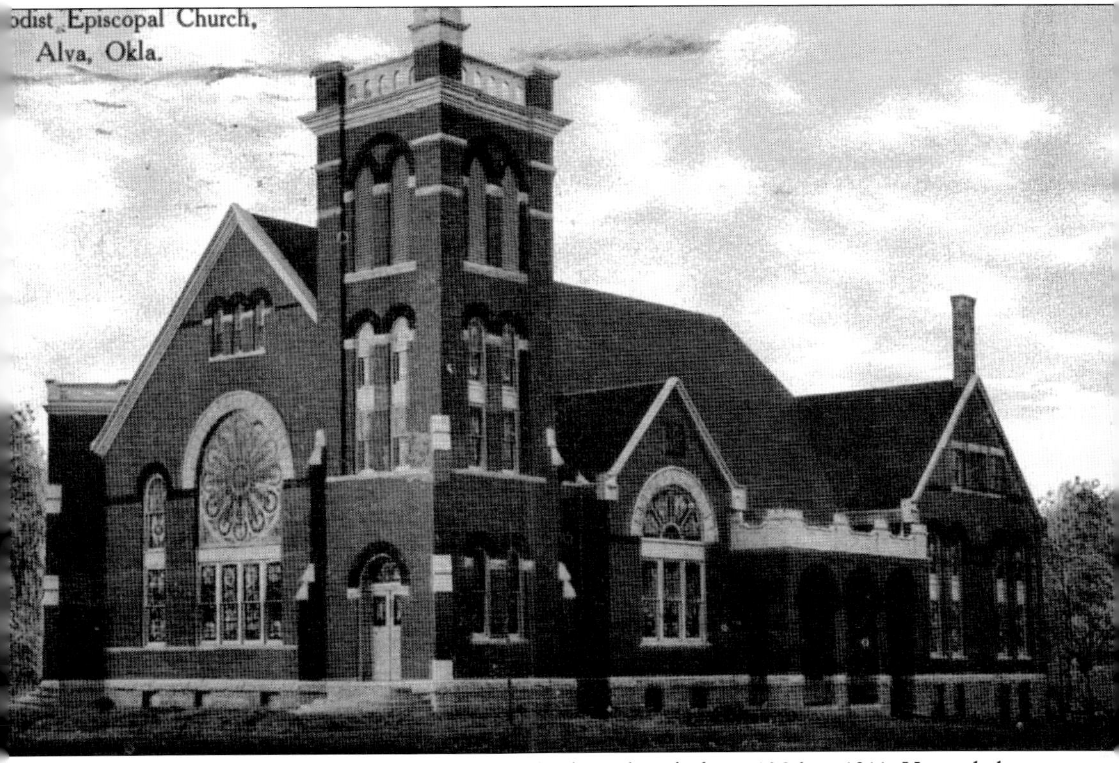

Rev. H.C. Case was the pastor of the First Methodist Church from 1906 to 1911. He and the congregation were responsible for this magnificent structure. The congregation has maintained the original church building and in 2010 celebrated its 100th anniversary. There is a history room there where more can be found about the church's past. (Courtesy of the First United Methodist Church.)

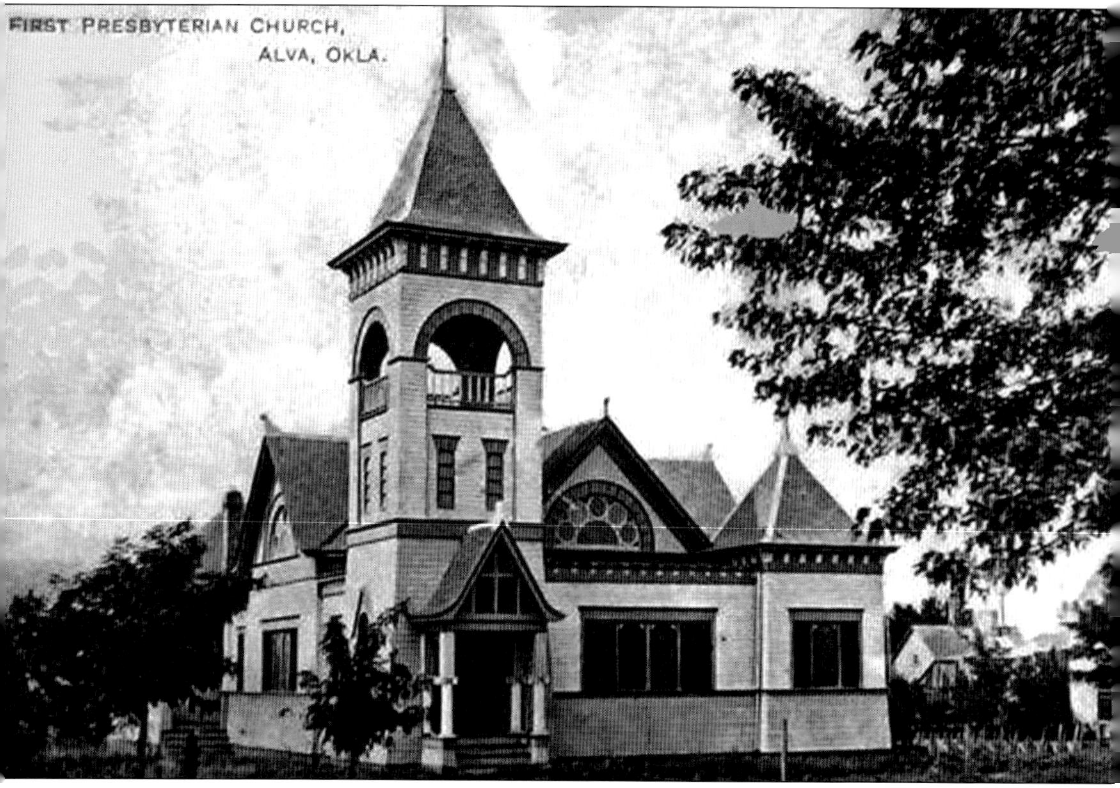

In 1899, the First Presbyterian Church was organized in Alva. The first project for the church was building a manse for the minister to live in. This was completed in 1901. Church services were held in Meads Hall, an upstairs room over a store, until 1902. Services were then held in an opera house until the church could be built. The church in the above image was built in 1903 and replaced in 1965.

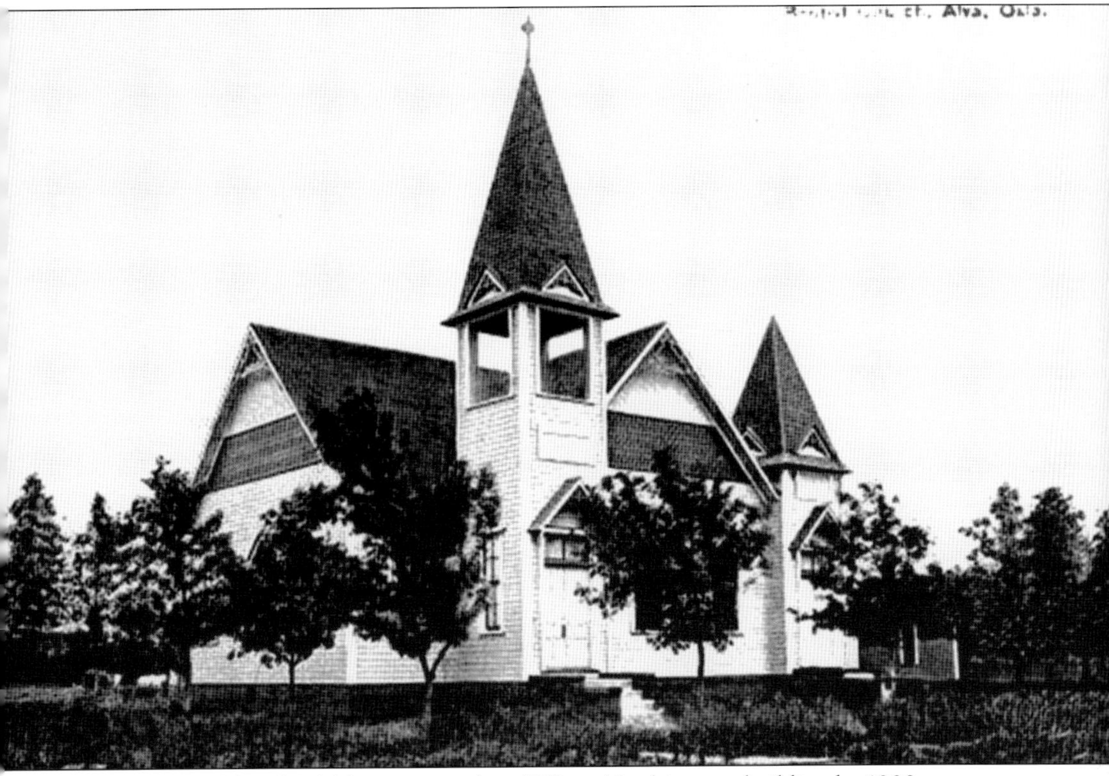

The First Baptist Church of Alva organized in 1893 and had its own building by 1900.

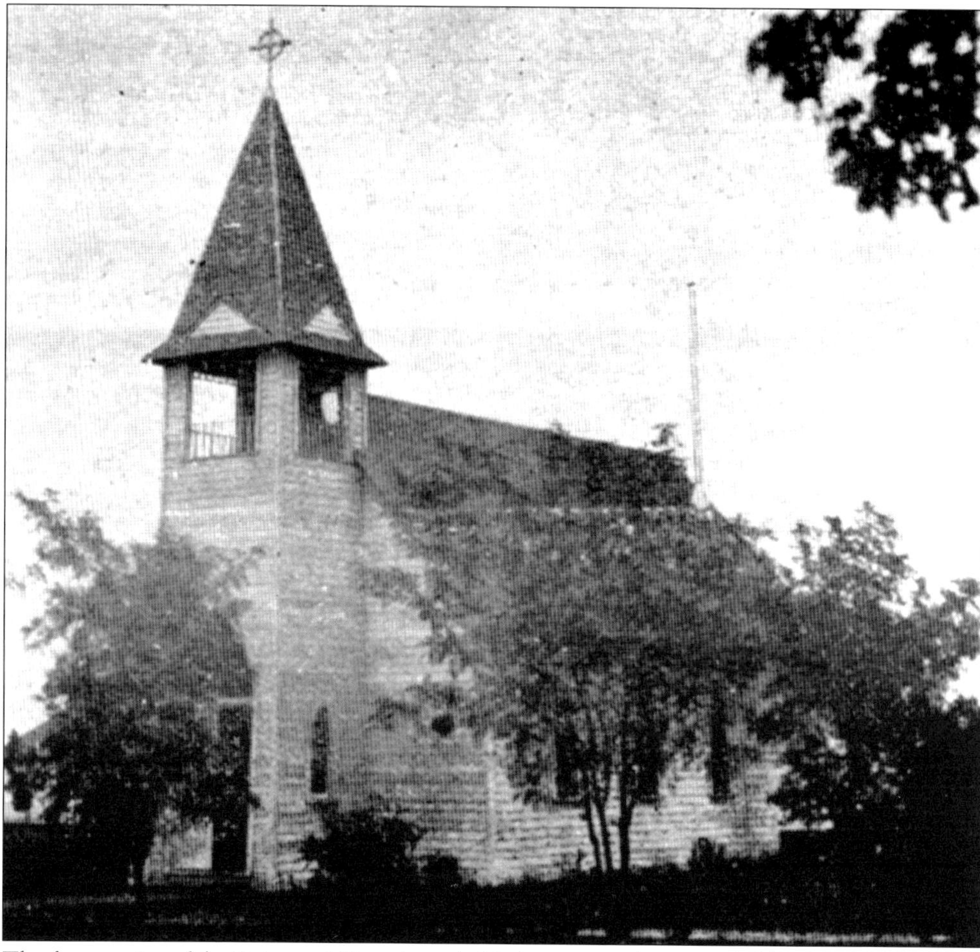

The first service of the Episcopal Church, with 34 charter members, was held on the third Sunday after the opening of the Cherokee Strip. In 1899, the Rev. Samuel G. Porter took charge of the congregation. In that year, under the reverend's administration, the present church building was erected. It still stands today, but is no longer an Episcopal church.

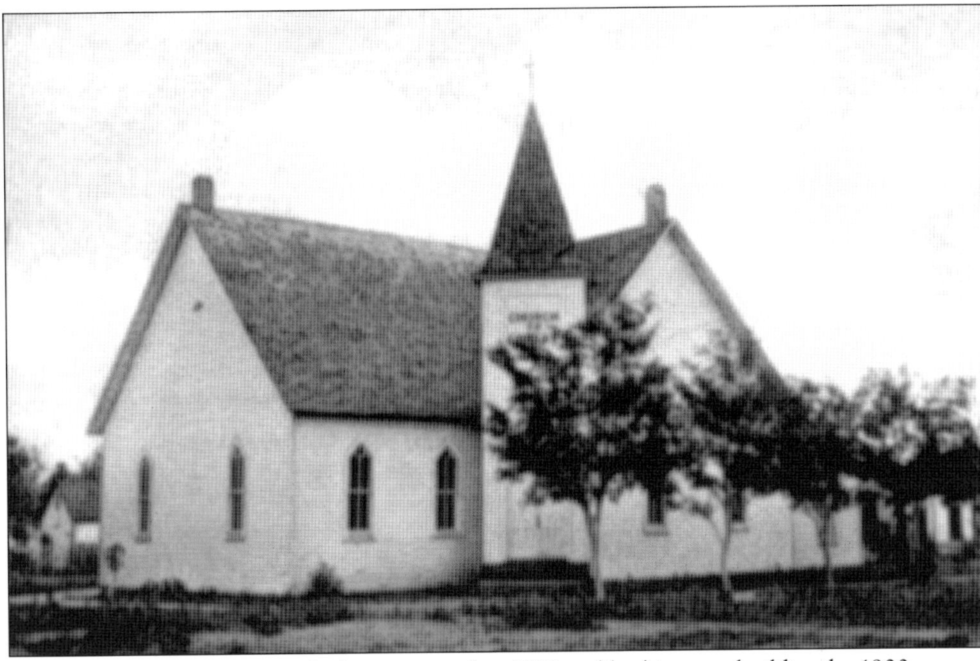

The First Church of Christ of Alva organized in 1893 and had its own building by 1900.

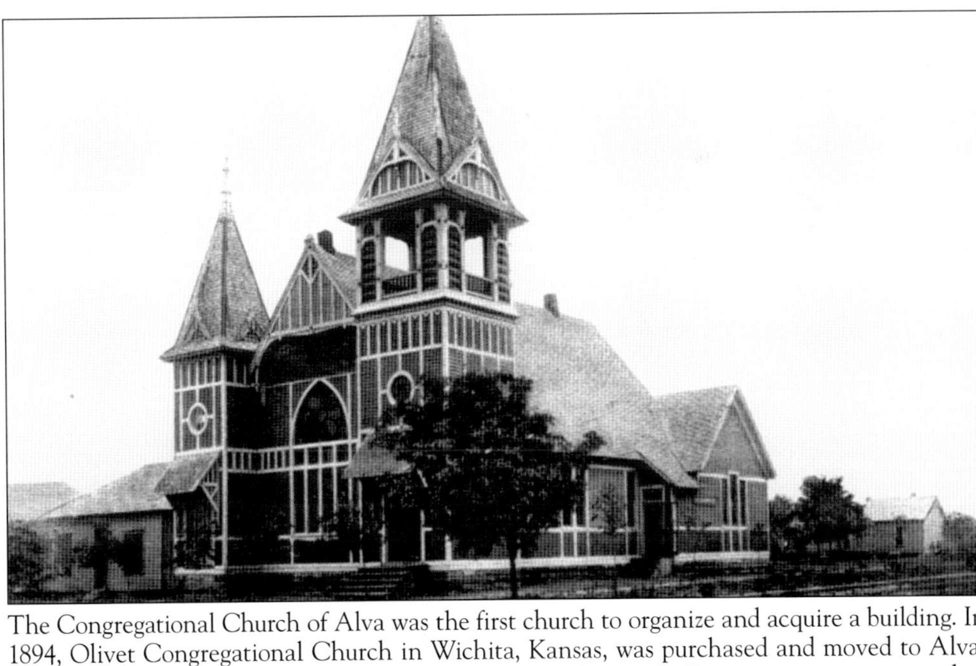

The Congregational Church of Alva was the first church to organize and acquire a building. In 1894, Olivet Congregational Church in Wichita, Kansas, was purchased and moved to Alva. Dedicated on May 12, 1895, the church served many functions. For two years, it was used as classrooms for the normal school. It housed the first term of the district court for "M" County. It was also used as the first library, high school, and for the first fair in Alva. It was sold to the Alva Friends Church in 1919 and is still used in that capacity today.

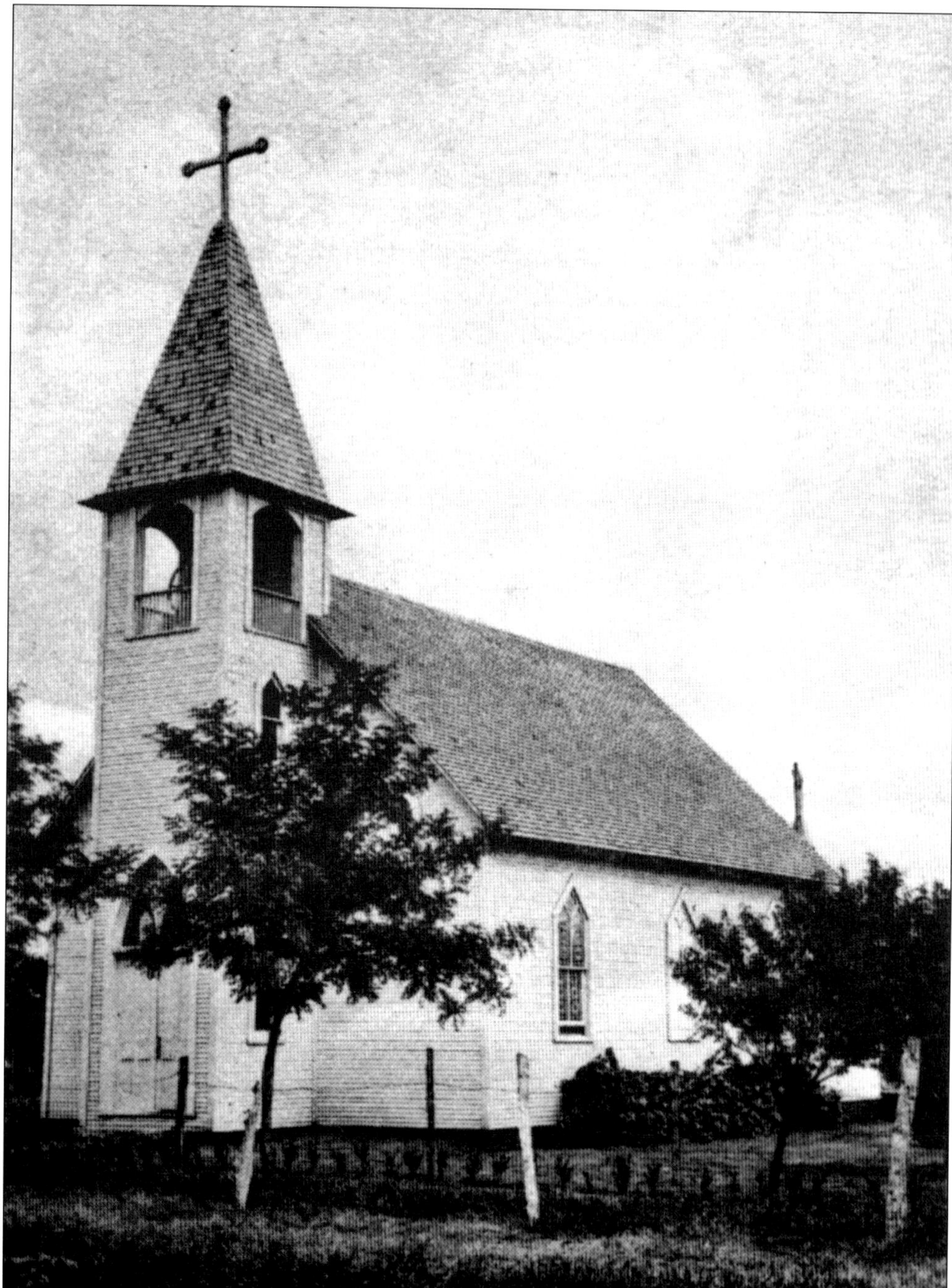

The Catholic Church was organized on October 9, 1899. The original church was located at the corner of Fourth and Choctaw Streets. A school was established on September 9, 1929. The Catholic Church is still strong in Alva, but the school closed a number of years ago.

Nine

Alva, People, and Buildings

The original town site extended three blocks east, two south, three north, and five west of the square. Much of the original town was located between the square and the Santa Fe Railroad. Everything south of Church Street was vacant lands and fields until the founding of the college in 1897.

Alva was one of the land offices established by the government to accommodate the filing of claims by homesteaders. The towns that had the land offices were also designated the county seats for that county. Alva's land office was built by W.H. Wiggins and his brother; they were carpenters from Hazelton, Kansas. The 1906 Atlas shows it located on the corner of the square where the City Hall is now. The first man to ride into Alva was Al Galbraith, also from Hazelton. He is said to have been a red-haired man riding a white horse covered with red dust, which made him a spectacular sight. He secured a town lot, which he later sold and on which the Alva National Bank was built.

Some came by wagon and train; many clung to the sides and roofs. A train left Kiowa 15 minutes behind the settlers who were on horseback and in wagons, stopping every now and then to let the horses and wagons catch up and let people off to find claims. By November, Alva boasted 113 businesses and houses, including several two-story structures.

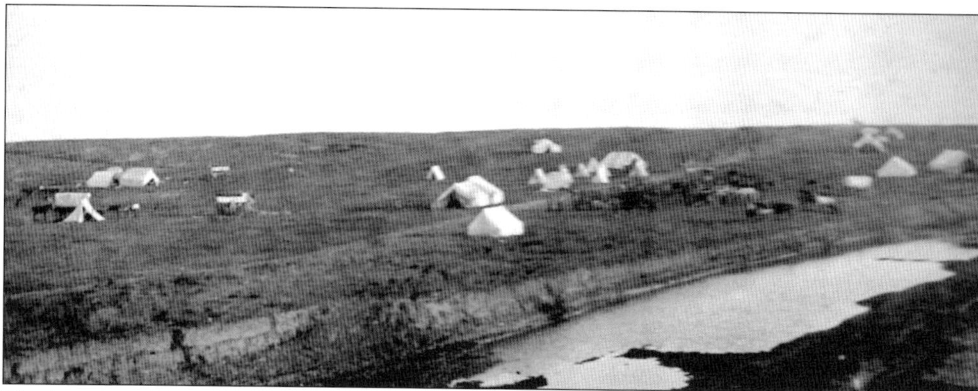

The location of this tent city is not known. Although there was a stream, this image clearly shows how barren "M" (Woods) County was. (Courtesy of Alva Cherokee Strip Museum.)

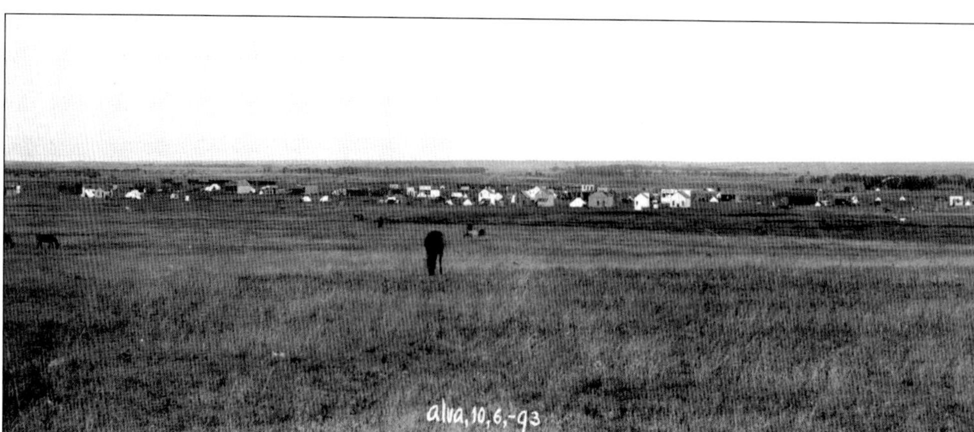

Alva, platted and staked by the government, lay on the south side of the Salt Fork. This photograph, taken 20 days after the run, shows both tents and hastily built structures, a sudden change from the lonely buffalo grass prairie a few days before. (Courtesy of Alva Cherokee Strip Museum.)

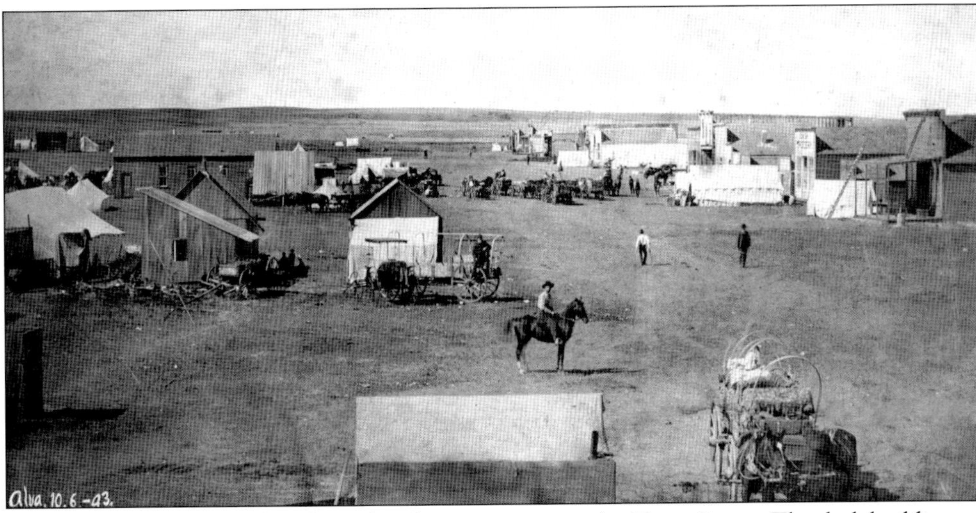

This street, photographed 20 days after the run, appears to be Flynn Street. The dark building on the left is the land office where the Alva Post Office is now. A 16-by-28-foot sod house, built in 1893, was one of the first dwellings built in Alva. It was used for nearly eight years as a residence. (Courtesy of Alva Cherokee Strip Museum.)

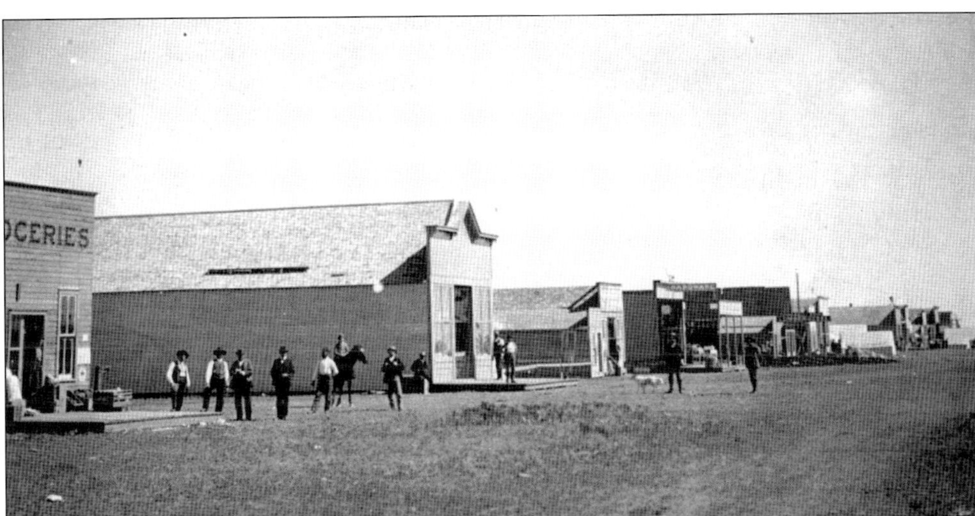

The north side of Alva's public square was photographed on October 6, 1893. Some of the businesses that can be seen are Alva National Bank, Green and Green's Hardware, Robert's Grocery, Matthews Hardware Store, and Hobbie's Grocery Store. Alva grew rapidly and many businesses were built. All through the new territory, land was cultivated and little towns sprung up, evidence of the pioneers' intention to stay. (Courtesy of Alva Cherokee Strip Museum.)

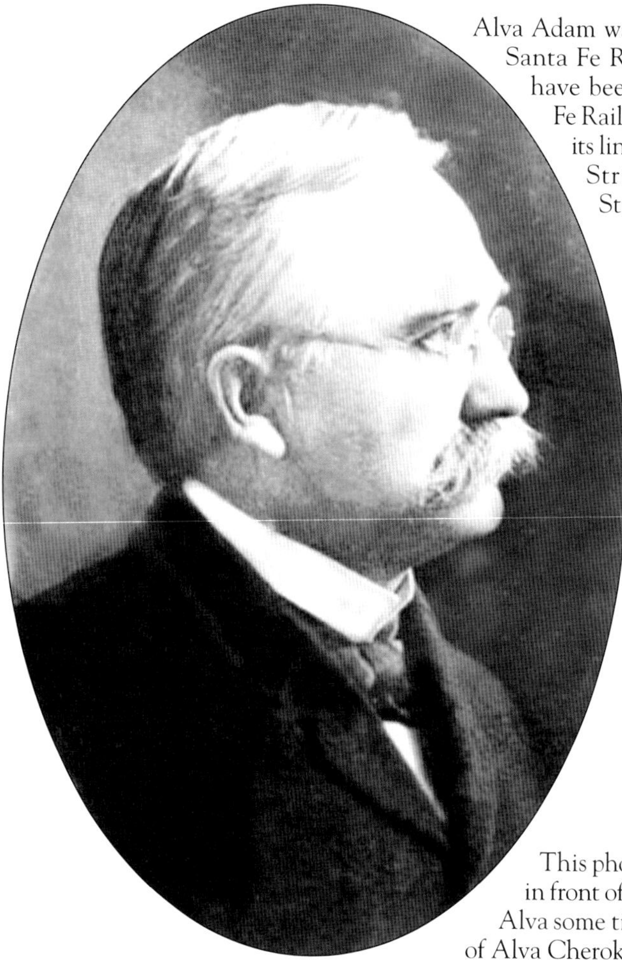

Alva Adam was at one time the attorney for the Santa Fe Railroad Company. Alva is said to have been named in his honor. The Santa Fe Railroad named a number of towns along its line before the opening of the Cherokee Strip. (Courtesy of Alva Cherokee Strip Museum.)

This photograph of National Guard soldiers in front of the Runnymede Hotel was taken in Alva some time after the run of 1893. (Courtesy of Alva Cherokee Strip Museum.)

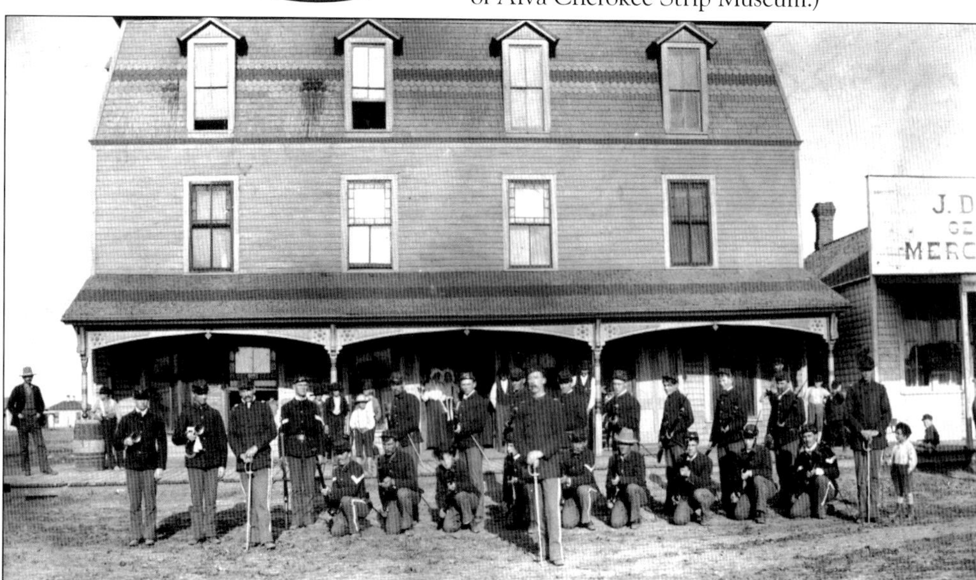

Established in 1894, Montfort's Drug Store carried a range of merchandise that included everything from drugs and paint to wallpaper and sporting goods. This wooden structure was replaced by a brick store that was destroyed by fire on May 22, 1953. (Courtesy of Alva Cherokee Strip Museum.)

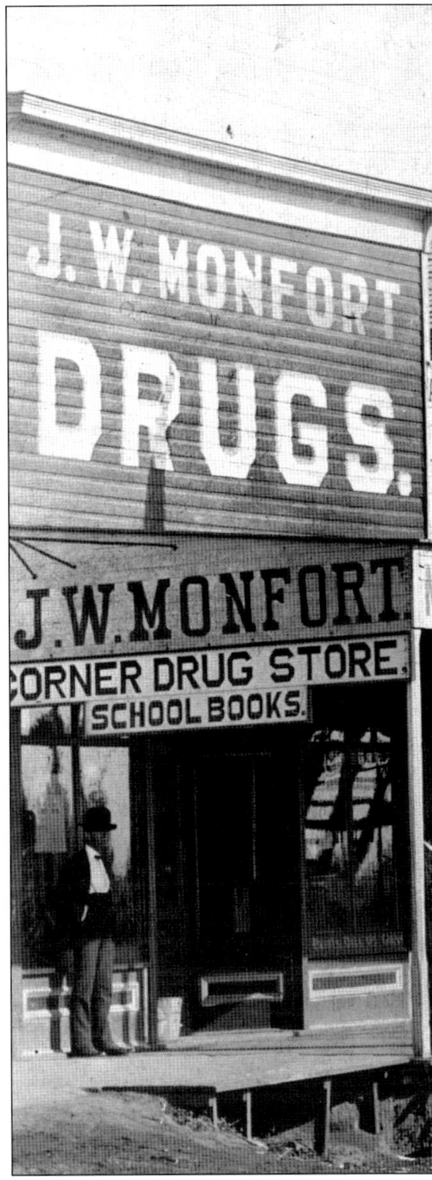

This is Alva as it was near the end of the 1800s. The *Alva Pioneer* newspaper building is on the left. It was the first two-story building in Alva. Runnymede Hotel was purchased in 1893 and moved intact from Runnymede, Kansas, to its present location. It was restored in 2007 to near original condition. (Courtesy of Alva Cherokee Strip Museum.)

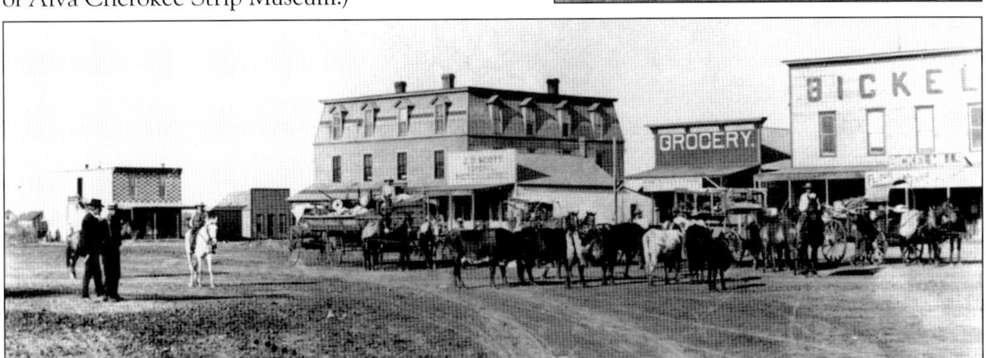

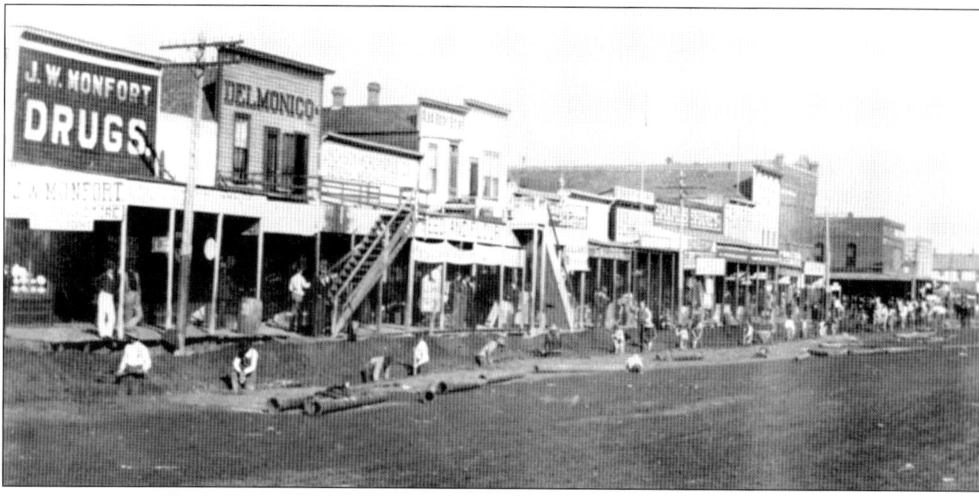

In 1903, a water line was laid from north to south on College Avenue to the normal school. Alva had an abundant supply of water that came by natural gravitational pull from springs 2.5 miles north. Water was brought to the reservoir, which was located north of the railroad viaduct on College Avenue. From the reservoir, the water was pumped a mile up the slope to the storage tank on the corner of the college campus. (Courtesy of Alva Cherokee Strip Museum.)

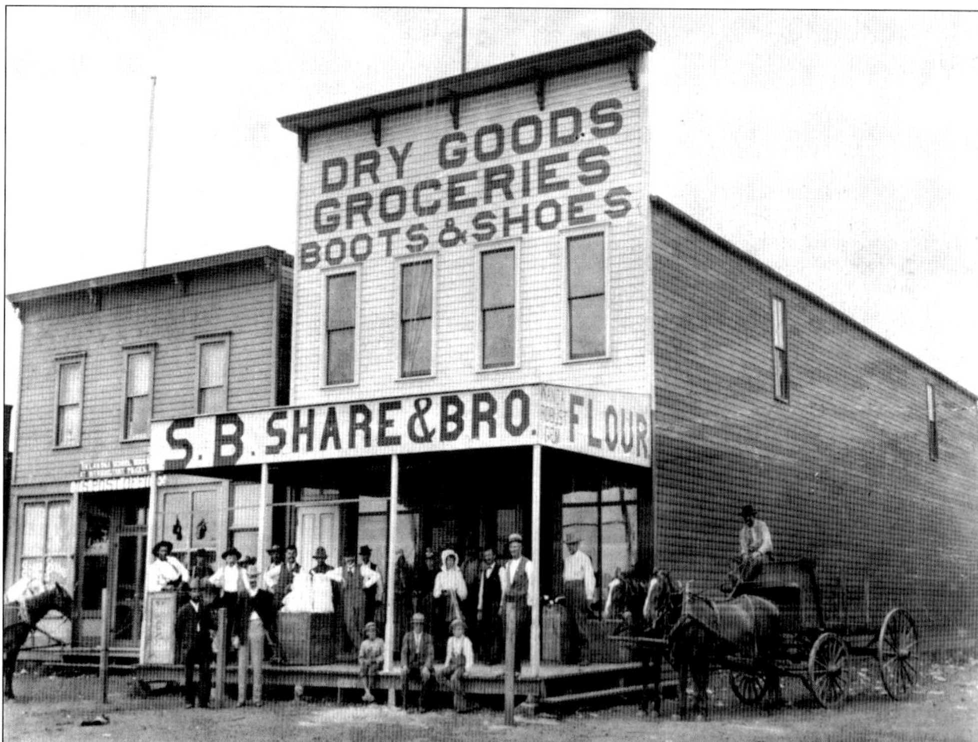

The Share brothers, J.D. and S.B., are standing on either side of the grain sacks. The brothers were natives of Michigan who came to Alva by way of Wellington, Kansas in 1895. J.D.'s son Corky continued to run the Share Brothers Store. Corky never had a family, and he left his wealth and land to Alva and Woods County to be used for the benefit of its people. (Courtesy of Alva Cherokee Strip Museum.)

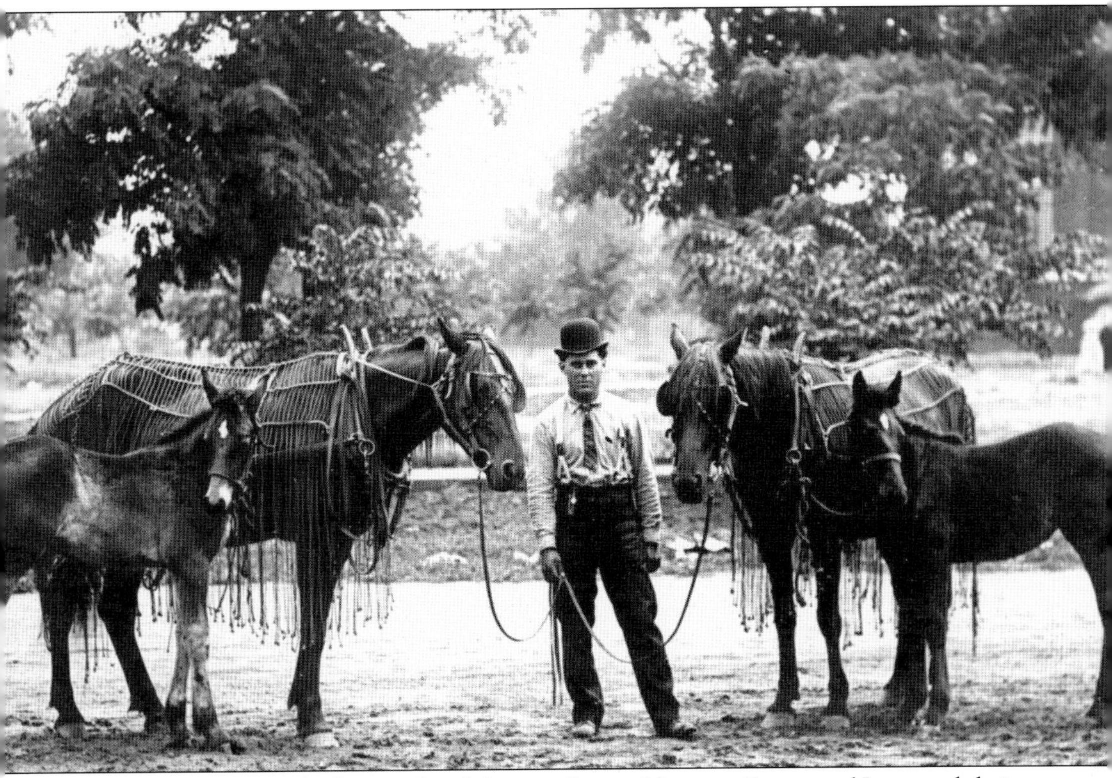

Guy Kinzie was photographed in 1905 with his two 5-year-old mares, Queen and Lucy, and their three-month-old colts. Kinzie always maintained that farmers were neglecting an opportunity when they failed to raise an annual crop of colts: "It is remarkable but true that as the prices of livestock or dairy products advance, many farmers drop out of these lines and take up other branches of agriculture. The claim is that the high price of grain makes raising stock prohibitive."

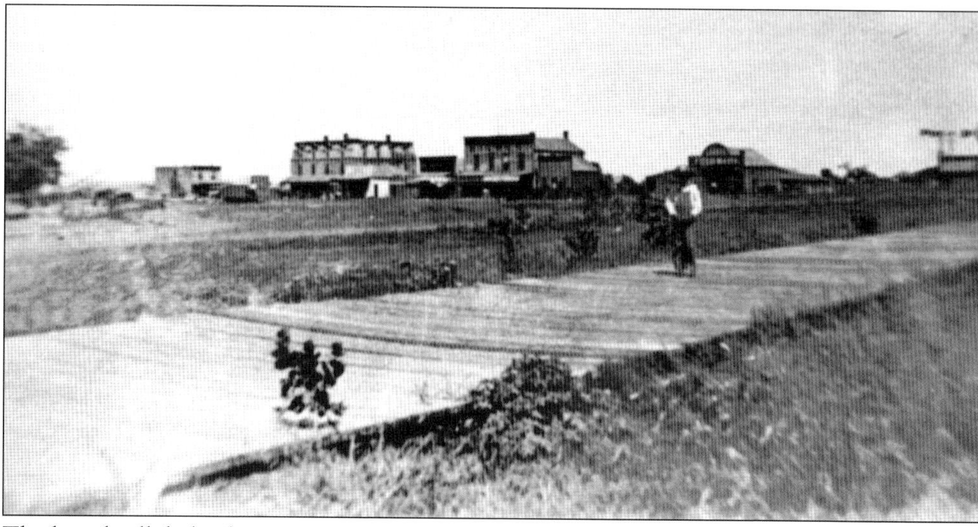

The boardwalk helped citizens get around Alva Square in the early days. In the background are two historic buildings. On the east side are the elegant Runnymede Hotel and the H.M. Bickel Building. (Courtesy of Alva Centennial Commission.)

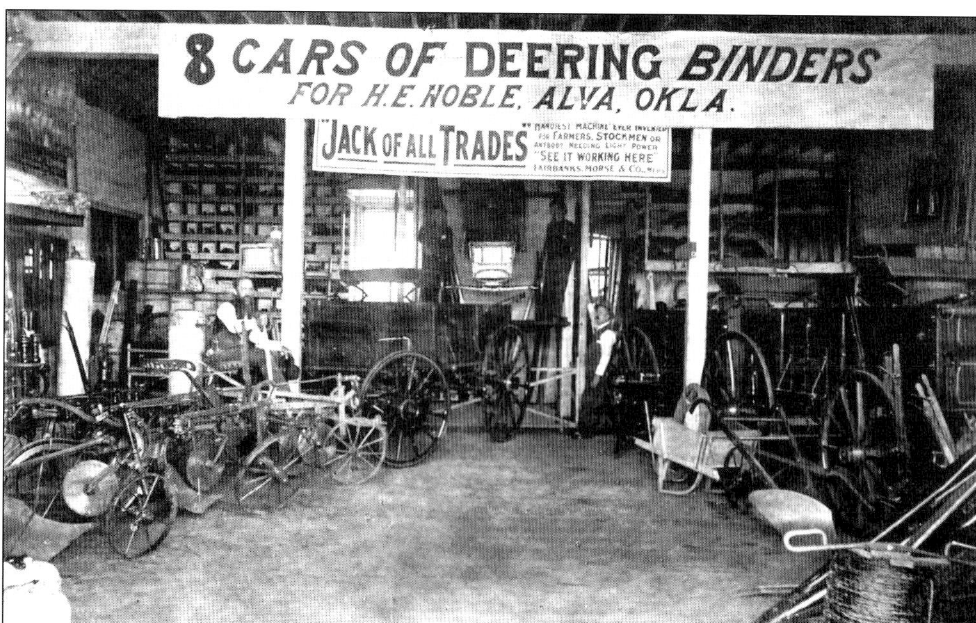

Deering Binders was located on the ground floor of Mr. Noble's hardware store. In the upper story of the building, he also had buggies for sale. This business was in downtown Alva before 1900. (Courtesy of Alva Cherokee Strip Museum.)

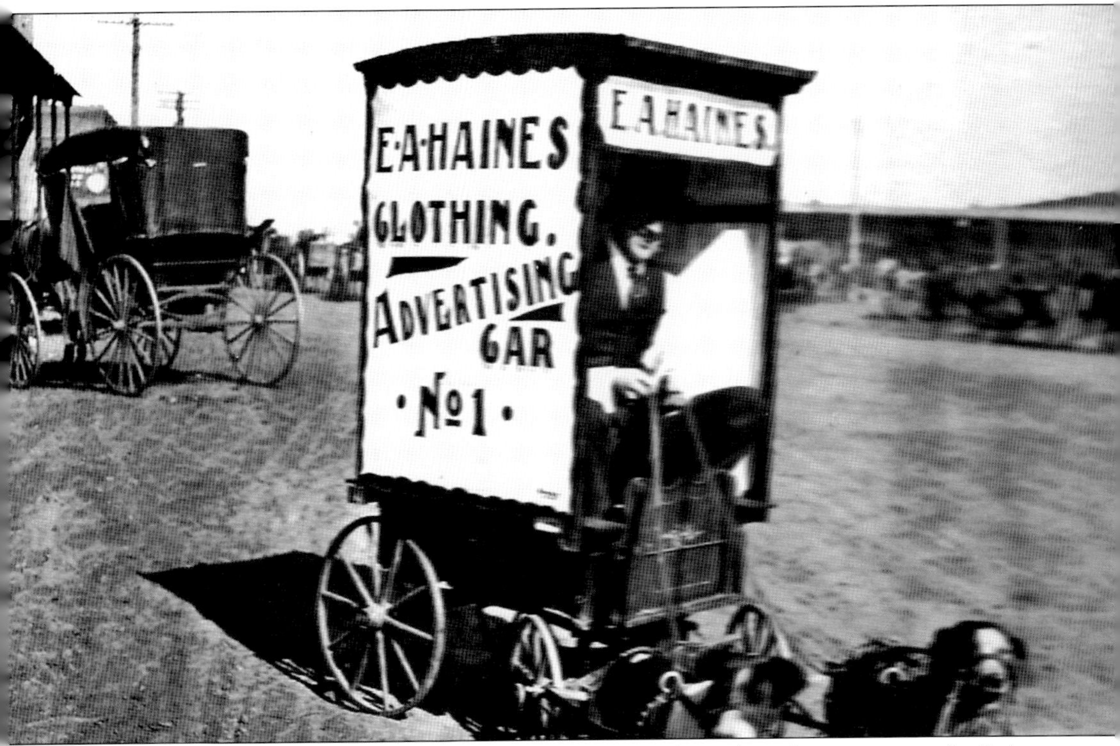

Advertising was as important in Alva's early days as it is today. This advertising cart for E.A. Haines was used to drum up business for his haberdashery. Notice the dogs pulling the cart. (Courtesy of Alva Cherokee Strip Museum.)

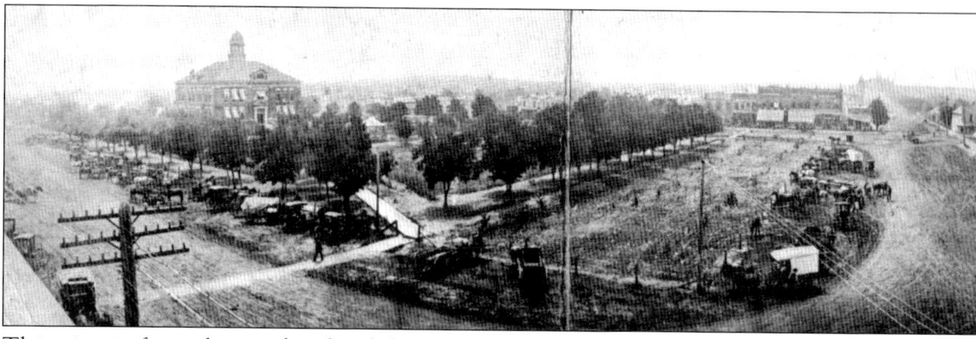

This view is from the north side of the square. When Alva obtained city water, it fenced the square and placed water tanks at the four corners to water horses. Setters were allowed to camp on the square when they came to town for business or to purchase supplies.

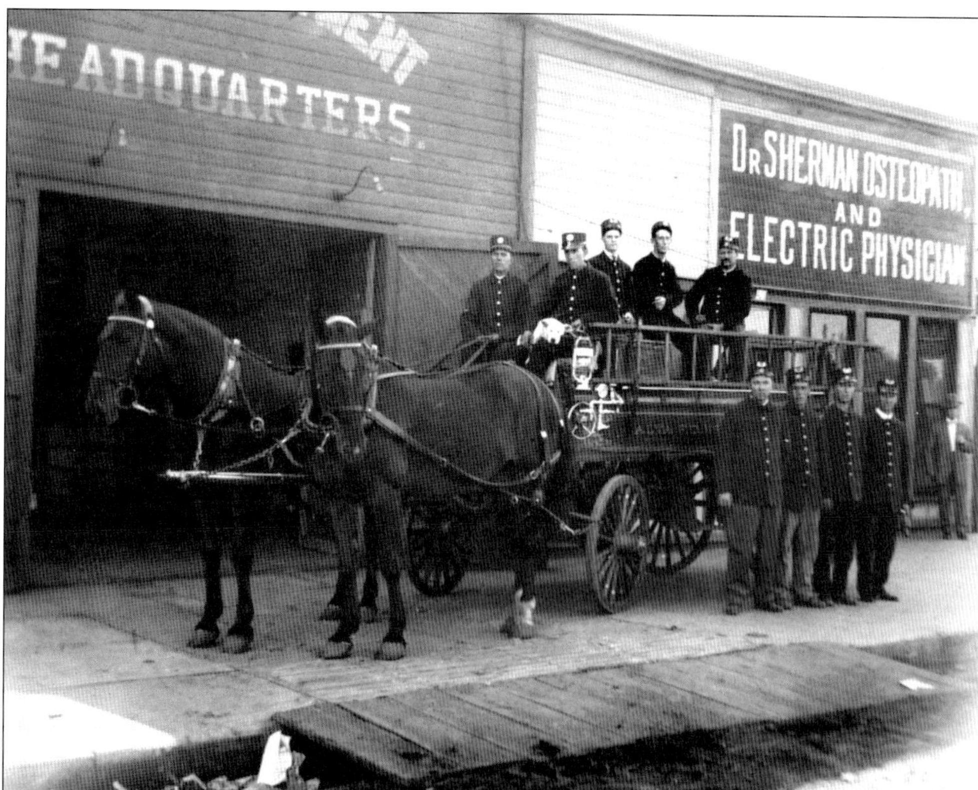

This fire vehicle was acquired sometime around 1903. The fire chief of Engine No. 1 was Wes Warren. Notice the building next door advertising an "electric physician." (Courtesy of Alva Cherokee Strip Museum.)

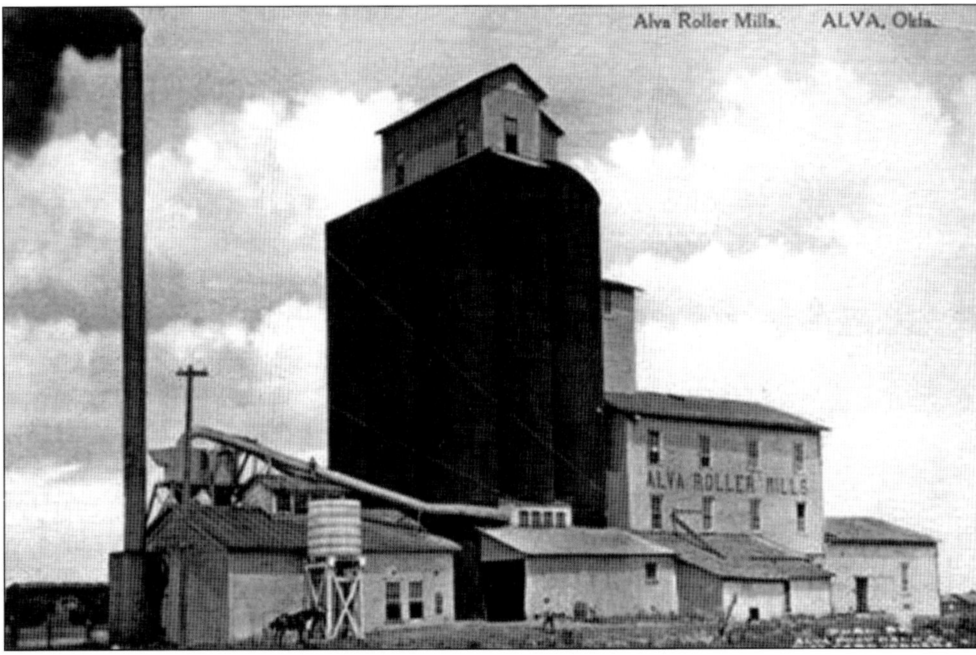

The first Alva Roller Mills was built in 1897 and burned down mysteriously in 1900. This building was erected in 1902 near the location of the previous roller mills. During World War II, it ran 24 hours a day and seven days a week to produce flour to be shipped around the country. (Courtesy of Alva Cherokee Strip Museum.)

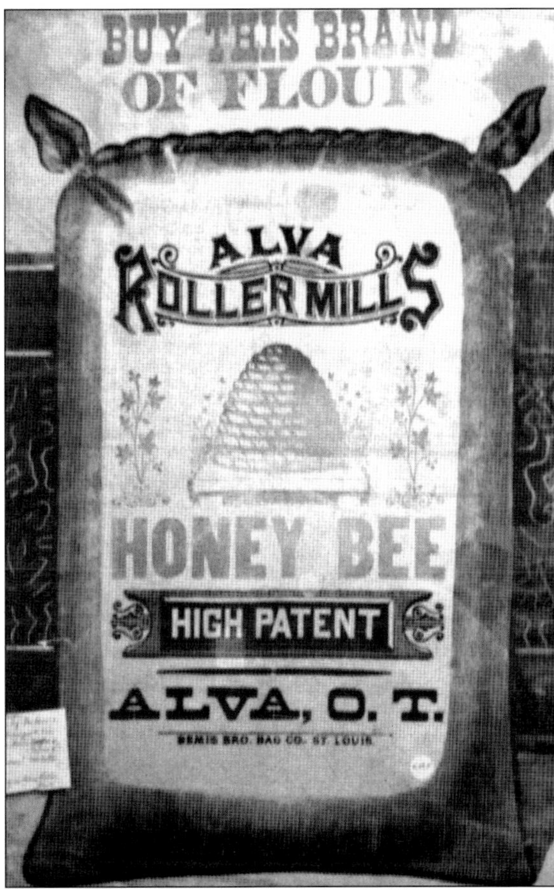

This photograph shows advertising printed on a flour bag for the Alva Roller Mills. Honey Bee Flour was their trademark. Their advertising slogan was "to get the best, don't experiment but buy the Honey Bee Flour and you will always have good bread." (Courtesy of Alva Cherokee Strip Museum.)

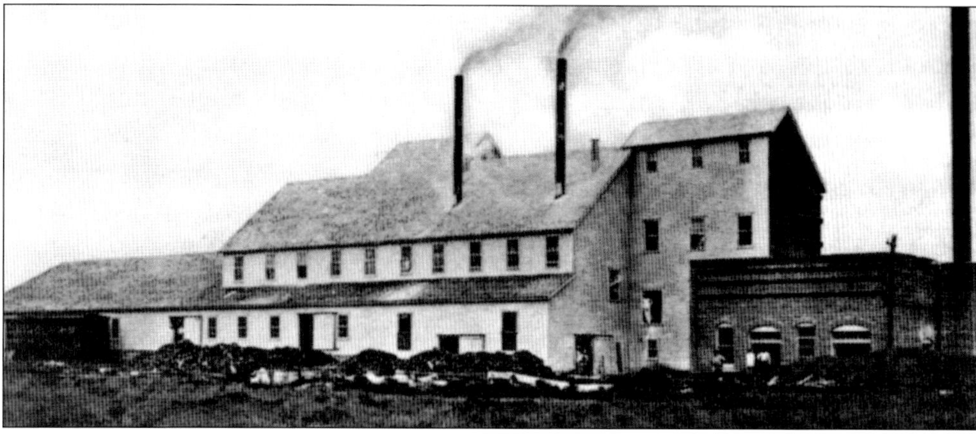

Alva Plaster Mills was located very near to Alva Roller Mills. (Courtesy of Alva Cherokee Strip Museum.)

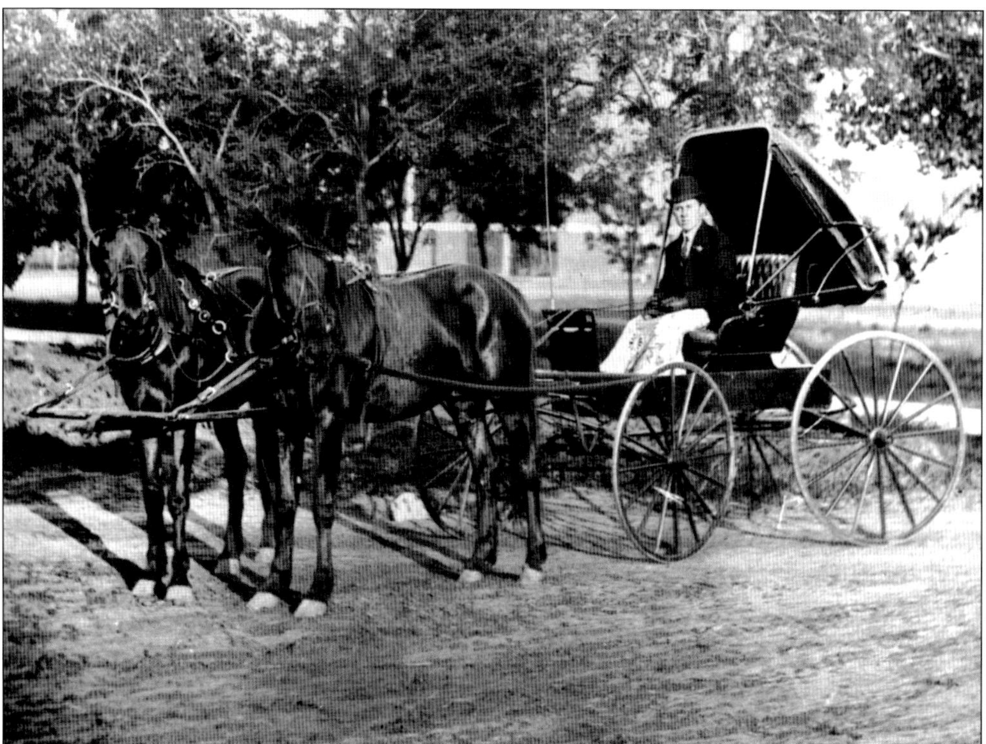

Guy Kinzie shows off his new mail-order buggy from Sears and Roebuck in this 1908 photograph. Guy moved to Alva from Indiana in 1905 and worked for C.E. Bainum farming and threshing. He bought his the mares Queen and Lucy at a local sale.

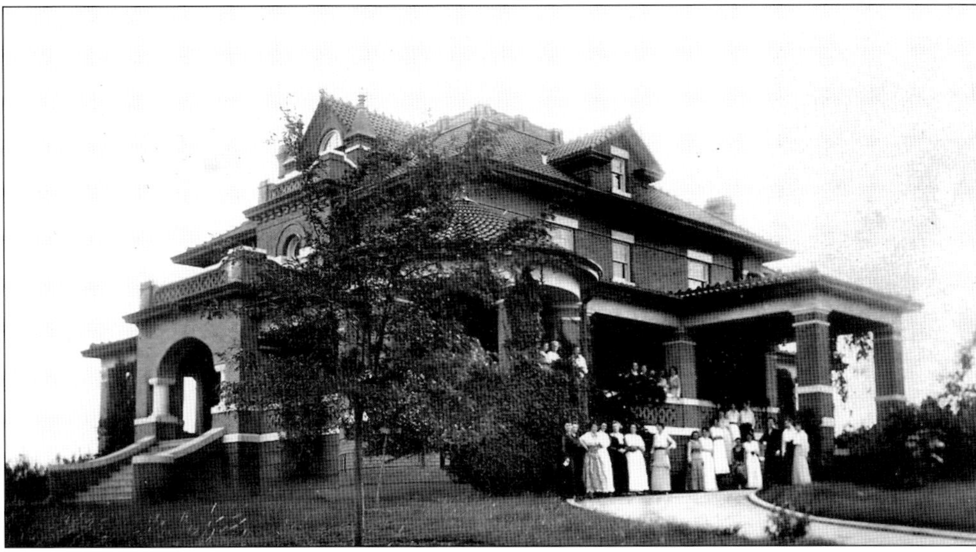

Mr. Nickels was an early-day Alva banker and businessman. His home was photographed in the early 1900s. The house still exists today and is undergoing restoration. (Courtesy of Alva Cherokee Strip Museum.)

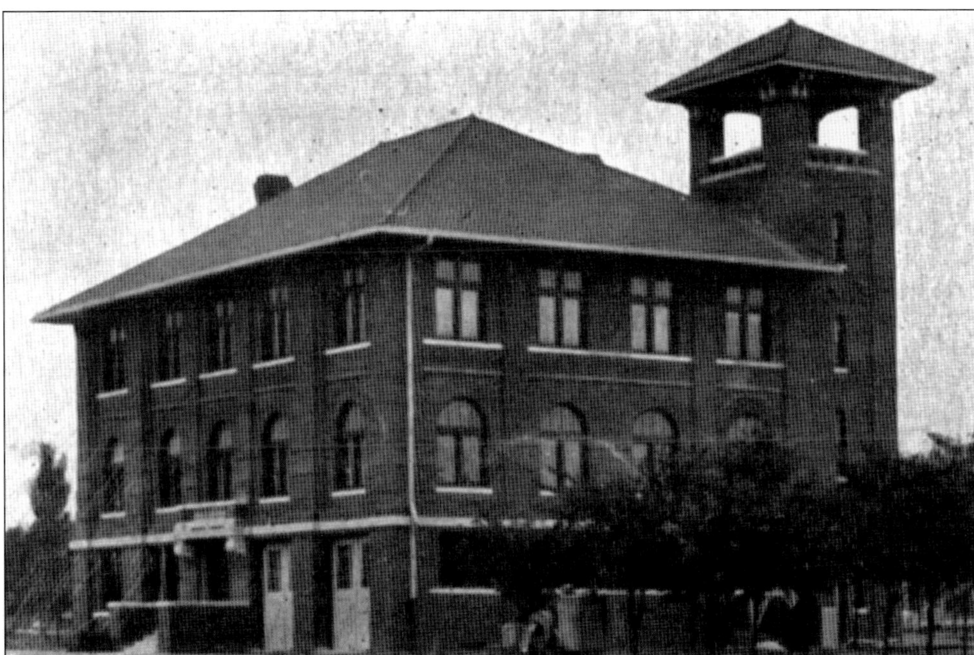

The first city hall was erected in 1903 as a one-story frame building. This structure, erected in approximately 1908, served until the present building was constructed on the same location. (Courtesy of Alva Cherokee Strip Museum.)

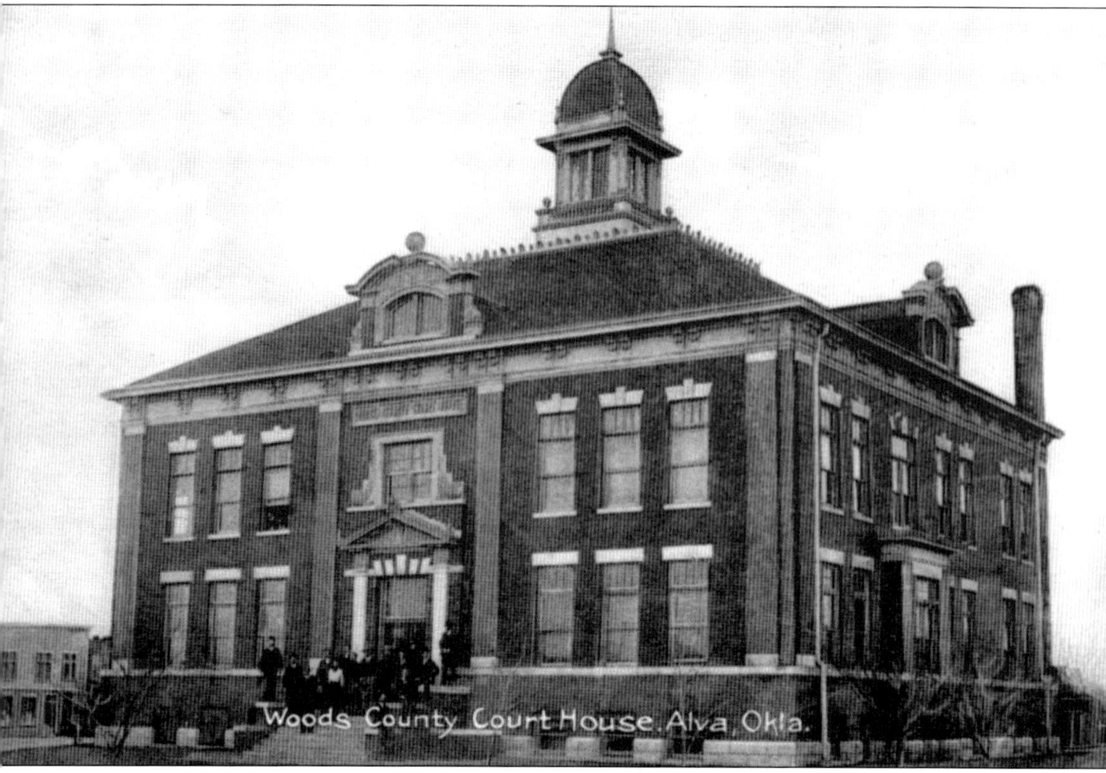

Alva could boast about its public buildings, including the old county courthouse. One of the stateliest public buildings in Oklahoma, it was built in 1904 after 10 years of controversy. Before statehood, "M" (Woods) County was larger than the states of Delaware and Rhode Island. In 2009, the Alva Mural Society commissioned a mural of the original courthouse to be depicted on the west side of the current courthouse. (Courtesy of Alva Cherokee Strip Museum.)

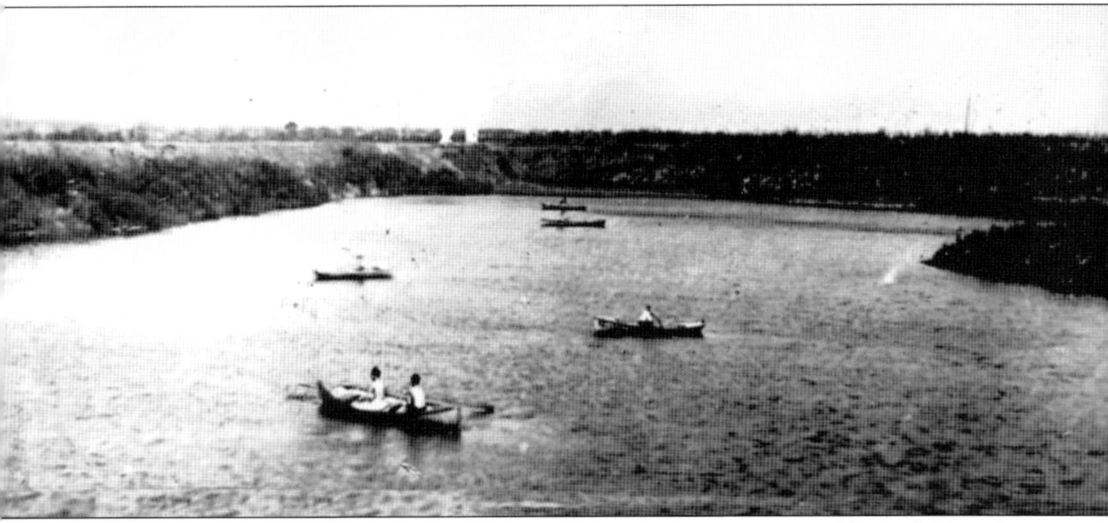

Hatfield Lake is part of the 58 acres deeded in 1906 to the city by W.F. Hatfield. Hatfield made the run and established the first Alva newspaper. He dammed up the stream on the property to make Hatfield Lake. In 1910, due to health reasons, he became the full-time manager of the park for the next 30 years. (Courtesy of Alva Cherokee Strip Museum.)

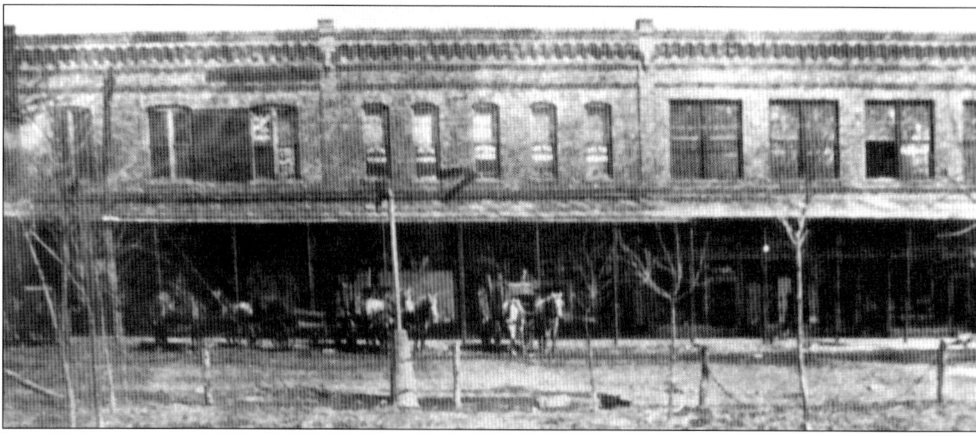

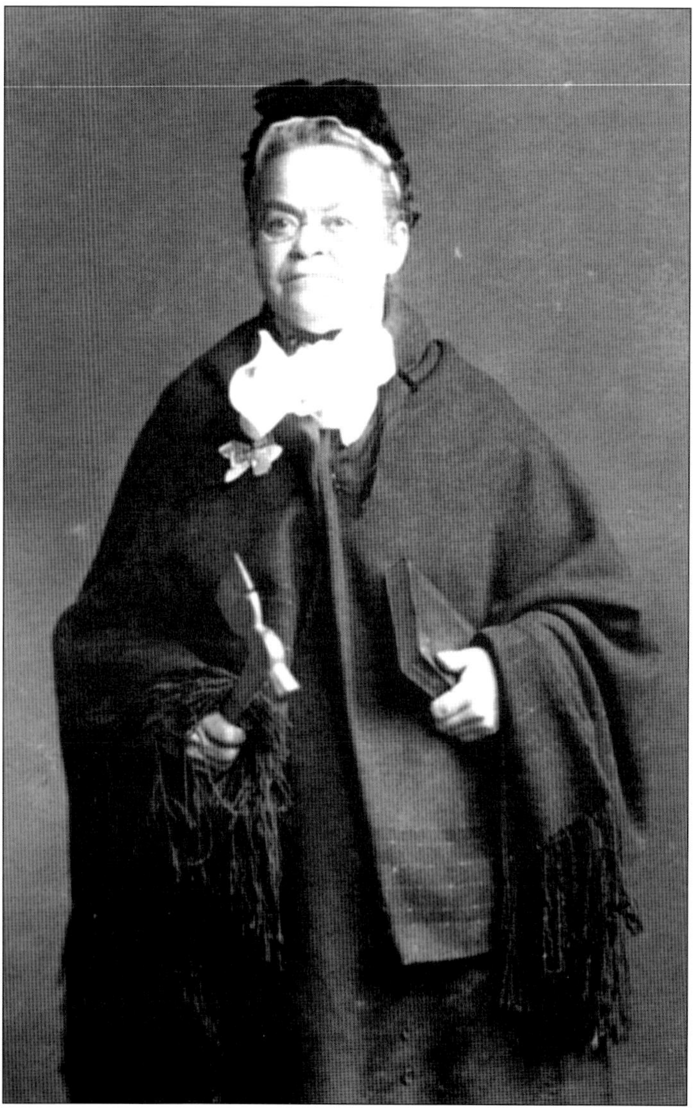

Carry Nation, the militant crusader against illegal saloons, came to Alva periodically from Kiowa, Kansas. She arrived with pocketfuls of rocks and threw them at saloons on the north side of Alva Square. (Courtesy of Alva Centennial Commission.)

This is Carry Nation as she appeared when she came to Alva. She had waged war against saloons all of her adult life, as her first husband had died from excessive drinking.

Ten

Towns of Woods County

Of the sixty-odd towns that were formed in "M" County before and after the run of 1893, only about six remain in Woods County. Throughout Woods County there are many communities that were originally school districts, churches, or stores. Times were hard in the early days and people could not travel great distance for supplies, so small communities thrived until transportation advanced.

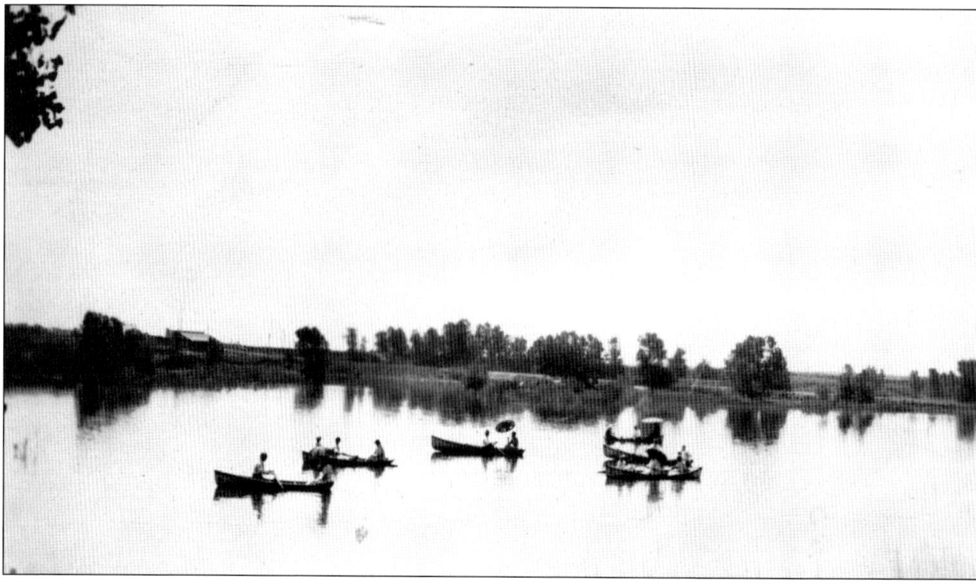

When the Frisco Railroad was first built in Avard, the tracks crossed those of the Santa Fe. Their turntable and water tank were west across the Eagle Chief Creek. The dam across the creek made a lake, which at that time covered about 25 acres. The Avard Lake was a popular place for picnicking and boating until it dried up during the 1930s.

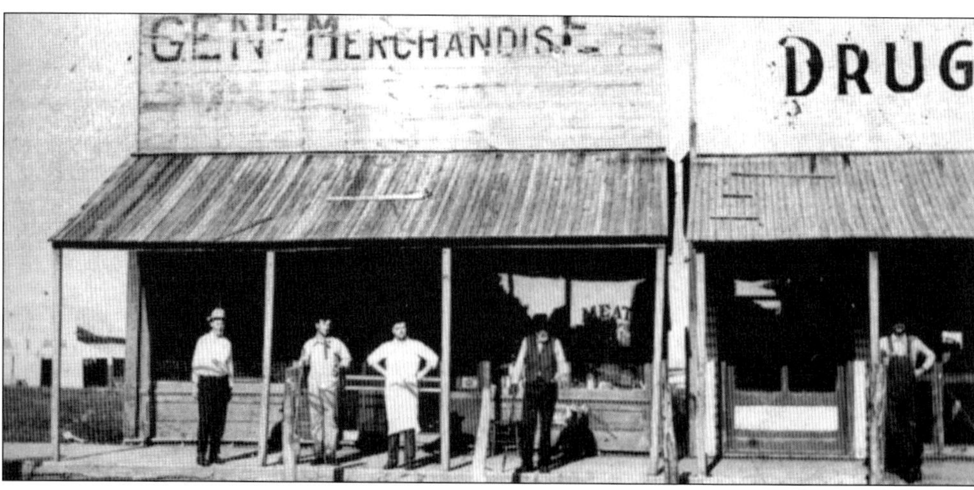

Pictured here are stores in Avard, which prospered as an agricultural center and railroad transfer point from its founding in 1904 until the mid-1930s. In that decade, Avard, like many farming towns, declined because of the Great Depression, devastating drought and dust storms, the resulting farm consolidation, and an improved national transportation system.

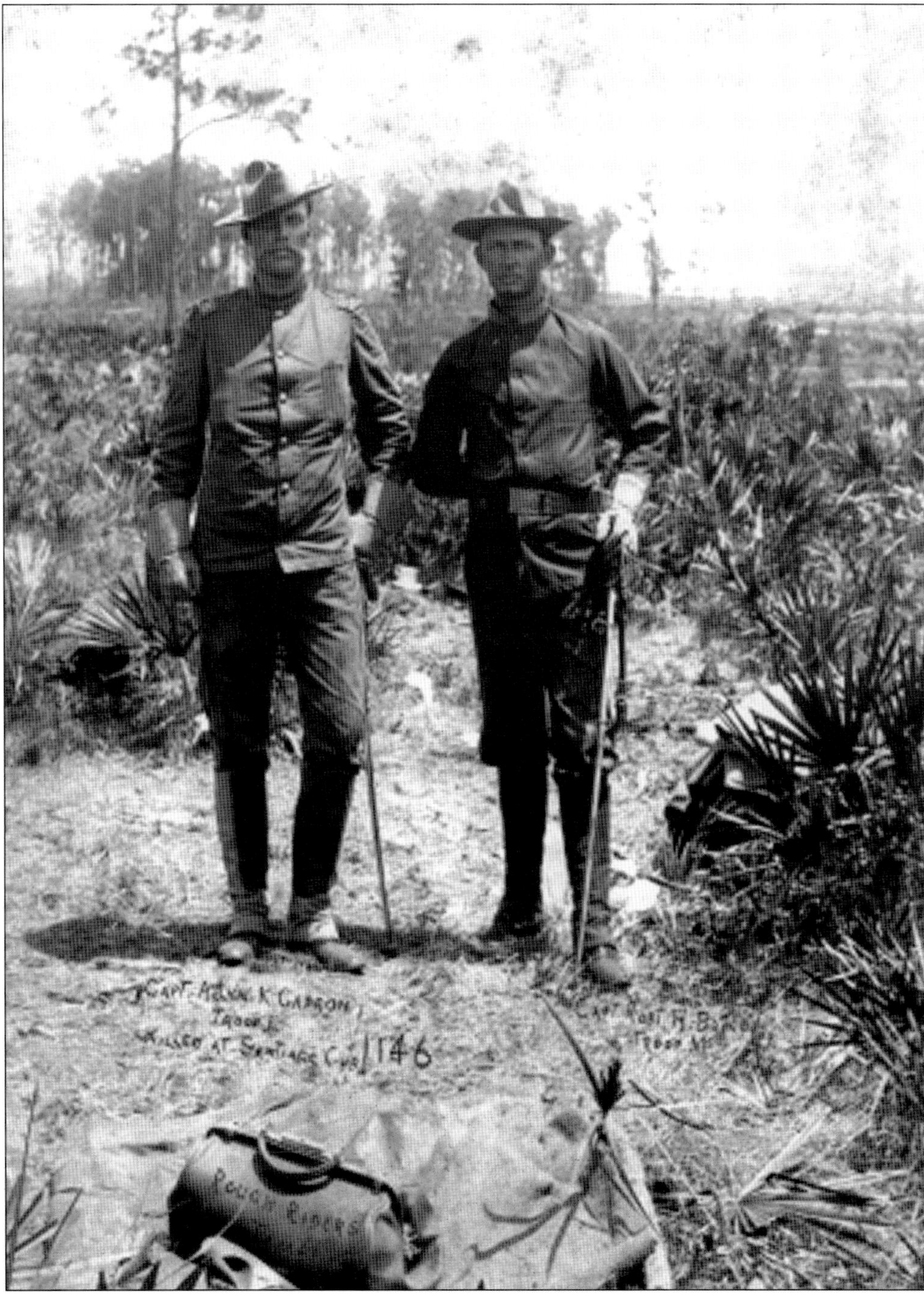

Capron received its name from Captain Allen Capron, a friend of Theodore Roosevelt and a distinguished officer of the Rough Rider Regiment. He is pictured here at left with Robert Bizo. Capron was established in 1895 by W.G. McClure, on whose quarter section of land it was located. Like Dacoma, Capron became famous and prosperous because it was surrounded by more than 250,000 acres of the finest wheat land in the state.

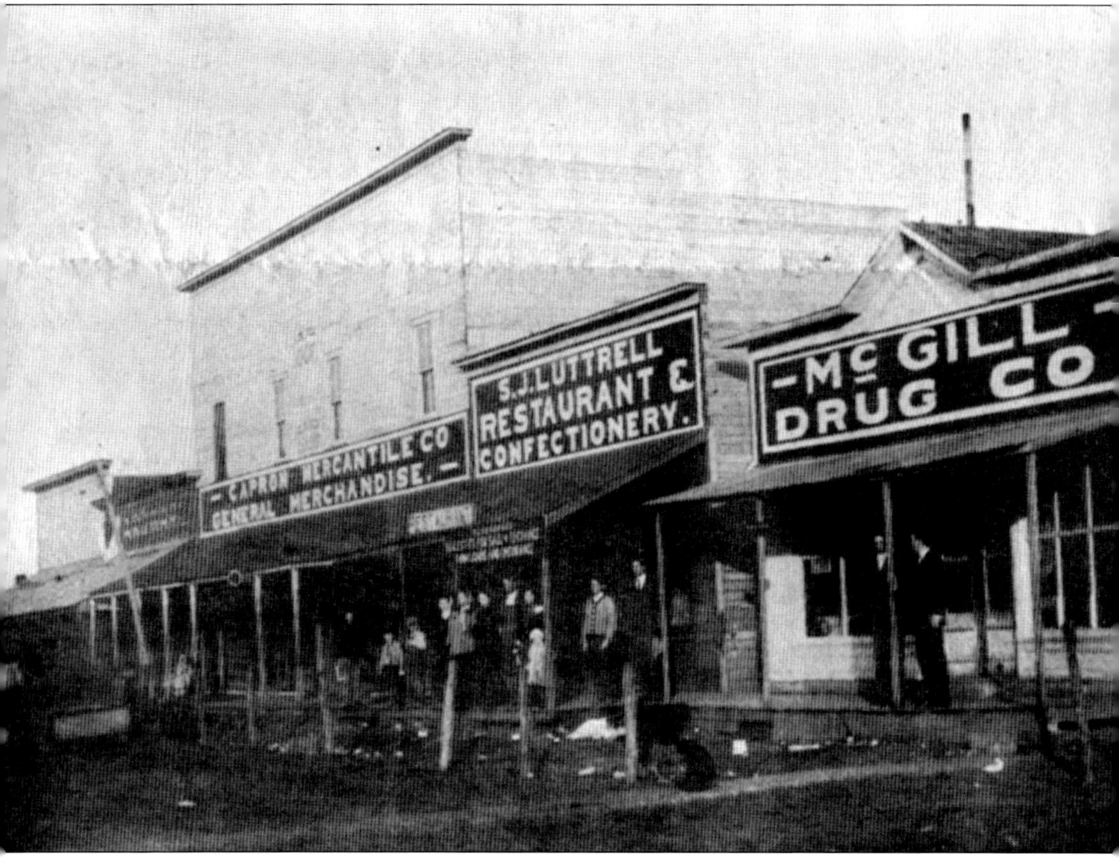

Capron was the first townsite on the Santa Fe Railroad when, in 1886, the railroad came south from Kiowa into what is now Woods County. Many settlers rushed there and thought it would become a major trade center. This photograph of Capron in early days includes McGill Drug Co., S.J. Luttrell Restaurant and Confectionery, Capron Mercantile Co., Wilson and Edwards Real Estate, Loans and Insurance, and a hardware store.

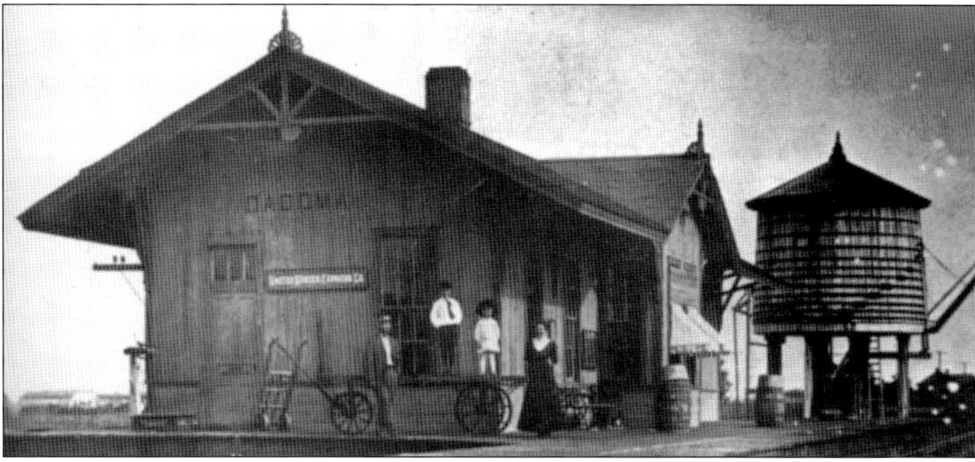

Dacoma tried other names before finally asking the US Post Office to give it the name of Dacoma. The extension of the Frisco Railroad to Avard created the demand for the town at its present location. Affecting the history and development of Dacoma the most was its fertile wheat-producing territory. Dacoma had large grain elevators that marketed annually more than 300,000 bushels of wheat.

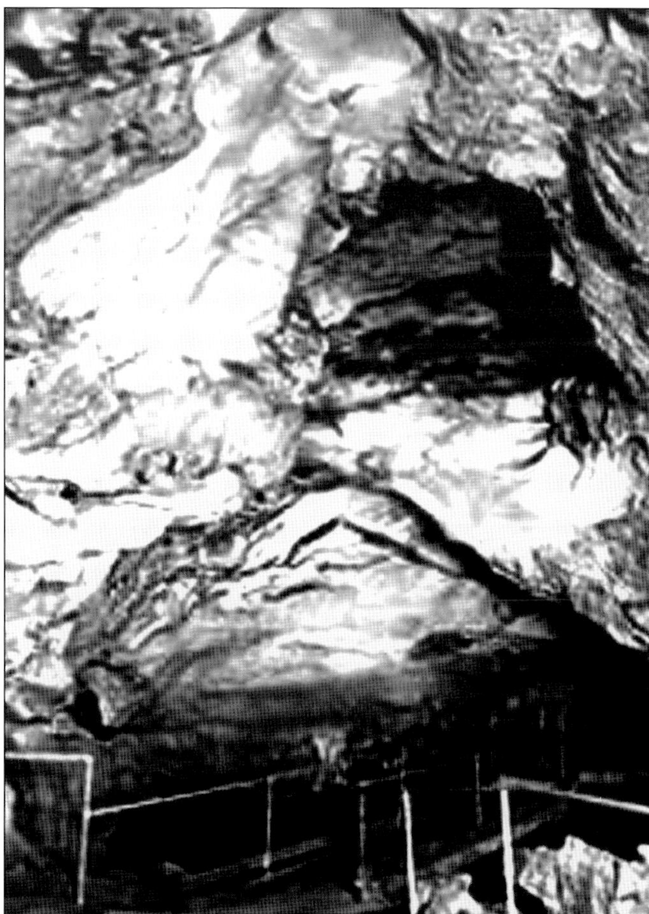

Freedom, established in 1901, has always been a ranching center with the appearance of a western town. Alabaster Caverns, located six miles south in Woodward County (originally in "M" County), has long been associated with Freedom. It is the nation's largest publicly held gypsum cave that is open to visitors and has been explored since the early 1900s. It is also believed to have been a hideout for outlaws such as Jesse James and the Dalton Gang.

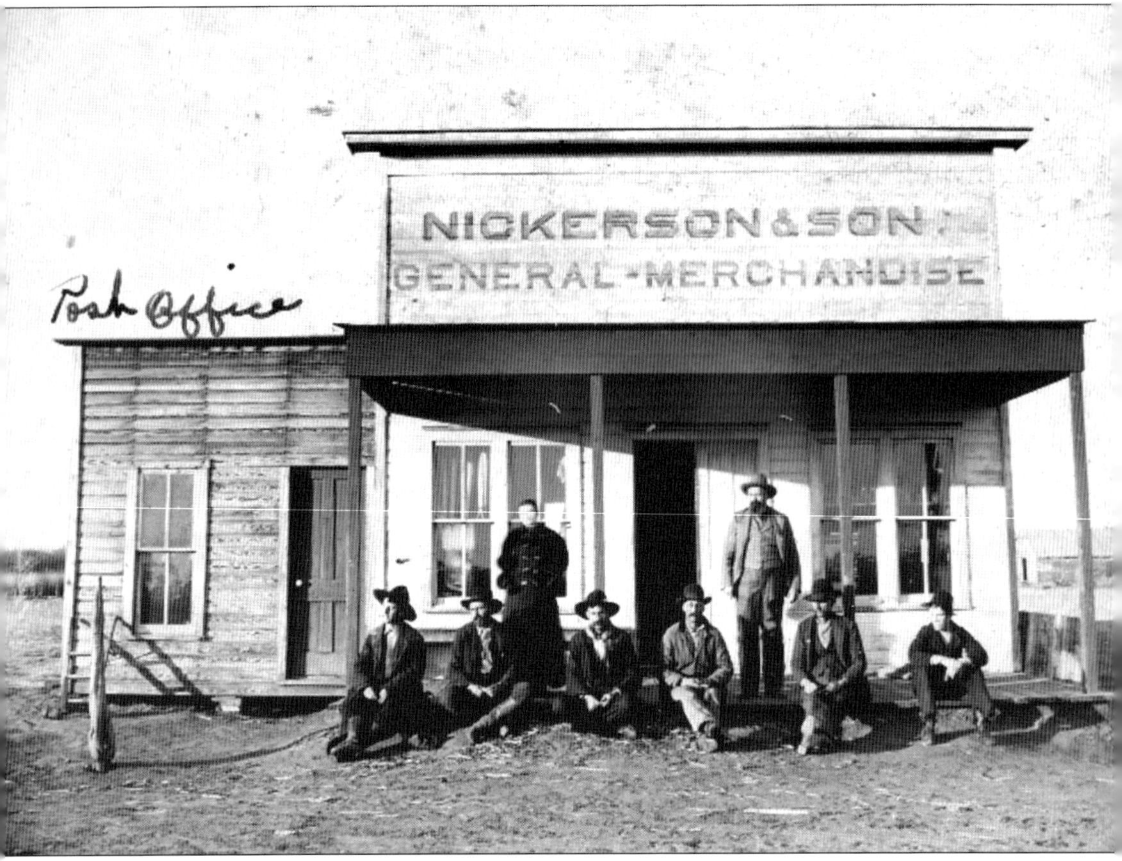

Pictured here is the Waynoka Post Office and general store before statehood. Waynoka is the second largest town in Woods County. Located 25 miles southwest of Alva, its name is of Indian origin and means "good water." When the Santa Fe Railroad was built through the county seven years before the opening of the Cherokee Strip, a shipping station and a section house were located there. This was an important crew change and service point during the steam era.

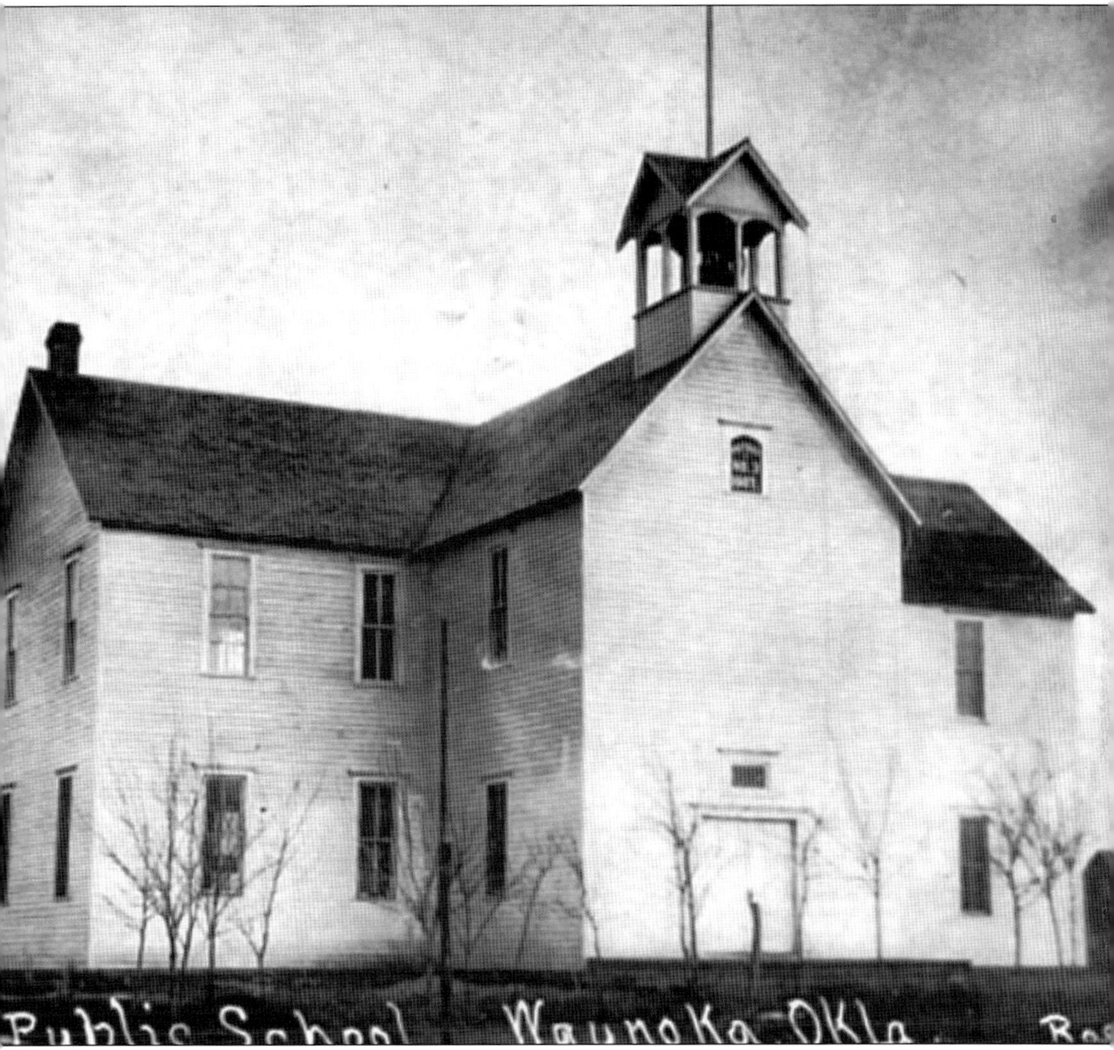

Waynoka built its first school in 1903. (Courtesy of the Waynoka Historical Society.)

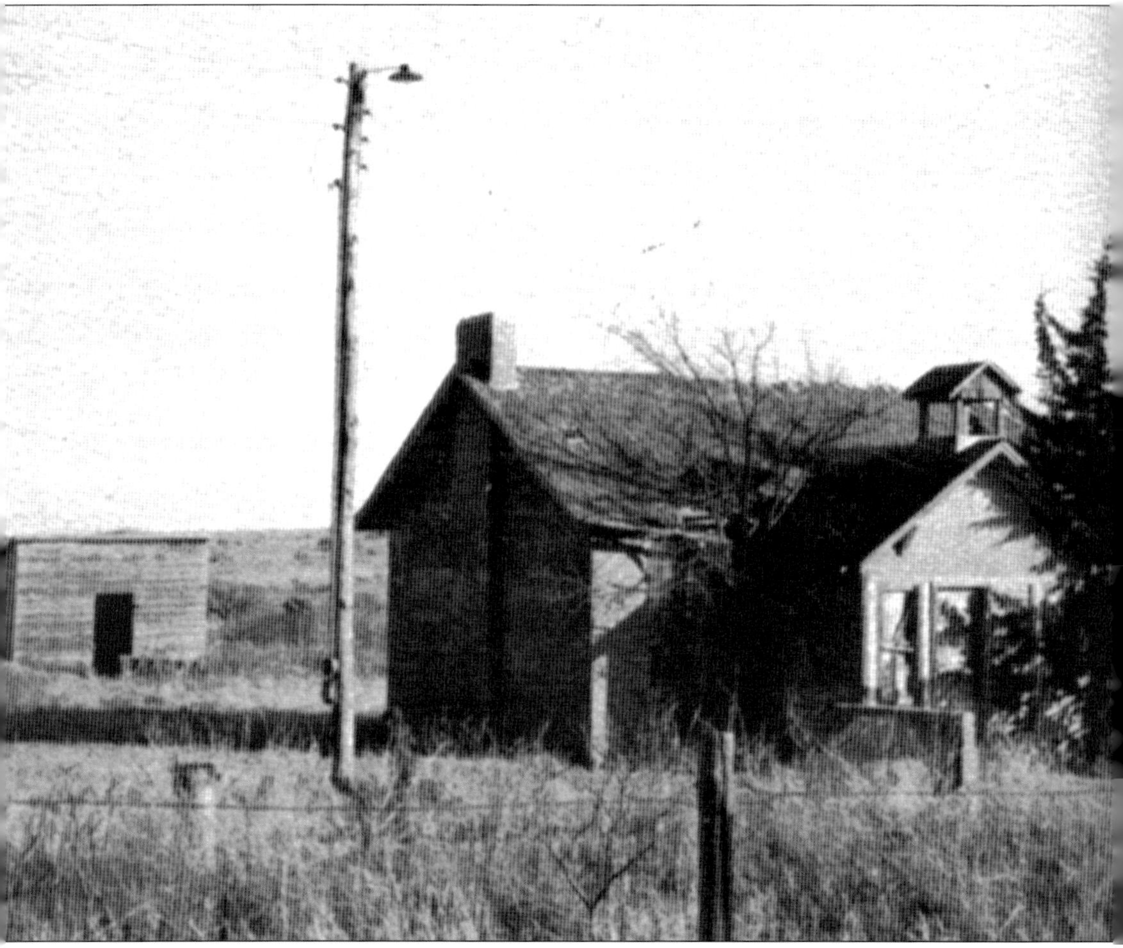

One of Oklahoma's ghost towns is Phroso, originally in "M" County and now part of Major County. It is 35 miles south and 10 miles west of Alva. Phroso is typical of numerous hamlets that developed in the drier and rougher western parts of the Cherokee Outlet. This area had no roads or transportation, but it had a small store that attracted other business until the 1920s. The population then moved to other areas and the town died.

SOURCES

Alva Pioneer. Alva, OK: 1893 to 1903.

Alva Centennial Commission. Alva, OK.

Newsom, D. Earl. *The Cherokee Strip*. Stillwater, OK: New Forums Press, 1992.

Oklahoma Historical Society. Oklahoma City, OK.

Western History Collection. Norman, OK: University of Oklahoma Press.